The Vitamix
Cookbook

The Vitamix Cookbook

250 Delicious Whole Food Recipes
to Make in Your Blender

Jodi Berg

WM

WILLIAM MORROW
An Imprint of HarperCollins*Publishers*

HarperCollins books may be purchased for educational, business, or sales promotional use. For information please e-mail the Special Markets Department at SPsales@harpercollins.com.

FIRST EDITION

Designed by Paula Russell Szafranski

All photographs by Allen Owens/Limoncello Productions, except pages viii, x, xiii, xiv, and xv from Jodi Berg's personal family collection and pages 8–9, 29, 44, 61, 66, 80, 102, 116, 165, 225, 226, 250, 255, 270, 272, 279, 282, 302, 328, 330, 346, and 355 © by Vitamix Corporation.

Library of Congress Cataloging-in-Publication Data has been applied for.

ISBN 978-0-06-240720-7

15 16 17 18 19 OV/RRD 10 9 8 7 6 5 4 3 2 1

To our dedicated and committed Vitamix team, who work tirelessly to help make the world a healthier place, and to our loyal fans.

Thank you for making a difference.

CONTENTS

William G. Barnard (Papa) on the Macfadden health walk.

Ruth M. Pellet Barnard with her family.

Papa Barnard.

Papa Barnard during the filming of "Home Miracles for 1950."

Nate Barnard demonstrating the Vitamix machine.

Introduction

I f you have ever had the opportunity to experience a Vitamix demonstration, you may not be surprised to know that demonstration has been the backbone of our company for generations. Our dedicated demonstrators whipping up smoothie, soup, and frozen dessert samples are both an iconic part of our brand and a tremendous teaching tool to help people successfully adopt a healthier lifestyle—a role that we have taken very seriously for over ninety years. In the 1940s, shortly after the first blender was invented, my great-grandfather was demonstrating the magic of blended whole foods in front of an audience equally eager to taste the rich flavors produced in mere moments. Hard to believe, right? My great-grandfather—our company's founder—had an incredible passion for whole foods, health, and wellness, as do our hundreds of Vitamix demonstrators in multiple countries around the world who carry on this tradition today.

I, Jodi Berg, am the current president and CEO of Vitamix, a fourth-generation family business. As a family entity, Vitamix can continue to focus on a purpose greater and more encompassing than the almighty sale; it is not just about the bottom line but about making a difference in improving the vitality of people's lives. We get to invite every employee and every customer to be a member of the greater Vitamix family and an advocate for healthy change. If you are already part of our family, you know that Vitamix is more than just a company, and more than a life-changing appliance. If you are just joining us, then welcome!

Prior to talking about the importance of whole foods, and before you start

Clockwise from left: William G. Barnard Jr. (Bill), William G. Barnard Sr. (Papa), Louie W. Barnard, Claire C. Charpentir Barnard.

looking at all of the delicious recipes, I want to tell you a bit of "our" family's story, because when you adopt a Vitamix lifestyle, this becomes your story too. And it's a good one! Full of laughter, hard work, a little log cabin, and a cast of wonderful characters, all deeply devoted to one another and to the business they were building together—all of them passionate about helping people increase their vitality. And it all started with a can opener.

Yes, a can opener and one skilled, charismatic, and resourceful salesman named William Grover Barnard. Living in Westpoint, Illinois, my great-grandfather, known affectionately to all as Papa Barnard, was a successful, ambitious jack-of-all-trades. Back in the early 1900s, Papa was a mayor, undertaker, railroad station agent, banker, and real estate investor to boot. He was the horse in a one-horse town, his son Bill once said. A workhorse, I would venture to say. But around 1921 his family, like many others, hit hard times. Papa had invested heavily in real estate, so when the land values plummeted, he had to reinvent himself. After all, he had a family to support, and he wasn't about to let them down. Papa tackled this challenge like many others: with tenacity, a twinkle in his eye, and a big dose of perseverance. For a natural showman like Papa, being a traveling salesman was a perfect fit. He got his start demonstrating small housewares like the can opener, long before the blender was even invented.

Papa was a gregarious, fun-loving man, and he always drew a crowd. He was a lot more than an entertainer—he was passionate about the value of his products. To Papa, the value to the customer had to be greater than the price paid. It *had to*. Twenty-five cents for a can opener was a lot of money in those days. Still, opening canned goods with a knife was dangerous. Unlike many can openers available in the late 1920s and early 1930s, the model Papa demonstrated had a small wheel to protect your fingers. Even in tight times, my great-grandfather was able to demonstrate that the value was well worth what one would spend. This cornerstone is foundational to this day.

As the country slid toward the Great Depression, Papa Barnard built up a successful business. Before too long, Papa's one-man show became a multigenerational business when his sons William Grove Jr. (Grandpa Bill) and Great-Uncle Louie came on board. Papa christened his growing business the Barnard Sales Company, and the three men took to the road in a Model T Ford, demonstrating in small towns across the United States to sell their wares.

Exploring Health and Whole Foods

In 1934, my grandpa Bill married his college sweetheart, Ruth. Her father, Frank C. Pellett, a well-respected naturalist and bee expert, was quite accomplished in his own right. As fate would have it, it was not Frank's strengths but his weaknesses that changed our family's history. You see, Frank had long suffered from digestive problems. Both the Barnard and the Pellett families rallied together to help him regain his health, and it was this quest that led them to wellness through whole foods. It was then that the Barnard family first became interested in health through diet, and Papa, Grandpa, and Grandma wanted very much to learn all they could.

Papa and my grandpa Bill became interested in the writings of Dr. John Harvey Kellogg, an early health food advocate, who later went on to found what would become the Kellogg's cereal company, and a health lecturer by the name of Dr. Bush. After a talk by Dr. Bush, Grandma wrote that Papa and Grandpa were inspired. "The philosophy of the thing got them, and Bill has refused to eat white flour, white sugar, and meat ever since." My grandpa hoped to eventually know enough about achieving wellness through a healthy diet to be able to lecture on it, but meanwhile, as Grandma wrote to her aunt Milly, "we live it."

The 1930s ended up being a very significant decade for our family. First, Papa and his sons demonstrated for two summers at the Great Lakes Exposition in Cleveland. During their time at the Expo, the Barnard family fell in love with the hardworking people of northeast Ohio. Deciding it was the best place to grow their families and their business, they moved to this great city in 1937, just after the Expo finished.

The second big event also happened around the hundred-day Expo. The Barnard family became aware of yet another new product, a blender. Many salesmen saw no use for the blender beyond bars and mixed drinks. But Papa saw the blender as the perfect tool to help himself, his family, and his customers add more whole food to their diets. Not only could you add more fruits and vegetables, but the foods you could make would be varied and delicious too. It was truly an aha moment for Papa. Great-Grandpa Pellett christened the new blender the "Vita-Mix," because *vita* in Latin means "life." The Barnards were then, as we are today, great livers of life, and the name fit perfectly with the product, the business, and the family too.

As you surely know, feeling good is an adrenaline rush that keeps you coming back for more. Papa and my grandparents were hooked on their new whole food diet. They wanted to share their discoveries with others. In 1939, they opened a health food store where they sold bulk food, supplements, and vitamins, quickly adding the blender to their product mix. Little did any of them know how iconic their blender would become in both residential and commercial kitchens all over the world.

As my grandparents and Papa continued to explore whole foods and learn about health, they came across the work of Bernarr Macfadden. Macfadden, a passionate advocate for exercise and nutrition, held weeklong hikes. Grandpa had written away for information about the walks, but as Grandma later wrote in a letter:

> I was the one who read the literature and decided it was just what I needed to make me strong and well again. Probably my future life depended on this. After two weeks of walking 265 miles from Cleveland to Dansville, New York, I was as fit and healthy and full of vim and vigor such as I had never before in my life experienced.

Grandma, who was then the mother of a three-year-old boy, Grove, and an eight-month-old baby, Ginny, recalled that the beginning of the walk was the most exciting day of her life. Papa, ever up for an adventure, came along to see her off and ended up walking right along with her—all the way to the Physical Culture Hotel in Dansville, New York. Grandma and Papa found a wonderful community on that walk. And since I get to tell you this story, I must tell you my favorite part: Some of the friends they made on that trip would one day introduce my dad, John, to my mom, Linda. Thank you, Bernarr Macfadden!

The House That Bill Built

In 1942, the country was emerging from the Great Depression and immersed in war. Grandpa, tiring of city life, bought twelve acres in Olmsted Township, Ohio, a little over eighteen miles from Cleveland. Today, the Olmsted community is bustling, but back in the early 1940s, it was little more than scattered farms and quite a few cows. The move was motivated, in part, by a desire to be outside. "We were never city people," my grandpa later recalled in an interview. To Grandpa and Papa, it was a beautiful oasis in the woods. Our family still loves being in nature.

William G. Barnard Jr. (Bill) and Ruth M. Pellet Barnard at the 1965 World's Fair.

My grandpa, like his father, had big dreams and boundless enthusiasm. Grandpa was a tall man with a booming voice, a terrific sense of humor, and a work ethic like no other. While my grandma and their three children lived in a tiny trailer, he set about building a house, growing the business, and contributing to the war efforts. Grandpa was a talented salesman like his father, but he was not particularly good with his hands. Not one to let this limitation be an obstacle, he tackled the house-building project with good cheer. My uncle Grove always laughed when he reminisced that his dad "didn't have any plans. He was just going to build the house." Grandma wisely insisted that there be plans. She had a real gift for giving Grandpa's dreams a solid foundation. It took some years, but the homestead was eventually finished. "The house that Bill built," as I call it, still stands today. A humble home with knotty pine walls, rather like a rustic cabin, sits at the entrance to our corporate headquarters. This simple home, along with another building Bill built that housed the first Vitamix offices, reminds us daily of our family roots, our focus on whole foods and wellness, and our purpose, which is to help customers achieve greater vitality.

Ginny, Grove, and John with Bootsie.

The Balancing Act

Balancing work and family is challenging at the best of times. My grandparents had their fair share of struggles: Raising six children, growing a business, and trying to change the way their fellow Americans thought about whole foods wasn't easy. Grandpa expected his family to be all hands on deck. As my aunt Ginny recalls, "Mom and Dad maybe sat down and played a game with us once or twice in our life. If we were with them, it was because we were working." All of my aunts and uncles were put to work in the family business, stuffing envelopes, packing mail-order boxes, or working in the office.

Vitamix continued to grow, and Grandpa made sure it continued to be a family venture, a family *adventure* in many cases. And oh, were there ever a lot of adventures! My grandparents loved children, laughter, nature, and hard work, and often there was some hilarious combination of these things all happening at once. For example, my aunts and uncles grew up with a whole menagerie of animals, including chickens, some rather unruly goats, a cow, ducks, and a horse. And of course, the house that Grandpa built was right next door to the Vitamix offices. My aunt Patty laughs remembering how the goats caused trouble for the Vitamix employees.

> I remember watching her [one of the goats, Bootsie] chase women around the property. The women that used to work at Vitamix . . . would be screaming and running down the driveway with their hands in the air, and the goat would be behind them, butting them.

Ruth and family out west.

My aunts and uncles say that Grandpa left most of the discipline to Grandma and focused, when he could, on the fun. He loved children and he loved to make them laugh. After the family moved to the Olmsted community, once a year he would clear a path to a place he called Mount Tooska-Ooska-Wooska-Choo, a name he chose because it got the most giggles from the kids. He would tromp his kids through the woods on the long, winding path to a clearing where they would have a picnic. When I think about these treks—to a destination that was probably not more than 350 feet away from the house—it reminds me that fun can be simple: as simple as packing so much silliness and wonder into a short walk in the woods!

In the summer, when other kids were lounging about, Grandpa and Grandma took to the road with all the kids in tow. While my grandpa may have been a fun-loving man, these trips were not a family vacation. Nope. They piled five of the six kids in the back of a big stake truck (the youngest got to ride up front) and traveled to shows and fairs around the country. My dad remembers sleeping on top of the Vitamix boxes in the back of the truck with all of his siblings, packed together like a row of logs. If one kid wanted to roll over, they all had to roll over.

Some years my grandparents were able to tow a little camper along behind their truck. Once they parked overnight in a public park—a fairly common practice at the time—and awoke to find a parade lining up around them. Grandpa, ever a showman, managed to time their departure so they were the first vehicle in the parade—hardly a coincidence, I am sure. He honked and smiled, while my aunts and uncles all waved. Poor Grandma was so embarrassed; she giggled as she told us how she willed herself to be invisible! Riding home to Ohio at the end of the summer, Aunt Ginny recalls, was a bit more comfortable since many of the Vitamix boxes had been sold, so the kids had a little more space.

A New Stage for Papa

Another big year for the Barnard family was 1949. Grandpa, always looking for new ways to share his whole foods message and the wonderful Vitamix with more people, got the idea that Papa should do his demonstration on television. Papa didn't agree. He was just as suspicious of this newfangled medium as Grandpa was passionate about its potential. After much coaxing, my grandpa convinced Papa to rent a studio in which to do a live demonstration. The program, considered the first infomercial, was an important move for the business. The phones started ringing about halfway through the segment, and the operator kept patching calls through until the middle of the night when she announced that she was going home. Grandpa remembers that "now we knew we had something big." The program really put the company on the map, and gave them a bigger stage for their whole foods message.

Marching to the Beat of a Different Drum

Committed to healthy living, Grandpa and Grandma raised their children as vegetarians, an unconventional practice at the time. My aunt Ginny says her friends didn't often know what being vegetarian meant, and my dad recalls being teased about the contents of his lunch box. My grandparents were dedicated to teaching others about whole foods and health, no matter how unfashionable it might be. They were definitely ahead of their time.

Grandpa continued to talk about health and how people could use the Vitamix to eat more whole food and set themselves on a path to vitality. Grandma was the glue that held it all together behind the scenes. For every ounce of passion and exuberance that Grandpa had, Grandma had a pound of common sense. She was also committed to developing new recipes and techniques for the Vitamix.

While Grandpa was on the road, Grandma was learning a lot about what the machine could do. She was the one who discovered that you could grind wheat berries and other ingredients into flour. She figured out how to knead bread dough in the Vitamix, so you could go from fresh whole wheat berries to bread rising in a pan in just three minutes. Grandma taught herself how to make frozen treats in the Vitamix, and she figured out that you could make hot soup without adding a heating element; the friction of the blades running at high speed would heat the soup. She taught us all of the different, tasty, and amazing ways we could *use* the machine to create nutritious and delicious food. We have carried on this tradition to today—with a state-of-the-art recipe development kitchen and a staff of talented chefs.

Both in the test kitchen and on the road, my grandparents were passionate about wellness—through whole foods. The Vitamix was an amazing kitchen tool but their goals were bigger—they wanted to make the world a healthier place. Even when it would have been easier to embrace the processed foods that were beginning to dominate the American diet, their commitment to healthy foods remained strong. They were not the first people to make the connection between diet and health, of course, but their dedication to healthy eating continues to inspire our family, our company, and hundreds of thousands of dedicated Vitamix owners around the world today.

It's All About Family

My own memories of my grandparents are strongly tied to family reunions because my dad had ventured out on his own and raised his family in Erie, Pennsylvania. For a long time, family reunions were held in the house that Bill built. When we would pull up to the house, all five of us kids would pile out of the car after the long trip, and my grandparents, aunts, uncles, over a dozen cousins, and all the family dogs would greet us at the door! If I shut my eyes, I can still hear the distinct clickety-clack of doggy feet, friendly barks, and all of those voices, talking and laughing. It was a boisterous, chaotic scene, not so different from the spirit of the house when my dad was growing up there.

After our reunions outgrew my grandparents' home in the 1970s, we held our ever-growing family get-togethers at the Vitamix offices. One of my most meaningful memories of Grandpa involves one of these gatherings. Like Papa, Grandpa believed passionately that our customers were the reason we existed, and that we were here for them. When the phones at Vitamix rang, they rang throughout the building, so that Grandpa could be sure the calls would be answered quickly. During one of these weekend reunions, Grandpa answered the phone. Being curious, I slipped into his office and listened as he spoke. He was patiently explaining, step-by-step, how to make bread in a Vitamix. A typically self-centered tween at the time, I was pretty riled that my beloved grandpa was working and not paying attention to us. When the call ended, I gave him a hard time for leaving the party.

And this part I remember very clearly. My grandpa, not a bit angry, looked straight at me and said, "Jodi, some day you will understand." He went on to say that we were not in the business to sell machines. We were changing the way people thought about food and how they ate. We're not successful, he told me, until our customers are successfully using their Vitamix. We want to help them use it or we want to take it back, so we can put it in the hands of someone who will. His commitment to our customers, to really making people's lives better, helping them be healthier, has really stuck with me and to this day remains one of our values.

While Vitamix is definitely more than just the Barnards now, it has remained an unwaveringly family-run and family-involved business. As my mother, Linda, says, "You cannot separate Vitamix from the [Barnard] family." In the 1960s, my uncle William Grover III ("Grove") left his dream of pursuing a master's degree in statistics to come back to the family business because his parents needed his help. Once he came back, he stayed; the company transferred to the third generation when Grove took on the role of president and CEO after Grandpa retired in 1985.

Over the years, several of my aunts and uncles came back into the business. In the early 1980s, my dad, John, returned to Ohio after years of being away. He brought a strong engineering background and years of different business experience. He worked with his brother Frank to bring first-class research and development to the company. My dad knew that when the opportunity came to enter the commercial food service market, Vitamix needed to prepare itself to become an international company, assuring the customers would be cared for. We continue this commitment of being a global company with a local feel to this day.

My father was also instrumental in introducing to the food-service industry a blender that was truly a reliable, lasting piece of equipment versus the disposable version that needed to be replaced every couple of months. Our goal was, and continues to be, to allow our food-service customers to focus on expanding their brand and enhancing their experience, rather than worrying about their blending equipment. This revolutionized the blending industry. Vitamix flourished under my father's leadership after Uncle Grove retired in 1999.

The Fourth Generation

Being part of a family business wasn't much more glamorous for my generation growing up than it was for my father's. Thankfully we didn't spend our summers bouncing around in the back of a stake truck. Instead we painted walls, cleaned toilets, and sorted mail. Because I had heard so much about the company as a child, it felt very familiar when I began working here myself after Dad moved the family to Ohio. Believe it or not, my favorite afterschool job ended up being answering phones! I discovered that I loved talking with our customers, answering their questions, and even helping people learn to make Vitamix bread.

Like my dad before me, I started my professional life without any intention of working at the family business long term. And also as with my dad, my work and my travels ultimately brought me home to Vitamix. When I came back several years after a different, yet successful, career, I transitioned from a minor character in the Vitamix story to one of the authors of its history. At that time, Vitamix was already a staple in many homes across the country, and we were really mixing it up in the food-service industry. I had the pleasure of setting up our international department, and I loved it. After several years, my father asked me to head up our household division, too, and I fell in love with it as well. This is where the story really gets interesting for me. As I dug in and did research in 2003, I started hearing a lot about whole foods, organics, and health. People were talking about natural, fresh, whole foods. *Real food.* People were starting to talk more about the ideas that we here at Vitamix had been talking about for decades. I could almost see the early generations of Barnards smiling down on all of us. At last it seemed people were ready to embrace whole food as a path to good health, and we at Vitamix were ready to help them. It was time to take generations of passion and commitment to whole food health and use them to help make the world a healthier place for generations to come. We simply needed to make sure our voice was heard.

The Road Ahead

I have given you a glimpse of the people and the philosophies that have shaped our family's past. But what of our future? The Barnard family directory is now more like a book, and our work family has grown significantly, too.

While we are a larger and even more diverse group now, our commitment to helping people lead healthier lives has never been stronger. We honor the memory of my grandparents by continuing to share a passion for health and nutrition. I have the honor and pleasure of working closely with my father and my cousin Loree Connors (our CFAO). Family is still a key value. We are thrilled when members of the next generation join Vitamix, whether they are Barnards or the children of our employees. We have found that our passion for wellness and our values of family, customer, quality, integrity, and teamwork are often carried down through the generations of our employees' families as well. With such a committed team around us, we will continue talking about whole foods, advocating for better health through diet whenever and wherever we can. We will proudly carry on with the work that Papa, Grandma, and Grandpa started so many years ago.

Part of the Barnard legacy is a healthy diet, of course. The Vitamix gives you hundreds of different ways to enjoy whole foods, many of which are highlighted in the following recipes. While green smoothies seem to be all the craze today, we've had a recipe for a Green Elixir, as it was called, since 1940. I crave this delightfully sweet and silky smooth beverage; there is no better way to start my day. My daughters and I are blessed to start our day with one made by my husband, Frank, our own personal "Green Smoothie Maker Extraordinaire." Whatever you make in your Vitamix, we Barnards and the rest of the Vitamix family raise a glass of a delicious, whole food drink to you. We hope that, with a little help from your Vitamix and the recipes and tips in this book, we contribute in some small way to your own vitality.

To your health!

The Vitamix Cookbook

Cashew Crema (page 249) is a wonderful, dairy-free topping for fresh fruit or desserts.

Chapter 1

Why Whole Foods?

With health, we have wealth!" declared Papa Barnard in the first Vitamix infomercial in 1949. "With our health, we're the richest person on Earth!" He went on to show us how, by using the Vitamix to blend the amazing flavors and nutrients of whole foods, we can consume more of already healthy foods: peels, seeds, and all. He showed us how we can improve our diets and our health without sacrificing flavor or convenience. Papa may have been more of a salesperson than a scientist, but over the years, the research in favor of whole food has stacked up. And however one defines wealth, there is no question that there is tremendous value to good health.

And yes, people may choose to define wealth differently, but there is no doubt that a lot of money is being spent on health care annually. According to the USDA, healthier diets could prevent at least $87 billion per year in medical costs, lost productivity, and lost lives.

But how do we get people eating a better diet? Here at Vitamix, we strongly believe that whole foods are key.

Whole Food Health Benefits

There is a lot of talk about whole foods, and for good reason. In 2014 in the *Annual Review of Public Health*, Dr. David Katz and Dr. Stephanie Meller from Yale University published a study comparing different popular diets. As the *Atlantic,* reporting on their work, concluded:

> A diet of minimally processed food close to nature, predominantly plants, is decisively associated with health promotion and disease prevention.
>
> [N]utritionally-complete, plant-based diets are supported by a wide array of favorable health outcomes, including fewer cancers and less heart disease. These diets ideally include not just fruits and vegetables, but whole grains, nuts, and seeds as well.

We can, it appears, make a positive impact on our health by eating more whole foods. Papa would not be surprised.

Before we talk about why we should eat more whole foods and how, let me clarify what we here at Vitamix believe they are. To us, whole foods are foods in, or very close to, their natural state, complete with most or all of their nutrients, fiber, phytochemicals, minerals, and the like. Fresh or frozen fruits and vegetables, nuts, and seeds are all whole foods. Whole grains—unprocessed whole grains such as oat groats, whole wheat kernels, and brown rice—are also whole foods. You get the idea.

Besides just plain tasting good, whole foods usually offer more nutrition. As a group, whole foods generally have higher nutrient density. What is nutrient density? It simply means that the foods have a large percentage of nutrients relative to the total number of calories. Blueberries and kale, for example, considered to be superfoods by some, have a very large number of nutrients relative to their calories. Not all whole foods are low in calories of course, but even foods like avocados and nuts are much more nutrient-dense than a serving of a more processed snack—even if you eat the same number of calories. Great taste and good nutrition together? Absolutely!

Whole foods are clearly very good for us, but do we eat enough of them? Sadly the answer is no, and we can't really say it is for lack of awareness about the health benefits of fruits and vegetables. This information was fairly common knowledge even back in Grandpa and Grandma's day, even if it was often ignored as people chose foods for convenience.

Research from the Centers for Disease Control and Prevention in 2013 showed that only about 37 percent of American adults eat fruit daily and only about 22 percent eat vegetables daily. Think about this. We need to do better—our health depends upon it! We logically know we should eat more produce, yet we don't. How can this be?

Processed Foods

Let's talk about processed food. If American adults are eating too few fruits and vegetables, we are arguably eating too many processed foods. According to a study conducted through UNC Chapel Hill, more than 60 percent of the calories in the food American consumers buy comes from overly processed food, which also tends to have more fat, sugar, and salt content than other foods. What counts as processed food? The Academy of Nutrition and Dietetics identifies a range. First, there are minimally processed foods like bagged greens. Next they identify foods processed at their peak to preserve nutrition, such as frozen vegetables. Then foods with ingredients—such as sweeteners, fats, or preservatives—added for flavor and texture. Finally, the last category of processed foods includes items like packaged baking mixes or bottled sauces and ready-to-eat foods like crackers and frozen meals.

Just as all whole foods are not created equal, not all processed foods are created equal either—nutritionally speaking. Cut and bagged vegetables or greens can make vegetables a more accessible, although slightly more expensive, option. Just be sure to check the labels. Some cut and bagged vegetables have added sugar, salt, or fat to enhance flavor or texture, so steer clear of those if your desire is for the least-processed whole foods.

The 2010 Dietary Guidelines for Americans, a report produced by the Departments of Agriculture and of Health and Human Services, explains the problem bluntly:

> Americans currently consume too much sodium and too many calories from solid fats, added sugars, and refined grains. These replace nutrient-dense foods and beverages and make it difficult for people to achieve recommended nutrient intake while controlling calorie and sodium intake.

The more a food is processed and refined, the more likely it is to lose its naturally occurring fiber, minerals, vitamins, and so forth.

WHOLE FOODS SUCCESS STORY

John Barnard

My dad, John Barnard, grew up as a vegetarian and in a family that emphasized the importance of eating whole foods at a time when neither practice was common.

After Dad left home for college, he says he turned his back on his childhood diet. In college and after he got married, he ate a pretty typical American diet. My family ate more fruits and vegetables than most when I was growing up, but we were not vegetarians like my dad's parents. Dad returned to Ohio and the family business in 1981. In 2004, after reading T. Colin Campbell and Thomas Campbell III's *The China Study*, which advocates a diet based primarily on plant foods, Dad decided to return to his healthier-eating roots.

Never much of a cook, my dad now loves to use his Vitamix to make green smoothies for himself and my mom. Dad's favorite smoothie often contains grapes, part of a whole lime, broccoli, pineapple, chia or flax seeds, a little water, and at least three different kinds of greens—filling up at least half of the container. Once blended, Dad adds even more greens to fill the container and continues to blend. Dad makes a big batch a few times a week and puts it in the refrigerator, so they can enjoy a delicious green smoothie every day.

My parents, now in their seventies, have more energy than people a fraction of their age. Dad even completed a forty-mile hike the day before his seventy-fourth birthday! Our goal at Vitamix is to increase our customers' vitality so they can live a long, full life. My dad and mom are walking, talking examples of this goal in action!

Health Benefits of Whole Foods

The health benefits of whole foods are vast. Because whole foods tend to have higher nutrient density, you can often eat more of them while taking in fewer calories overall, which in turn support maintaining a healthy ideal weight. Fresh fruits and vegetables usually contain fiber, so you are likely to feel fuller for longer, an added advantage.

Cooking and eating whole foods can also be important if you are on a restricted diet. When you prepare whole foods at home, you know *exactly* what is going into your food. If you put spinach, grapes, banana, berries, and ice in your blender for a smoothie, you will simply get a delicious drink, with no hidden ingredients, preservatives, or other such surprises.

By preparing foods at home, you can also control the amounts of salt and sugar added to your food. There may very well be a health benefit to the peace of mind that comes with knowing exactly what you are putting into your body, but the scientists have not discovered this yet!

We know that whole foods are important to good health, so the question becomes not *why* should we eat a more whole-foods-focused diet, but *how*? If flavor and convenience are important, we here at Vitamix have great news. With this cookbook in hand, you will quickly discover that healthy cooking can be both simple *and* delicious.

Better Nutrition Made Simple

As we learned in the introduction, Papa was thrilled after he first encountered the blender. *This* was the way to bring more whole foods into people's diets! He was clearly onto something. Similarly, just as my grandma realized back in 1937, a sustainable whole foods diet needs to taste good and have variety. To meet the demands of our busy lives, we strongly believe it's important that food be simple and quick to prepare. You may not want to sit down to a big bowl of leafy greens first thing in the morning, but drop those greens in a Vitamix with fresh fruit, whip up a delicious smoothie, and suddenly you have a nutritious and delicious breakfast on the go. Especially for the kids; try giving toddlers a smoothie in their sippy cups and they may not let you take it away.

As our Vitamix nutritionist Anne Thacker notes, you can hide a lot of greens in a smoothie—up to 4 or 5 cups—to get all of the good nutrition that comes

the **Dirty Dozen** and

Often when we reflect on what we are consuming, the subject of eating organic comes up. Many of us have to strike a compromise between what we might like to eat and what is financially and logistically possible. If you want to buy some organic produce, but are unable or unwilling to buy all organic, there is a great resource to guide your choices.

Every year, the Environmental Working Group (EWG) compiles the "Dirty Dozen" and "Clean Fifteen" lists, ranking common produce on the amounts of pesticide residue found on conventionally grown produce even after it had been washed. The EWG website (www .ewg.org/foodnews/index.php) publishes the two lists annually, and it is worth taking a few minutes to read the full report. For example, leafy greens and hot peppers were on the "Dirty Dozen" list recently even though the number of pesticides found after washing was low, the vegetables contained residues from particularly toxic insecticides that can damage the nervous system. The EWG recommended that customers who frequently eat these vegetables buy organic if possible. The two lists from 2015 are presented opposite.

the Clean Fifteen

The EWG encourages us to try to limit our exposure to pesticides but states, "The health benefits of a diet rich in fruits and vegetables outweigh the risks of pesticide exposure. Use EWG's Shopper's Guide to reduce your exposures as much as possible, but eating conventionally grown produce is better than not eating fruits and vegetables at all." Papa Barnard would doubtless agree.

Dirty Dozen Plus

1. Apples
2. Peaches
3. Nectarines
4. Strawberries
5. Grapes
6. Celery
7. Spinach
8. Sweet bell peppers
9. Cucumbers
10. Cherry tomatoes
11. Imported snap peas
12. Potatoes
13. Hot peppers
14. Kale / collard greens

Clean Fifteen

1. Avocado
2. Sweet corn
3. Pineapple
4. Cabbage
5. Sweet peas (frozen)
6. Onions
7. Asparagus
8. Mangoes
9. Papaya
10. Kiwi
11. Eggplant
12. Grapefruit
13. Cantaloupe
14. Cauliflower
15. Sweet potatoes

with them without altering the flavor of the other ingredients. Combining leafy greens with fruit brings out the sweetness in the greens, allowing the flavors to blend right in. That's a lot of nutrient-dense foods first thing in the morning, making for a powerful way to prepare your body for anything that fills your day! Smoothies are a great place to start, but they aren't the only easy way to add more whole foods to your diet. Tomato Vinaigrette (page 231) has half a pound of raw tomatoes in it. Imagine, getting a healthy dose of vegetables in both the dressing and the salad!

Want more whole foods in your diet but worry that you don't have the culinary skills or the time? With a Vitamix, vegetables for soups and salads can be chopped in seconds. Fruit and vegetables can be whipped into tasty, silky drinks in under a minute. (You can even make a large batch of your favorite smoothie every few days and store it in the refrigerator as my dad does. Just stir or shake it to reemulsify, and enjoy.) Whole-grain cereals, quick breads, savory soups, and hearty tomato sauces come together in a snap. Each recipe contains lots of nutrient-dense whole foods and most come together in less than 30 minutes, including prep and cleanup.

Why Blended Recipes?

There are lots of ways that you can incorporate whole foods into your diet, but it is quite a challenge to eat the volume of whole food and get the nutrition your body needs without a Vitamix blender. Vitamix machines allow you to use the *whole* food so you retain all the nutrients within the food. The sweet pineapple core is too fibrous to chew but can be blended up into a juice, smoothie, or sauce. You can puree a whole tomato—skin, seeds, and all—and make a soup or hearty tomato sauce. You can't chew up an orange seed or a flax seed very easily, but a Vitamix blender can pulverize it almost instantly, where other blenders may struggle with these tougher ingredients. Using the whole food lets you consume all of the available nutrients, and preparing it quickly allows you to squeeze healthy eating into even the busiest day. We don't just talk the talk here at Vitamix. It is not uncommon to see one of our employees bring a bag of vegetables into the office and whip up a hot, steaming soup for lunch in a matter of minutes. Of course it helps to work for a company that has a Vitamix station in every break room.

When We Say Delicious

It is easier to eat healthier foods when they taste delicious, and all of the nearly 250 recipes in this book will not disappoint! Our culinary team, registered dietician nutritionist Anne Thacker and chef and manager of recipe development Bev Shaffer, worked together to create recipes that were tasty and met our rigorous nutritional standards. They created delicious and nutritious recipes with little to no refined sugar, little added salt, and no more than 15 grams of total fat. In this book you will find a huge variety of tempting treats, savory soups, and hearty entrées for every meal. Our goal is to help you eat more whole foods. Our sincere hope is that these recipes will allow you to eat healthier in an efficient and delicious way.

How to Use This Book

All the recipes in this book are intended to be made in the Vitamix. Although some recipes may also work in another blender, the Vitamix engineering allows us to do a lot of things other blenders may not be able to do as well, if at all. The instructions for blending speeds and times have been created with optimal taste and texture in mind. A Vitamix blender is powerful and built to be reliable and durable. Don't worry about using it on its highest speeds or using the tamper—the machine is made for it! The end product will be worth it.

Our culinary team created these recipes to demonstrate how easy it is to get healthy whole food into the foods you already love to eat, as well as foods you may not have tried before. The focus of this book is whole foods, so some recipes do include dairy or meat products, but feel free to experiment on your own with substitutions if you choose not to use these ingredients.

Artichoke, Red Pepper, and
Parmesan Frittata (page 26)

Chapter 2

Breakfast and Brunch

The alarm clock sounds. The children wake up hungry for breakfast. Pets want food and attention. There are showers to take, teeth to brush, shoes and socks to find. There are workouts to squeeze in, lunches to pack, and jobs to get to. Sound familiar? Most of us are *busy* from the moment our feet hit the ground. My family is no exception. Even the weekends, which can be a respite from the usual hustle and bustle, are usually hectic. Saturday and Sunday quickly fill up with softball and volleyball practice, yard work, errands galore, and time with family and friends. It is hard to imagine we have time for any sort of breakfast, much less a healthy one.

Many of us are told from a tender age that breakfast is the most important meal of the day. The link between children who eat breakfast, particularly a healthy one with nutrients and fiber, and academic success is well established. Research aside, starting the day with a healthy meal, complete with whole foods, may just *feel* good to you as it does to me, as right and proper as a hot shower and a cup of coffee. Enter a Vitamix blender! In this chapter, we explore all of the healthy, delicious, and *fast* ways that you can start your day.

Drink Your Breakfast

When you think about making breakfast in your Vitamix, many of you will think first of making a smoothie or whole-fruit or whole-vegetable juice. This sort of drink can be quickly assembled and can use whatever produce you have in your fruit bowl, crisper, or freezer. You can even put portioned smoothie ingredients into bags for easy morning prep! The potential combinations are nearly endless. We've included a handful of delicious smoothies here, but chapter 8, "Drinks," offers many other recipes you may want to consider for your morning meal.

More Than Just Smoothies

Smoothies aren't the only healthy breakfast choice, of course. In this chapter, you will also find delicious recipes for quick breads, muffins, and breakfast cakes. How do you use Vitamix blenders to make foods like these? Vitamix machines have always been more than blenders. Dry ingredients can be chopped and ground, and wet ingredients are whipped, blended, or mixed together in the Vitamix. Wet ingredients get stirred into dry, and presto! The batter gets poured into a loaf pan, a cake pan, or muffin tins and into the oven it goes. (You will also learn how to make your own flours for some of these recipes in a Vitamix dry grains container.) In almost no time at all, your kitchen will smell amazing, and your stomach will be rumbling!

After they have cooled, the quick breads and muffins in this chapter freeze beautifully. Consider making an extra batch of your favorite recipe, so you have a healthy breakfast or snack on hand even on your busiest days, especially when slathered with a homemade nut butter or fruit spread. To freeze quick breads, cool the bread completely. Wrap the slices individually in foil and store in a freezer-safe bag or a container with a tight-fitting lid to prevent freezer burn. Slices can be thawed at room temperature. Leave a wrapped slice or two on the counter before you go to sleep, and they will be thawed and ready to eat by morning.

Homemade Granola and Hot Cereals

The cereal aisle in your local grocery store has an endless bounty of options, from the marshmallow-sprinkled to the flax-seed-ful. Our homemade granola is a delicious alternative to these processed options, and you can adjust the recipe to include the nuts, seeds, and dried fruits that you like best. Egg whites, honey, brown sugar, a little canola oil, cinnamon, and a pinch of sea salt can be blended together in a Vitamix machine and poured over a bowl of oats, nuts, and seeds. Toasty, crunchy clusters emerge from the oven, ready to be mixed with your favorite dried fruits. This granola is delicious on yogurt, with milk, or straight out of the jar for a healthy snack.

On the mornings you crave a hot, hearty, whole-grain cereal, try Apple Raisin Cracked Wheat Cereal (page 19), Oat Porridge (page 22), or Creamy Rice Cereal (page 20). Extras will keep in the refrigerator for up to 4 days, so once again consider making enough for leftovers.

Pancakes, Waffles, and More

Some mornings we crave something heartier for breakfast. The many pancake, waffle, and crepe recipes in this book will be sure to please. Try Curried Sweet Potato Pancakes (page 31), Breakfast Crepes (page 43), or Buttermilk Cornmeal Waffles (page 37), to name just a few. Oatmeal Pancakes (page 32) will fill you up, and paired with our dried cranberry compote so delicious that you will find yourself making extra, just to have it on hand for oatmeal, yogurt, or maybe even a smoothie. Vegan French Toast (page 42) will tempt breakfast lovers everywhere, even those who are not avoiding animal products. These delicious dishes come together quickly enough to be a weekday-morning staple and yet are tempting enough to be welcome at a leisurely brunch.

Pancakes and waffles also freeze well, and extras can be put aside for busier mornings. Cool the cooked items and store them in a freezer-safe bag. Frozen pancakes and waffles can be easily warmed up in a toaster or microwave.

Toast and Toppings

Grandpa and Grandma loved to make their famous Vitamix whole wheat bread for their children and grandchildren during our family reunions in Ohio. I remember how my grandfather used to make dozens of loaves of bread at a time. He would put his yeast into warm water, and while that developed, he would grind his wheat berries into fresh flour. Adding the yeast mixture and any other ingredients, possibly raisins for sweetness, he would knead the bread dough in the Vitamix and have a bread pan of dough ready to rise in 3 minutes flat. We used to time him. He would do it over and over again. The only time it took longer than 3 minutes was when we would distract him and cause him to break out in a belly laugh or remind him of a joke.

Few scents can match the heavenly aroma of baking bread, and if you like to start your mornings with a slice of toast, consider using your Vitamix blender to make the dough for your own hearty, healthy whole wheat bread, just as my grandpa loved to do. This bread is delicious toasted or for sandwiches. Top it with homemade nut butter or Raisin Almond Breakfast Spread (page 245) for a tasty and protein-packed treat.

Grind Your Own Flours for a Reliably Gluten-Free Morning

Our scrumptious Gluten-Free Buttermilk Pancake Mix (page 33)—along with two delicious variations—will delight those who avoid gluten as well as those who don't. You can purchase the appropriate flours, or you can quickly grind your own in a Vitamix dry grains container, which was designed with specially angled and spaced blades that efficiently grind dry ingredients with excellent results time after time. In this chapter, you will also learn how to make your own Cornmeal (page 40) and Whole-Grain Flour (page 44). Both begin to lose nutritional value once they are ground, so use them immediately if possible. If not, store in the freezer for up to one month.

Vitamix Containers

When you bought your Vitamix blender, it likely came with one container—the standard Wet container (stamped "W" on the blades). Designed to pull ingredients into the blades and then circulate the ingredients around the blade and back up the sides of the container, this container is great for almost all purposes. However, a few years ago the Vitamix team engineered a separate container for dry grains (stamped with a "D" on the blades). This container was created with blades specially designed to grind even small quantities of spices, grains, and other dry ingredients to a very fine texture. The blades are also ideal for kneading doughs, simulating the kneading process by bouncing ingredients off the blades instead of circulating them underneath and sending them back up the sides of the container. The dry grains container is also great for creating your own fresh flours regularly, and is a great tool to keep separate for grinding rice and other wheat-free grains into flours if you or someone in your house follows a gluten-free diet.

LET'S EAT!

Cracked Wheat Cereal

With a whopping 9 grams of fiber, 8 grams of protein, and a delicious nutty flavor, you will find yourself making this cracked wheat cereal again and again. Delicious on its own or topped with fresh or dried fruit, toasted nuts, maple syrup, or your favorite milk.

PREPARATION: 10 minutes   PROCESSING: 15 seconds   COOK TIME: 15 to 20 minutes
YIELD: 3 cups (720 g) cooked cereal

1 cup (180 g) whole wheat kernels

3 cups (720 ml) water

½ teaspoon salt

1. Place the whole wheat kernels into the Vitamix dry grains container and secure the lid. Select Variable 1. Turn the machine on and slowly increase the speed to Variable 7 or 8. Grind to desired degree of fineness, or for about 15 seconds.

2. Combine the water and salt in a saucepan and bring to a boil. Slowly add the cracked wheat to the boiling water, whisking constantly. Reduce the heat to low, cover, and simmer until cooked, 15 to 20 minutes.

AMOUNT PER 1 CUP (240 ML) SERVING: calories 210, total fat 1.5 g, saturated fat 0 g, cholesterol 0 mg, sodium 400 mg, total carbohydrate 45 g, dietary fiber 9 g, sugars 0 g, protein 8 g

Apple Raisin Cracked Wheat Cereal

In the late 1930s, my grandma Ruth and my papa participated in one of Bernarr Macfadden's 265-mile hikes from Cleveland, Ohio, to Dansville, New York. These walks were sometimes called "cracked wheat derbies" because of the limited and healthy diet that the participants were fed. You don't need to go on a long walk to appreciate this hearty cracked wheat cereal in the morning, but we suspect that this delicious dish would have been popular on Macfadden's hikes!

PREPARATION: 15 minutes   PROCESSING: 25 seconds   COOK TIME: 15 to 20 minutes
YIELD: 3 cups (720 g) cooked cereal

1 cup (180 g) whole wheat kernels

1½ cups (360 ml) water

¼ teaspoon salt

1 tart apple (170 g), quartered and seeded

⅛ teaspoon ground cinnamon

½ cup (72 g) raisins

2 tablespoons (18 g) sunflower seeds

1. Place the whole wheat kernels into the Vitamix dry grains container and secure the lid. Select Variable 1. Turn the machine on and slowly increase the speed to Variable 7. Grind to the desired degree of fineness (ideally a coarse texture), about 15 seconds.

2. Combine the water and salt in a saucepan and bring to a boil. Slowly add the cracked wheat to the boiling water, whisking constantly. Reduce the heat to low, cover, and simmer, stirring frequently, until cooked but still al dente, 15 to 20 minutes.

3. Meanwhile, switch to the standard Vitamix container. Secure the lid and remove the lid plug. Select Variable 1. Turn the machine on and slowly increase the speed to Variable 4. With the machine running, drop the apple quarters through the lid plug opening (using the tamper as needed) and chop the apples, about 10 seconds.

4. Remove the pan from the heat and stir in the chopped apple, cinnamon, raisins, and sunflower seeds.

5. Cover and let stand for 5 minutes before serving.

AMOUNT PER 1 CUP (240 ML) SERVING: calories 360, total fat 3.5 g, saturated fat 0 g, cholesterol 0 mg, sodium 210 mg, total carbohydrate 75 g, dietary fiber 13 g, sugars 25 g, protein 10 g

Creamy Rice Cereal

This creamy, soothing cereal is the perfect use for that last ½ cup of rice. You can make the cereal with pretty much any variety of rice that you have on hand, and you won't lose a bit of the nutritional goodness because you are grinding it yourself. Brown rice will take slightly longer to cook, but the nutty, hearty flavor will be worth the wait!

PREPARATION: **10 minutes**　　PROCESSING: **10 seconds**　　COOK TIME: **8 to 10 minutes**
YIELD: **1¾ cups (420 ml) cooked cereal**

½ cup (93 g) uncooked rice

2 cups (480 ml) water

¼ teaspoon salt (optional)

1. Place the rice into the Vitamix dry grains container and secure the lid. Select Variable 1. Turn the machine on and slowly increase the speed to Variable 7 or 8. Grind to the desired degree of fineness, about 10 seconds to create cracked rice. If a finer cereal is desired, grind longer.

2. Combine the water and salt (if using) in a saucepan and bring to a boil. Slowly add the cracked rice to the boiling water, whisking constantly. Reduce the heat to low, cover, and simmer, stirring frequently, until cooked, 8 to 10 minutes (slightly longer for brown rice).

AMOUNT PER 1 CUP (240 ML) SERVING: calories 170, total fat 0 g, saturated fat 0 g, cholesterol 0 mg, sodium 340 mg, total carbohydrate 40 g, dietary fiber 0 g, sugars 0 g, protein 3 g

Apricot Brown Rice Cereal

Why limit delicious and undeniably nutritious brown rice to lunch or dinner? This hearty cereal, complete with dried apricots and sunflower seeds, will encourage you to see this healthy grain's good-morning potential.

PREPARATION: **10 minutes**   PROCESSING: **13 to 25 seconds**   COOK TIME: **20 minutes**
YIELD: **3½ cups (840 ml) cooked cereal**

1 cup (185 g) uncooked brown rice

3½ cups (840 ml) water

½ teaspoon salt

8 unsweetened dried apricots

2 tablespoons (18 g) sunflower seeds

¼ teaspoon almond extract (optional)

1. Place the brown rice into the Vitamix dry grains container and secure the lid. Select Variable 1. Turn the machine on and slowly increase the speed to Variable 7 or 8. Grind to the desired degree of fineness, about 10 seconds to create cracked rice, longer for finer cereal.

2. Combine the water and salt in a saucepan and bring to a boil. Slowly add the cracked rice to the boiling water, whisking constantly. Reduce the heat to low, cover, and simmer, stirring frequently, until cooked, about 20 minutes.

3. Meanwhile, switch to the standard Vitamix container. Select Variable 1. Secure the lid and remove the lid plug. Turn the machine on and slowly increase the speed to Variable 5. With the machine running, drop the apricots through the lid plug opening, processing to your desired texture. If necessary, adjust the Variable speed for a finer chop.

4. Remove the saucepan from the heat, add the chopped apricots, sunflower seeds, and almond extract (if using), and stir to combine.

5. Cover and let the mixture stand for 5 minutes before serving.

AMOUNT PER 1 CUP (240 ML) SERVING: calories 260, total fat 3 g, saturated fat 0.5 g, cholesterol 0 mg, sodium 350 mg, total carbohydrate 52 g, dietary fiber 4 g, sugars 8 g, protein 5 g

Oat Porridge

Oat groats—oats with the inedible outermost hull removed—are the least processed form of oat that you can buy at the grocery store. (Steel-cut oats are oat groats that have been cut just enough to reduce their cooking time.) This porridge will sustain you on even the most blustery of winter days!

PREPARATION: 10 minutes   PROCESSING: 10 seconds   COOK TIME: 35 minutes

YIELD: 3½ cups (840 ml) cooked cereal

1 cup (160 g) oat groats (NOT oatmeal)

4 cups (960 ml) water

½ teaspoon salt (optional, to taste)

1. Place the oat groats into the Vitamix dry grains container and secure the lid. Select Variable 1. Turn the machine on and slowly increase the speed to Variable 7. Grind to the desired degree of fineness, about 10 seconds. If a finer cereal is desired, grind longer.

2. Combine the water and salt (if using) in a saucepan and bring to a boil. Slowly add the cracked groats to the boiling water, whisking constantly. Reduce the heat to low, cover, and simmer, stirring frequently until cooked, about 30 minutes.

AMOUNT PER 1 CUP (240 ML) SERVING: calories 130, total fat 3 g, saturated fat 0 g, cholesterol 0 mg, sodium 340 mg, total carbohydrate 31 g, dietary fiber 5 g, sugars 1 g, protein 8 g

Crunchy Customized Granola

Once you start making this wonderful, crunchy granola you may wonder why you ever bought it! Feel free to get creative and use whatever nuts and seeds you have on hand. It is also delicious as a cereal with homemade Almond Milk (see page 354).

PREPARATION: **15 minutes**   PROCESSING: **20 seconds**   BAKE TIME: **40 to 55 minutes**
YIELD: **7 cups (1.7 liters)**

2 large egg whites

⅓ cup (80 ml) honey

¼ cup (60 ml) canola or vegetable oil

2 tablespoons (28 g) light brown sugar

½ teaspoon sea salt

1 teaspoon ground cinnamon

3 cups (240 g) rolled oats

½ cup (72 g) almonds

½ cup (60 g) pecan pieces

½ cup (58 g) walnut pieces

1 cup (80 g) unsweetened shredded coconut

½ cup (80 g) pumpkin seeds

¼ cup (40 g) golden flax seeds

1 cup (130 g) assorted unsweetened dried fruit (such as apricots, tart cherries, cranberries), cut into pieces

1. Preheat the oven to 300°F (150°C). Line 1 or 2 rimmed baking sheets (the mixture needs to be in a single layer) with parchment paper or silicone baking mats.

2. Place the egg whites, honey, canola oil, brown sugar, salt, and cinnamon into the Vitamix container in the order listed and secure the lid. Select Variable 1. Turn the machine on and slowly increase the speed to Variable 10, then to High. Blend for 20 seconds, or until well blended.

3. Combine the oats, nuts, coconut, pumpkin seeds, and flax seeds in a large bowl. Pour in the egg white mixture and stir well to combine.

4. Spread the mixture on the baking sheet(s) and bake for 40 to 55 minutes, stirring every 10 or 15 minutes, until light golden brown.

5. Cool the baking sheet(s) on a wire rack for 10 minutes, then transfer the granola to a large bowl and stir in the dried fruit pieces. (The granola will crisp as it cools.)

6. Store in an airtight container at room temperature.

AMOUNT PER ¼ CUP (60 ML) SERVING: calories 170, total fat 11 g, saturated fat 2.5 g, cholesterol 0 mg, sodium 50 mg, total carbohydrate 16 g, dietary fiber 3 g, sugars 7 g, protein 4 g

Vitamix Granola Bars

These granola bars are full of grains, nuts, and fruit (both fresh and dried), and they are destined to become a staple in your household! They have terrific flavor with much less fat and sugar than many other granola bars.

PREPARATION: 10 minutes   PROCESSING: 1 minute 10 seconds   BAKE TIME: 25 minutes
YIELD: 12 bars

¼ cup (50 g) wheat berries, or ½ cup (60 g) whole wheat flour, preferably homemade (page 44)

¼ cup (28 g) wheat germ

½ cup (70 g) raw almonds

1 cup (155 g) rolled oats

1 medium to large apple, cubed, or 1 cup plus 2 tablespoons (210 g) unsweetened applesauce

¼ teaspoon salt

1 teaspoon ground cinnamon

1 teaspoon vanilla extract

3 tablespoons (45 ml) honey or agave nectar

½ cup (60 g) dried unsweetened cranberries

1. Preheat the oven to 350°F (180°C). Grease an 8-inch (20-cm) square baking pan.

2. Place the wheat berries, wheat germ, almonds, and oats into the Vitamix dry grains container and secure the lid. Select Variable 1. Turn the machine on and slowly increase the speed to Variable 10, then to High. Blend for 30 seconds.

3. Turn the machine off and pour the mixture into a bowl.

4. If using an apple, place it into the standard Vitamix container and secure the lid. Select Variable 1. Turn the machine on and slowly increase the speed to Variable 10, then to High. Blend for 35 to 40 seconds, until the fruit has the consistency of applesauce, using the tamper to press the apple into the blades.

5. Add the applesauce to the bowl with the dry ingredients. Add the salt, cinnamon, vanilla, honey, and cranberries to the mixture. Mix gently by hand to combine.

6. Spread the mixture into the baking pan. Bake for 25 minutes.

7. Cool completely on a wire rack, then cut into bars in the pan.

AMOUNT PER BAR: calories 120, total fat 4 g, saturated fat 0 g, cholesterol 0 mg, sodium 50 mg, total carbohydrate 21 g, dietary fiber 3 g, sugars 10 g, protein 3 g

Artichoke, Red Pepper, and Parmesan Frittata

You may already be adding vegetables to your morning smoothie, but don't forget to add a few servings to your frittata. Here, the marinated artichokes and roasted red peppers are pureed in the Vitamix along with eggs, garlic, milk, and spices to produce a breakfast bursting with flavor. With only 10 to 15 minutes of cooking time, it is fast enough for a quick breakfast or dinner.

PREPARATION: **10 minutes**   PROCESSING: **20 seconds**   COOK TIME: **10 to 15 minutes**
YIELD: **5 servings**

2 tablespoons (30 ml) olive oil

¼ cup (60 ml) skim milk

3 large eggs

3 large egg whites

1 garlic clove, roasted and peeled

¼ teaspoon red pepper flakes

¼ teaspoon freshly cracked black pepper

One 7.5-ounce (213-g) jar grilled marinated artichoke hearts, drained

½ cup (100 g) marinated roasted red peppers, drained

⅓ cup (33 g) freshly grated Parmesan

Sea salt (optional)

1. Heat an 8-inch (20-cm) ovenproof skillet over medium heat. Add the olive oil.

2. Meanwhile, place the milk, whole eggs, egg whites, garlic, red pepper flakes, and black pepper into the Vitamix container in the order listed and secure the lid. Select Variable 1. Turn the machine on and slowly increase the speed to Variable 4. Blend for 10 seconds, or until smooth.

3. Stop the machine and remove the lid. Add the artichoke hearts and roasted red peppers and secure the lid. Select Variable 1. Turn the machine on and slowly increase the speed to Variable 3. Blend for 10 seconds.

4. Pour the egg mixture into the skillet. Cook over medium heat until the edges are lightly browned, 8 to 10 minutes. Sprinkle with the Parmesan.

5. Place the skillet under the broiler set on high. Broil for 1 to 2 minutes, until the top is lightly browned and no longer wet. Season with sea salt, if desired.

AMOUNT PER SERVING: calories 190, total fat 14 g, saturated fat 3 g, cholesterol 115 mg, sodium 410 mg, total carbohydrate 5 g, dietary fiber 2 g, sugars 1 g, protein 9 g

Corned Beef Hash

Chopping the ingredients for this tasty hash in your Vitamix blender makes the dish come together in a flash. Adding water with your vegetables—wet-chopping—helps the ingredients float above the blades, resulting in more evenly sized pieces. A few quick pulses and everything is ready! Drain the chopped food and proceed with the recipe as directed.

PREPARATION: **15 minutes**   PROCESSING: **pulsing**   COOK TIME: **20 minutes**   YIELD: **5 servings**

1¼ pounds (568 g) small red potatoes, halved

½ small onion, halved

1 small green bell pepper, cut into eighths

¼ pound (110 g) store-bought corned beef (sliced ½ inch / 1.3 cm thick), cut into 1½-inch (4-cm) pieces

2 tablespoons (30 ml) olive oil

¼ teaspoon ground black pepper

5 large eggs (optional)

1. Place the potatoes, onion, and bell pepper into the Vitamix container. Add water to just cover the vegetables and secure the lid. Select Variable 4. Use the On/Off switch to quickly pulse 5 times.

2. Pour the contents into a colander and drain well.

3. Add the corned beef to the Vitamix container and secure the lid. Select Variable 5. Use the On/Off switch to quickly pulse 4 times.

4. Heat the oil in a heavy 12-inch nonstick skillet over medium heat. Add the potato mixture and the corned beef. Stir in the black pepper. Cook, turning the mixture over with a spatula 2 or 3 times, until browned and crisp, 8 to 10 minutes.

5. If desired, make 5 depressions in the surface of the hash and crack an egg into each depression. Cover, reduce the heat to low, and cook until the potatoes are tender (and the eggs are cooked to the desired doneness), 8 to 10 minutes.

AMOUNT PER SERVING (WITHOUT EGGS): calories 130, total fat 4 g, saturated fat 1 g, sodium 280 mg, total carbohydrate 20 g, dietary fiber 3 g, sugars 3 g, protein 6 g

Apple Pancakes

An apple a day may or may not keep the doctor away, but apples do add wonderful flavor, moisture, and sweetness to these delicious pancakes. Try them topped with homemade Applesauce (page 246).

PREPARATION: 15 minutes   PROCESSING: 15 seconds   YIELD: enough batter for 10 pancakes

1 cup (120 g) whole wheat flour, preferably homemade (page 44)

1 tablespoon baking powder

½ teaspoon baking soda

½ teaspoon salt

3 tablespoons (38 g) sugar

¼ teaspoon ground nutmeg

1 cup (240 ml) skim milk

1 large egg

1½ teaspoons unsalted butter

1½ teaspoons vanilla extract

½ medium apple (3 oz / 85 g), cut into chunks

1. Combine the flour, baking powder, baking soda, salt, sugar, and nutmeg in a medium bowl and stir lightly. Set aside.

2. Place the milk, egg, butter, vanilla, and apple into the Vitamix container in the order listed and secure the lid. Select Variable 1. Turn the machine on and slowly increase the speed to Variable 8. Blend for 15 seconds.

3. Pour the milk mixture into the flour mixture and mix by hand just until combined.

4. For the best texture and flavor, let the batter sit for 5 to 10 minutes before using.

AMOUNT PER PANCAKE: calories 80, total fat 1.5 g, saturated fat 0.5 g, cholesterol 20 mg, sodium 340 mg, total carbohydrate 15 g, dietary fiber 2 g, sugars 6 g, protein 3 g

Oatmeal Cranberry Pancakes

After you whip up this tasty pancake batter, be sure to let it rest for 5 to 10 minutes on the counter before cooking. The resting time allows the oats and flax meal to soften a bit, resulting in a more delicious and tender pancake.

PREPARATION: 15 minutes   PROCESSING: 35 seconds   YIELD: 10 pancakes

1½ cups (360 ml) skim milk

¾ cup (90 g) whole wheat flour, preferably homemade (page 44)

2 teaspoons baking powder

½ teaspoon baking soda

½ teaspoon salt (optional)

¼ cup (40 g) flax meal

¾ cup (60 g) rolled oats

¼ cup (30 g) fresh cranberries

2 tablespoons (20 g) unsalted sunflower seeds

1. Place the milk, flour, baking powder, baking soda, and salt (if using) into the Vitamix container in the order listed and secure the lid. Select Variable 1. Turn the machine on and slowly increase the speed to Variable 10, then to High. Blend for 20 seconds.

2. Stop the machine and remove the lid. Add the flax meal, oats, cranberries, and sunflower seeds and secure the lid. Select Variable 2. Turn the machine on and blend for 15 seconds, using the tamper if necessary to press the ingredients into the blades.

3. For the best texture, let the batter sit for 5 to 10 minutes before using.

4. Drop ¼ cup (60 ml) batter for each pancake onto a nonstick griddle or skillet, and cook until golden brown, or about 3 minutes per side.

AMOUNT PER PANCAKE: calories 110, total fat 2.5 g, saturated fat 0 g, cholesterol 0 mg, sodium 180 mg, total carbohydrate 18 g, dietary fiber 3 g, sugars 4 g, protein 4 g

Curried Sweet Potato Pancakes

These pancakes are perfect for the mornings when you want something warm but aren't hungry for something sweet. Not only will you be able to skip the maple syrup here, but you will get a serving of vegetables too.

PREPARATION: **15 minutes**   PROCESSING: **35 seconds**   COOK TIME: **45 minutes**   YIELD: **12 pancakes**

2 large eggs

¼ cup (60 ml) low-fat (1%) milk

2 tablespoons (30 ml) light olive oil or vegetable oil

¼ cup (26 g) flax meal

2 tablespoons (5 g) fresh thyme leaves

2 cups (480 ml) grated peeled sweet potato (about 1 medium to large sweet potato)

2 tablespoons (30 ml) grated yellow onion

⅓ cup (40 g) whole wheat flour, preferably homemade (page 44)

1 teaspoon baking powder

½ teaspoon salt

½ teaspoon curry powder

1. Place the eggs, milk, olive oil, and flax meal into the Vitamix container in the order listed and secure the lid. Select Variable 1. Turn the machine on and slowly increase the speed to Variable 10. Blend for 20 seconds.

2. Stop the machine and remove the lid. Add the thyme to the container and secure the lid. Select Variable 1. Turn the machine on and slowly increase the speed to Variable 4. Blend for 15 seconds.

3. Combine the sweet potato, onion, flour, baking powder, salt, and curry powder in a medium bowl.

4. Pour the egg mixture into the sweet potato mixture and stir by hand just until combined.

5. Drop 2 tablespoons (30 ml) batter for each pancake onto a hot nonstick griddle. Cook until golden on the bottom, about 5 minutes. Flip, then press lightly and continue to cook until golden and cooked through, about 8 minutes longer.

AMOUNT PER PANCAKE: calories 80, total fat 4 g, saturated fat 0.5 g, cholesterol 30 mg, sodium 160 mg, total carbohydrate 8 g, dietary fiber 2 g, sugars 1 g, protein 3 g

Oatmeal Pancakes with Dried Cranberry Topping

These hearty pancakes give you another great way to add oats to your morning meal. The dried cranberry topping comes together in a snap and is so delicious you will find yourself spooning it on everything—a turkey sandwich, a dish of yogurt, maybe even a fall-inspired smoothie!

PREPARATION: **15 minutes**   PROCESSING: **15 seconds**   YIELD: **18 pancakes (2 per serving)**

TOPPING:

¼ cup (60 ml) water

2 tablespoons (30 ml) pure maple syrup

¾ cup (95 g) unsweetened dried cranberries

PANCAKES:

2 large eggs

2 cups (480 ml) skim milk

2 tablespoons (30 ml) vegetable oil

1½ tablespoons light brown sugar

1 cup (125 g) unbleached all-purpose flour

¾ cup (90 g) whole wheat flour, preferably homemade (page 44)

2 teaspoons baking powder

½ teaspoon ground cinnamon

¼ teaspoon salt

1 cup (84 g) rolled oats

1. For the topping: Combine the water, maple syrup, and cranberries in a small saucepan and bring to a boil. Remove from the heat and set aside, covered, until ready to serve.

2. For the pancakes: Place the eggs, milk, oil, and brown sugar into the Vitamix container in the order listed and secure the lid. Select Variable 1. Turn the machine on and slowly increase the speed to Variable 8. Blend for 15 seconds, until the mixture is creamy.

3. Combine the flours, baking powder, cinnamon, salt, and oats in a medium bowl.

4. Pour the milk mixture into the flour mixture and fold by hand just until blended.

5. Pour ¼ cup batter onto a nonstick skillet or griddle over medium-high heat, turning after 3 minutes or once the bottom side is golden brown. Cook until both sides are golden brown and firm to the touch.

6. Serve hot with the topping.

AMOUNT PER SERVING: calories 210, total fat 5 g, saturated fat 1 g, cholesterol 40 mg, sodium 210 mg, total carbohydrate 35 g, dietary fiber 3 g, sugars 9 g, protein 7 g

Gluten-Free Buttermilk Pancake Mix

Whip up this delicious gluten-free pancake mix in your Vitamix and you can have pancakes for breakfast or dinner at a moment's notice. Consider grinding your own brown rice and white rice flours too. (See page 36 for instructions.)

PREPARATION: 15 minutes   PROCESSING: 15 seconds
YIELD: 5 cups (1.2 liters), enough to make 20 pancakes

2½ cups (368 g) brown rice flour*

1 cup (160 g) potato starch

½ cup (60 g) amaranth flour

¼ cup (42 g) white rice flour*

1 cup (120 g) low-fat buttermilk powder

¼ cup (50 g) granulated sugar

4 teaspoons gluten-free baking powder

1 tablespoon baking soda

½ teaspoon salt

1½ teaspoons xanthan gum

*Make brown or white rice flour in your Vitamix (see page 36).

1. Place all the ingredients into the Vitamix container and secure the lid. Select Variable 1. Turn the machine on and slowly increase the speed to Variable 2 or 3. Blend for 15 seconds, or until combined, using the tamper as needed.

2. Use immediately or store the leftover mix, tightly covered in an airtight container and refrigerated, for up to 3 months. Whisk thoroughly to recombine before each use.

AMOUNT PER ¼ CUP (60 ML) SERVING: calories 150, total fat 1 g, saturated fat 0 g, cholesterol 5 mg, sodium 280 mg, total carbohydrate 31 g, dietary fiber 2 g, sugars 3 g, protein 4 g

Gluten-Free Pancakes

Once you have homemade gluten-free buttermilk pancake mix on hand, you can whip up these delicious pancakes anytime using basic pantry staples. Serve them with fresh fruit or maple syrup for a dish that will delight everyone at the table.

PREPARATION: 10 minutes   PROCESSING: 20 seconds

YIELD: 12 pancakes (about 3 pancakes per serving)

2 large eggs

1½ cups (360 ml) water

2 tablespoons (30 ml) vegetable oil

1⅓ cups (194 g) Gluten-Free Buttermilk Pancake Mix (page 33)

1. Place the eggs, water, and oil into the Vitamix container in the order listed and secure the lid. Select Variable 1. Turn the machine on and slowly increase the speed to Variable 5. Blend for 20 seconds.

2. Place the pancake mix in a medium bowl. Pour the egg mixture into the pancake mix and combine by hand until blended.

3. Let the batter rest for 5 minutes while a nonstick griddle or skillet heats.

4. Drop ¼ cup (60 ml) batter for each pancake onto the griddle or skillet and cook until golden on both sides.

AMOUNT PER SERVING: calories 360, total fat 14 g, saturated fat 2.5 g, cholesterol 130 mg, sodium 490 mg, total carbohydrate 49 g, dietary fiber 2 g, sugars 4 g, protein 11 g

Gluten-Free Ricotta Pancakes

The most delicious, aromatic, light, and fluffy pancakes you have ever tasted! And gluten-free too. Wonderful with blueberries or without.

PREPARATION: 15 minutes   PROCESSING: 20 seconds   YIELD: 12 pancakes

½ cup (120 ml) skim milk

2 tablespoons (30 ml) vegetable oil

4 large egg whites, lightly beaten

½ cup (120 ml) part-skim ricotta

½ cup (120 ml) plain 0% Greek yogurt, stirred

⅓ cup (73 g) firmly packed light brown sugar

Grated zest of 1 lemon

⅔ cup (89 g) gluten-free all-purpose flour mix

¼ teaspoon xanthan gum

1 teaspoon gluten-free baking powder

½ cup (74 g) blueberries, washed and patted completely dry

1. Place the milk, oil, egg whites, ricotta, yogurt, brown sugar, and lemon zest into the Vitamix container in the order listed and secure the lid. Select Variable 1. Turn the machine on and slowly increase the speed to Variable 10, then to High. Blend for 20 seconds.

2. Combine the gluten-free flour mix, xanthan gum, and baking powder in a medium bowl and whisk by hand.

3. Pour the ricotta mixture into the flour mixture and whisk together until well blended. Fold in the blueberries.

4. Let the batter rest for 5 minutes while heating a nonstick griddle or skillet. Lightly coat the griddle or skillet with cooking spray.

5. Scoop ¼ cup (60 ml) batter for each pancake onto the griddle and cook over medium-low heat until cooked through and golden on both sides, flipping once.

AMOUNT PER PANCAKE: calories 100, total fat 3.5 g, saturated fat 1 g, cholesterol 5 mg, sodium 80 mg, total carbohydrate 14 g, dietary fiber 1 g, sugars 8 g, protein 4 g

Gluten-Free Flour Mix

You can buy gluten-free flours, of course, but if you have the dry grains container for your Vitamix blender, you should consider grinding your own. This mix comes together quickly and will keep well in an airtight container in the refrigerator (for several months) or in the freezer (for 6 to 8 months).

PREPARATION: 10 minutes   PROCESSING: 30 seconds   YIELD: 7 cups (1.7 liters)

3 cups (556 g) white or brown rice

2½ cups (320 g) cornstarch

1½ cups (180 g) tapioca flour

1. Place the brown rice into the Vitamix dry grains container and secure the lid. Select Variable 1. Turn the machine on and slowly increase the speed to Variable 10, then to High. Blend for 30 seconds, or until the desired flour consistency is reached.

2. Pour into a large bowl and whisk in the cornstarch and tapioca flour until completely blended.

3. Store in an airtight container and whisk before each use.

AMOUNT PER ¼ CUP SERVING: calories 110, total fat 0 g, saturated fat 0 g, cholesterol 0 mg, sodium 0 mg, total carbohydrate 24 g, dietary fiber 1 g, sugars 0 g, protein 1 g

Buttermilk Cornmeal Waffles

Tempted by this recipe but out of buttermilk? Pour a scant 2 cups of 1% or 2% milk into a bowl or measuring cup. Add 2 tablespoons lemon juice or vinegar to the milk and allow it to thicken at room temperature for 10 to 15 minutes. Proceed with the recipe as directed!

PREPARATION: **10 minutes**   PROCESSING: **15 seconds**   YIELD: **10 waffles**

2 large eggs

2 cups (480 ml) low-fat buttermilk

¼ cup (60 ml) canola or vegetable oil

1 tablespoon light brown sugar

¾ cup (94 g) unbleached all-purpose flour

1¼ cups (150 g) whole wheat flour, preferably homemade (page 44)

¾ cup (118 g) cornmeal, preferably homemade (page 40)

2 teaspoons baking powder

1 teaspoon baking soda

¼ teaspoon salt

¼ teaspoon ground cinnamon

⅓ teaspoon ground ginger

1. Place the eggs, buttermilk, canola oil, and brown sugar into the Vitamix container in the order listed and secure the lid. Select Variable 1. Turn the machine on and slowly increase the speed to Variable 10, then to High. Blend for 15 seconds.

2. Combine the flours, cornmeal, baking powder, baking soda, salt, cinnamon, and ginger in a medium bowl.

3. Pour the buttermilk mixture into the flour mixture and fold by hand just until combined.

4. Preheat a waffle iron.

5. Pour the batter into the preheated waffle iron and cook for 2 to 3 minutes, or until the waffle maker indicates they are ready.

AMOUNT PER WAFFLE: calories 220, total fat 8 g, saturated fat 1 g, cholesterol 40 mg, sodium 350 mg, total carbohydrate 32 g, dietary fiber 2 g, sugars 4 g, protein 7 g

Banana Waffles

Like banana bread in your waffle maker! These sweet waffles, loaded with potassium, are lovely plain, as the bread for a peanut butter sandwich, or simply topped with maple syrup or fresh fruit.

PREPARATION: **10 minutes**   PROCESSING: **40 seconds**   YIELD: **10 waffles**

2 cups (240 g) whole wheat flour, preferably homemade (page 44)

1 tablespoon baking powder

1 teaspoon salt

3 large eggs

1½ cups (360 ml) skim milk

2 ripe bananas

3 tablespoons (40 g) unsalted butter

1. Combine the flour, baking powder, and salt in a medium bowl and stir lightly. Set aside.

2. Place the eggs, milk, bananas, and butter into the Vitamix container in the order listed and secure the lid. Select Variable 1. Turn the machine on and slowly increase the speed to Variable 6. Blend for 20 seconds.

3. Stop the machine and remove the lid. Add the flour mixture and secure the lid. Select Variable 1. Turn the machine on and slowly increase the speed to Variable 6. Blend for 20 seconds, using the tamper to press the ingredients into the blades.

4. For best texture and flavor, let the batter sit for 5 to 10 minutes before using.

5. Preheat a waffle iron.

6. Pour the batter into the preheated waffle iron and cook for 2 to 3 minutes, or until the waffle maker indicates they are ready.

AMOUNT PER WAFFLE: calories 170, total fat 6 g, saturated fat 3 g, cholesterol 65 mg, sodium 420 mg, total carbohydrate 25 g, dietary fiber 3 g, sugars 5 g, protein 7 g

Cornmeal

Making homemade flours, like this fresh cornmeal, is a snap in your Vitamix. Whip up a batch to use in the Cornmeal Pumpkin Spice Loaf (page 59) and save any leftover cornmeal in a tightly sealed container for another use.

PREPARATION: **5 minutes**   PROCESSING: **1 minute**   YIELD: **2⅔ cups (640 ml)**

2 cups (390 g) unpopped popcorn kernels

Place the popcorn kernels into the Vitamix container and secure the lid. Select Variable 1. Start the machine and slowly increase the speed to Variable 10, then to High. Grind to the desired degree of fineness, up to 1 minute. The longer the machine runs, the finer the consistency of the cornmeal.

AMOUNT PER ¼ CUP (60 ML) SERVING: calories 130, total fat 1.5 g, saturated fat 0 g, cholesterol 0 mg, sodium 0 mg, total carbohydrate 26 g, dietary fiber 4 g, sugars 0 g, protein 4 g

Baked Whole Wheat French Toast

Fragrant with vanilla, cinnamon, and nutmeg, this whole wheat French toast will quickly become a regular at your breakfast table! Baking the French toast gives you a golden brown, crispy result without any added oil.

PREPARATION: **10 minutes**   PROCESSING: **15 seconds**   BAKE TIME: **8 minutes**   YIELD: **6 servings**

1 large egg

2 large egg whites

¾ cup (180 ml) skim milk

1 tablespoon honey

1 teaspoon vanilla extract

¼ teaspoon ground cinnamon

⅓ teaspoon ground nutmeg

½ teaspoon baking powder

6 slices whole wheat bread, preferably homemade (page 47)

Fresh seasonal fruit (optional)

1. Place the whole egg, egg whites, milk, honey, vanilla, cinnamon, nutmeg, and baking powder into the Vitamix container in the order listed and secure the lid. Select Variable 1. Turn the machine on and slowly increase the speed to Variable 6. Blend for 15 seconds.

2. Place the bread slices in a single layer in a large, deep baking dish. Pour the egg mixture over the bread, cover, and refrigerate for 30 minutes.

3. Preheat the oven to 425°F (220°C). Line a large baking sheet with parchment paper or a silicone baking mat.

4. Remove the bread slices from the egg mixture and arrange them on the baking sheet. Bake for 8 minutes, flip, and bake for 8 minutes longer, or until crisp and golden.

5. Serve hot, topped with fresh fruit, if desired.

AMOUNT PER SERVING: calories 140, total fat 2 g, saturated fat 0 g, cholesterol 30 mg, sodium 200 mg, total carbohydrate 24 g, dietary fiber 3 g, sugars 7 g, protein 8 g

Vegan French Toast

This delicious vegan French toast is fast to make and full of flavor!

PREPARATION: **10 minutes**   PROCESSING: **30 seconds**   BAKE TIME: **25 minutes**   YIELD: **4 servings**

8 ounces (227 g) silken tofu, medium firmness

¾ cup (180 ml) water

1 teaspoon maple syrup

½ teaspoon ground cinnamon

1 tablespoon flax meal

1 medium banana

8 slices whole wheat bread, preferably homemade (page 47)

Fresh seasonal berries and maple syrup, for serving (optional)

1. Preheat the oven to 375°F (190°C). Line a baking sheet with parchment paper or a silicone baking mat.

2. Place the tofu, water, maple syrup, cinnamon, flax meal, and banana into the Vitamix container in the order listed and secure the lid. Select Variable 1. Turn the machine on and slowly increase the speed to Variable 10, then to High. Blend for 30 seconds.

3. Pour the mixture into a 9 × 13-inch (23 × 33-cm) baking dish. Place the bread in the batter and turn to coat both sides. Arrange the bread on the baking sheet.

4. Bake for 25 minutes, or until golden. Serve with fresh berries and maple syrup, if desired.

Baking French toast helps you make a tasty breakfast without adding any oil.

AMOUNT PER SERVING: calories 250, total fat 4 g, saturated fat 0 g, cholesterol 0 mg, sodium 270 mg, total carbohydrate 42 g, dietary fiber 5 g, sugars 9 g, protein 11 g

Breakfast Crepes

These nutty breakfast crepes are wonderfully adaptable. Fill the cooked crepes with your favorite sweet or savory filling, depending on your mood and the contents of your pantry. Cooked crepes keep, covered, in the refrigerator for 2 days.

PREPARATION: 10 minutes plus resting time   PROCESSING TIME: 25 seconds   YIELD: 8 large crepes

3 large eggs

½ cup (120 ml) low-fat (1%) milk

2 teaspoons canola oil

¾ cup (90 g) whole wheat flour, preferably homemade (page 44)

¼ cup (31 g) unbleached all-purpose flour

¼ teaspoon sea salt

½ cup (120 ml) seltzer water

1. Place the eggs, milk, canola oil, flours, and salt into the Vitamix container in the order listed and secure the lid. Select Variable 1. Turn the machine on and slowly increase the speed to Variable 10, then to High. Blend for 25 seconds, until smooth. Stop the machine, remove the lid, and scrape the sides of the container as needed.

2. Transfer the batter to a bowl. Cover and refrigerate for at least 1 hour and up to overnight.

3. When ready to cook, whisk the seltzer water into the batter.

4. Coat a medium skillet with cooking spray. Heat over medium-high heat.

5. Ladle ¼ cup (60 ml) to ⅓ cup (80 ml) batter into the center of the pan and immediately tilt and rotate the pan to spread the batter evenly over the bottom. Cook until the underside is lightly browned, 30 seconds to 1 minute. Flip the crepe and cook until lightly browned on the second side, about 20 seconds.

AMOUNT PER SERVING: calories 100, total fat 3.5 g, saturated fat 1 g, cholesterol 70 mg, sodium 105 mg, total carbohydrate 12 g, dietary fiber 1 g, sugars 1 g, protein 5 g

Whole-Grain Flour

PREPARATION: **5 minutes**   PROCESSING: **1 minute**
YIELD: **¼ to 2 cups (50 to 400 g) whole-kernel grains**

1. Place up to 2 cups (400 g) whole-kernel grain into the Vitamix dry grains container and secure the lid. Select Variable 1.

2. Turn the machine on and slowly increase the speed to Variable 10, then to High. Grind to the desired degree of fineness, up to 1 minute. The longer the machine runs, the finer the consistency of the flour.

The Benefits of Whole-Grain Flour

Talking about the benefits of whole-grain flours, Adam Wilson, our Senior Culinary Manager at Vitamix, says, "A grain kernel consists of three parts: the inner-most germ, the endosperm that surrounds the germ, and the bran that envelops both. Most of the kernel's nutrients are locked into the germ and bran. Whole-grain products, therefore, provide us with the full nutrient content of the grain kernel."

By grinding your own flour, you keep all of the nutrition of the whole grain, even after the grain is processed. But if we can buy whole-grain flours, why should we grind our own? There are a number of reasons. The flavor and aroma of ground flour are something special, and these qualities come through when you use the flour. If you are using a lot of specialty flours—teff, millet, and oat, for example—grinding your own flours from whole grains can be less expensive and taste better, too. Homemade flours can also be safer if you are avoiding gluten, because you can reduce the risk of cross-contamination. Please do note that, because the fresh flour will contain some oil, plan on either using the flour within a day or two or storing it in the refrigerator, so the flour does not become rancid.

Read the Whole Foods Success Stories about Shauna Ahern (page 60) and Janice Summers (page 254) for more about grinding your own flours.

Whole Wheat Muffins

These delicious, homey muffins can be enjoyed plain or split, toasted, and spread with your favorite topping. If you want to add a little extra flavor, fold in 1 cup of chopped dried fruit or chocolate chips once the wet and dry ingredients have been combined for an extra tasty treat!

PREPARATION: 10 minutes   PROCESSING: 30 seconds   BAKE TIME: 18 to 25 minutes
YIELD: 12 muffins

1½ cups (180 g) whole wheat flour, preferably homemade (page 44)

2 teaspoons baking powder

½ teaspoon salt

1 large egg

½ cup (120 ml) low-fat (1%) milk

½ cup (120 ml) unsweetened applesauce, preferably homemade (page 246)

¼ cup firmly packed (55 g) light brown sugar

¼ cup (60 ml) light olive oil

1 tablespoon maple syrup

1 tablespoon water

1¼ cups (200 g) pitted dates

1. Preheat the oven to 375°F (190°C). Line 12 cups of a muffin tin with paper liners.

2. Combine the flour, baking powder, and salt in a medium bowl.

3. Place the egg, milk, applesauce, brown sugar, olive oil, maple syrup, water, and dates into the Vitamix container in the order listed and secure the lid. Select Variable 1. Turn the machine on and slowly increase the speed to Variable 10, then to High. Blend for 30 seconds, or until well blended and creamy.

4. Pour the wet mixture into the flour mixture and fold by hand just until blended. Fill the muffin cups three-fourths full.

5. Bake for 18 to 25 minutes, until a toothpick inserted into the center of a muffin comes out clean.

6. Immediately transfer to a wire rack to cool.

AMOUNT PER MUFFIN: calories 180, total fat 6 g, saturated fat 1 g, cholesterol 15 mg, sodium 190 mg, total carbohydrate 32 g, dietary fiber 3 g, sugars 19 g, protein 3 g

Whole Wheat Bread

In the introduction, you read a story about my grandpa Bill taking time away from a family reunion to explain to a customer, step-by-step, how to make Vitamix bread. Grandpa Bill taught us the basics but Vitamix chef and recipe developer Bev Shaffer has added some advice of her own.

Pay careful attention to the instructions for this delicious bread. Not significantly more difficult than making a smoothie, but definitely more precise! Shaffer says that the most common mistake is overworking the dough once the liquid is added. Mixing the dough too long will overdevelop the gluten, and the resulting bread will be tough. Making bread in the Vitamix, just as without, takes practice. If at first you don't succeed, try and try again! The results are worth it.

PREPARATION: **10 minutes**   PROCESSING: **5 seconds to 1 minute plus pulsing**   BAKE TIME: **35 minutes**
YIELD: **1 loaf (10 slices)**

1¼ cups (300 ml) warm water (105° to 115°F / 40° to 46°C)

1 tablespoon honey

1 tablespoon active dry yeast

1½ cups (270 g) whole-kernel wheat, or 2¼ cups (270 g) whole wheat flour, preferably homemade (page 44)

1 teaspoon salt (optional)

1 tablespoon light olive or grapeseed oil

1 teaspoon fresh lemon juice

1 egg white mixed with 1 tablespoon water, for brushing dough (optional)

1. Combine the warm water, honey, and yeast in a bowl and stir quickly to combine. Set aside for 5 minutes to proof.

2. When starting with whole-kernel wheat: Place the wheat and salt (if using) into the Vitamix dry grains container and secure the lid. Select Variable 1. Turn the machine on and slowly increase the speed to Variable 10, then to High. Grind the wheat for 1 minute. (Do not overprocess.) Stop the machine to allow the flour to cool for a few minutes.

3. When starting with whole wheat flour: Place the flour and salt (if using) into the Vitamix dry grains container and secure the lid. Select Variable 1. Turn the machine on and slowly increase the speed to Variable 6. Blend until a hole forms in the center of the mixture, about 5 seconds.

4. Select Variable 3. Turn the machine on and remove the lid plug. Pour the oil, lemon juice, and yeast mixture through the lid plug opening. Stop the machine.

5. Replace the lid plug. Select High speed. Use the On/Off switch to quickly pulse 2 times. Stop the machine and remove the lid. Let the dough rest while greasing the pan.

6. Lightly coat an 8½ × 4½-inch (22 × 11-cm) loaf pan with cooking spray.

7. Use a spatula to scrape the sides of the Vitamix container. Pull the dough away from the container sides and into the center of the mixture. Replace the lid. Select High speed. Use the On/Off switch to quickly pulse 5 times. (Add additional water, 1 tablespoon at a time, only if the dough seems exceptionally dry.) Repeat the process 5 times, scraping the sides of the container each time, until the dough binds together into a soft, elastic mixture.

8. To remove the dough from the container, use the On/Off switch to quickly pulse 5 times (to assist in lifting the dough up and away from the blades). Invert the container over the loaf pan and let the dough fall into the pan. Use a wet spatula to remove any remaining dough from the container.

9. Use a wet or oiled spatula (or lightly floured fingers) to shape the loaf. Allow the dough to rise, covered with a clean, dry kitchen towel, until it is flush with the top of the bread pan, 20 to 25 minutes.

10. Meanwhile, preheat the oven to 350°F (180°C).

11. If desired, brush the loaf quickly and gently with the egg white wash. Using a sharp serrated knife, make 3 or 4 diagonal slits about ¼ inch deep on the top of the loaf.

12. Bake for 35 minutes, or until the bread is well browned and reaches an internal temperature of 190°F (88°C) when tested with an instant-read thermometer.

13. Cool in the pan on a wire rack for 10 minutes, then carefully turn out of the pan onto the rack to cool completely before slicing.

AMOUNT PER SLICE: calories 140, total fat 2 g, saturated fat 0 g, cholesterol 0 mg, sodium 240 mg, total carbohydrate 26 g, dietary fiber 4 g, sugars 2 g, protein 5 g

Wholesome Hearty Grain Breakfast "Cake"

What could be more exciting than cake for breakfast! True, this cake is not dripping with chocolate frosting or sprinkles, but it's full of hearty, nutty flavor that will keep you coming back for more.

PREPARATION: **20 minutes**   PROCESSING: **15 seconds**   BAKE TIME: **35 to 45 minutes**
YIELD: **10 servings**

1 cup (125 g) unbleached all-purpose flour

2 cups (240 g) whole wheat flour, preferably homemade (page 44)

½ cup (42 g) quick-cooking oats, plus 1 to 2 tablespoons for garnish

1 tablespoon baking powder

½ teaspoon sea salt

1½ cups (360 ml) low-fat (1%) milk

3 tablespoons (45 ml) vegetable oil

¼ cup firmly packed (55 g) light brown sugar

1 large egg

1. Preheat the oven to 350°F (180°C). Lightly coat the bottom only of an 8-inch (20-cm) round cake pan with cooking spray.

2. Combine the flours, ½ cup oats, baking powder, and salt in a medium bowl.

3. Place the milk, vegetable oil, brown sugar, and egg into the Vitamix container in the order listed and secure the lid. Select Variable 1. Turn the machine on and slowly increase the speed to Variable 8. Blend for 15 seconds, until a smooth, creamy consistency is reached.

4. Pour the milk mixture into the flour mixture and fold by hand just until moistened. Spread the batter in the pan and sprinkle with the remaining oats for garnish.

5. Bake for 35 to 45 minutes, until golden brown and a toothpick inserted into the center comes out clean.

6. Cool for 15 minutes in the pan, then turn out of the pan onto a wire rack to cool. Once cool, cut into 10 wedges before serving.

AMOUNT PER SERVING: calories 230, total fat 6 g, saturated fat 1 g, cholesterol 20 mg, sodium 290 mg, total carbohydrate 38 g, dietary fiber 3 g, sugars 8 g, protein 7 g

Breakfast and Brunch

Yogurt Bread with Fruit and Nuts

This moist, flavorful bread is full of grains (both whole wheat flour and bran flakes), dried fruit, and crunchy chopped nuts. Just sweet enough to taste like a treat, but with enough nutritional oomph to feel like a treat that you could have every day.

PREPARATION: **15 minutes**   PROCESSING: **10 to 15 seconds**   BAKE TIME: **45 minutes**

YIELD: **2 loaves (16 slices per loaf)**

1 cup (240 ml) low-fat buttermilk

¾ cup firmly packed (165 g) light brown sugar

½ cup (120 ml) plain 0% Greek yogurt, stirred

2 tablespoons (30 g) unsalted butter, melted

1 large egg

1¼ cups (150 g) whole wheat flour, preferably homemade (page 44)

1 cup (125 g) unbleached all-purpose flour

2 cups (77 g) bran flake cereal

2 teaspoons baking powder

2 teaspoons ground cinnamon

1 teaspoon baking soda

¼ teaspoon sea salt

1 cup (138 g) chopped almonds

1 cup (160 g) unsweetened dried fruit (such as raisins or chopped apricots, pineapple, or apples)

1. Preheat the oven to 350°F (180°C). Lightly coat two 8½ × 4½-inch (22 × 11-cm) loaf pans with cooking spray.

2. Place the buttermilk, brown sugar, yogurt, melted butter, and egg into the Vitamix container in the order listed and secure the lid. Select Variable 1. Turn the machine on and slowly increase the speed to Variable 10. Blend for 10 to 15 seconds, until a creamy consistency is reached.

3. Combine the flours, cereal, baking powder, cinnamon, baking soda, and salt in a large bowl.

4. Pour the buttermilk mixture into the flour mixture and stir by hand just until combined. Stir in the almonds and dried fruit. Divide the batter between the pans.

5. Bake for 45 minutes, or until a toothpick inserted into the center comes out clean.

6. Cool for 10 minutes in the pans, then turn out onto a wire rack to cool completely before slicing.

AMOUNT PER SLICE: calories 110, total fat 3.5 g, saturated fat 1 g, cholesterol 10 mg, sodium 120 mg, total carbohydrate 19 g, dietary fiber 2 g, sugars 10 g, protein 3 g

Bran Cherry Muffins

With crunchy toasted almonds, chewy dried cherries, and spices, these bran muffins are great for a quick breakfast or an afterschool snack. Enjoy these along with the knowledge that you are getting a good dose of calcium, protein, and fiber along with an unbeatable taste!

PREPARATION: **10 minutes**   PROCESSING: **15 seconds**   BAKE TIME: **20 to 25 minutes**
YIELD: **12 muffins**

1½ cups (90 g) wheat bran

1¼ cups (300 ml) skim milk

2 large eggs

⅓ cup (80 ml) molasses

4 to 5 tablespoons (60 to 75 ml) plain 0% Greek yogurt, stirred

1 tablespoon light brown sugar

1½ cups (180 g) whole wheat flour, preferably homemade (page 44)

1 tablespoon baking powder

½ teaspoon baking soda

1 teaspoon ground cinnamon

¾ teaspoon ground ginger

¼ teaspoon sea salt

¾ cup (103 g) coarsely chopped almonds, toasted

⅔ cup (80 g) unsweetened dried tart cherries

1. Preheat the oven to 350°F (180°C). Lightly coat 12 cups of a muffin tin with cooking spray or line with paper liners.

2. Combine the wheat bran and milk in a medium bowl. Let stand for 10 minutes, or until most of the milk is absorbed.

3. Transfer the milk and bran to the Vitamix container. Add the eggs, molasses, 4 tablespoons (60 ml) of the yogurt, and the brown sugar in the order listed and secure the lid. Select Variable 1. Turn the machine on and slowly increase the speed to Variable 10, then to High. Blend for 15 seconds. If the batter is too dry, add additional yogurt.

4. Combine the flour, baking powder, baking soda, cinnamon, ginger, and salt in a medium bowl.

5. Pour the egg mixture into the flour mixture and fold by hand just until combined. Stir in the almonds and cherries.

6. Scrape the batter into the muffin cups and bake for 20 to 25 minutes, or until a toothpick inserted into the center comes out with a few moist crumbs. Serve warm.

AMOUNT PER MUFFIN: calories 200, total fat 6 g, saturated fat 0.5 g, cholesterol 30 mg, sodium 260 mg, total carbohydrate 33 g, dietary fiber 6 g, sugars 14 g, protein 7 g

Individual Orange Cranberry Biscuits

Perfect for a fall brunch or a breakfast treat for Thanksgiving houseguests, these tender biscuits are bursting with tart cranberries, orange zest, and the gentle perfume of vanilla.

PREPARATION: **15 minutes**   PROCESSING: **20 seconds**   BAKE TIME: **30 to 35 minutes**
YIELD: **12 biscuits**

1¼ cups (150 g) whole wheat flour, preferably homemade (page 44)

1 cup (125 g) unbleached all-purpose flour

2¼ teaspoons baking powder

½ teaspoon baking soda

¼ teaspoon sea salt

1¼ cups (300 ml) plain 0% Greek yogurt, stirred

¼ cup (60 ml) fresh orange juice (page 301)

⅓ cup firmly packed (73 g) light brown sugar

1 tablespoon grated orange zest

1 teaspoon vanilla extract

1 cup (100 g) frozen cranberries, coarsely chopped

¼ cup (60 ml) reduced-fat (2%) milk

1. Preheat the oven to 400°F (200°C). Line a baking sheet with parchment paper or a silicone baking mat.

2. Combine the flours, baking powder, baking soda, and salt in a medium bowl.

3. Place the yogurt, orange juice, brown sugar, orange zest, and vanilla into the Vitamix container in the order listed and secure the lid. Select Variable 1. Turn the machine on and slowly increase the speed to Variable 10, then to High. Blend for 20 seconds.

4. Pour the yogurt mixture into the flour mixture and fold in the cranberries.

5. On a floured surface, pat the dough into a 9-inch (23-cm) round about ½ inch (1.3 cm) thick. Cut into 12 wedges.

6. Place the wedges on the baking sheet and brush the tops with the milk. Bake for 30 to 35 minutes, until lightly browned.

7. Remove from the baking sheet and cool on a wire rack.

AMOUNT PER BISCUIT: calories 130, total fat 0.5 g, saturated fat 0 g, cholesterol 0 mg, sodium 210 mg, total carbohydrate 26 g, dietary fiber 2 g, sugars 8 g, protein 5 g

Oatmeal Breakfast Muffins with Raisins

All of the wonderful and cozy flavors we love in a bowl of oatmeal—the raisins, cinnamon, and brown sugar—in a convenient, handheld package. Perfect with a cup of tea or tucked in a lunch box for a not-too-sweet dessert.

PREPARATION: **15 minutes**   PROCESSING: **20 seconds**   BAKE TIME: **18 to 20 minutes**

YIELD: **12 muffins**

1 cup (80 g) rolled oats

1 cup (240 ml) low-fat buttermilk

¾ cup (90 g) whole wheat flour, preferably homemade (page 44)

¾ teaspoon baking soda

½ teaspoon baking powder

¼ teaspoon salt

½ teaspoon ground cinnamon

2 large eggs

⅓ cup firmly packed (73 g) light brown sugar

3 tablespoons (45 ml) plain 0% Greek yogurt, stirred

3 tablespoons (45 ml) olive oil

⅓ cup (53 g) raisins

1. Combine the oats and buttermilk in a bowl and set aside to soften for 15 minutes.

2. Preheat the oven to 375°F (190°C). Coat 12 cups of a muffin tin with cooking spray or line with paper liners.

3. Combine the flour, baking soda, baking powder, salt, and cinnamon in a medium bowl.

4. Place the eggs, brown sugar, yogurt, and olive oil into the Vitamix container in the order listed and secure the lid. Select Variable 1. Turn the machine on and slowly increase the speed to Variable 10, then to High. Blend for 20 seconds, or until a creamy consistency is reached.

5. Stir the soaked oats and any remaining liquid into the flour mixture. Pour in the egg mixture and stir just until combined. Fold in the raisins.

6. Spoon the batter into the muffin cups, filling them about two-thirds full. Bake for 18 to 20 minutes, or until a toothpick inserted into the center of a muffin comes out with a few moist crumbs.

7. Let the muffins cool in the pan for 10 minutes, then transfer to a wire rack to cool.

AMOUNT PER MUFFIN: calories 140, total fat 5 g, saturated fat 1 g, cholesterol 30 mg, sodium 190 mg, total carbohydrate 21 g, dietary fiber 2 g, sugars 11 g, protein 4 g

Pumpkin Puree

This homemade pumpkin puree is a snap to make and perfect for quick breads like Pumpkin Bread (page 57) or Cornmeal Pumpkin Spice Loaf (page 59). We like to make a double or even triple batch of this puree and freeze the leftovers. Simply thaw the puree as you need it for soups, quick breads, or muffins.

PREPARATION: **5 minutes**   PROCESSING: **30 seconds**   YIELD: **2½ cups (600 ml)**

2 cups (440 g) cubed roasted fresh pumpkin

½ cup (120 ml) low-sodium vegetable broth

¼ teaspoon ground ginger

¼ teaspoon ground cinnamon

Place all the ingredients into the Vitamix container in the order listed and secure the lid. Select Variable 1. Turn the machine on and slowly increase the speed to Variable 10, then to High. Blend for 30 seconds, using the tamper to push the ingredients into the blade.

Use this simple recipe in place of canned pumpkin. The average can of pumpkin puree is 15 ounces. This recipe yields 20 ounces.

AMOUNT PER ½ CUP (120 ML) SERVING: calories 20, total fat 0 g, saturated fat 0 g, cholesterol 0 mg, sodium 25 mg, total carbohydrate 5 g, dietary fiber 1 g, sugars 2 g, protein 1 g

Pumpkin Bread

The recipe for this delicious, tender, lightly spiced pumpkin bread makes two loaves: one to enjoy now, the other to share or freeze. Be sure to try toasting the thickly sliced bread and serving it with your favorite spread.

PREPARATION: **15 minutes**   PROCESSING: **30 seconds**   BAKE TIME: **45 to 55 minutes**

YIELD: **2 loaves (16 slices per loaf)**

½ cup (120 ml) low-fat (1%) milk

⅔ cup (160 ml) unsweetened applesauce, preferably homemade (page 246)

One 15-ounce (425-g) can unsweetened pumpkin puree, or 2 cups homemade pumpkin puree (page 55)

2 teaspoons vanilla extract

2 large eggs

4 large egg whites

¼ cup (60 ml) honey

½ cup firmly packed (110 g) dark brown sugar

2 cups (240 g) whole wheat flour, preferably homemade (page 44)

1 cup (125 g) unbleached all-purpose flour

2 teaspoons baking soda

½ teaspoon baking powder

1 teaspoon salt

1 teaspoon ground cinnamon

½ teaspoon ground cloves

Crystallized ginger, for garnish

1. Preheat the oven to 350°F (180°C). Lightly coat the bottoms only of two 8½ × 4½-inch (22 × 11-cm) loaf pans with cooking spray.

2. Place the milk, applesauce, pumpkin puree, vanilla, whole eggs, egg whites, honey, and brown sugar into the Vitamix container in the order listed and secure the lid. Select Variable 1. Turn the machine on and slowly increase the speed to Variable 10, then to High. Blend for 30 seconds, or until the mixture is creamy and smooth.

3. Combine the flours, baking soda, baking powder, salt, cinnamon, and cloves in a large bowl.

4. Pour the pumpkin mixture into the flour mixture and fold by hand just until blended.

5. Scrape the batter into the pans and bake for 45 to 55 minutes, until a toothpick inserted into the center comes out clean.

6. Cool in the pans for 20 minutes, then turn out of the pans onto a wire rack. Garnish with crystallized ginger if desired.

AMOUNT PER SLICE: calories 80, total fat 0.5 g, saturated fat 0 g, cholesterol 10 mg, sodium 170 mg, total carbohydrate 16 g, dietary fiber 2 g, sugars 7 g, protein 3 g

Flecks of Zucchini Cornbread

A perfect recipe for the days when gardens, grocery stores, and farmstands are overflowing with zucchini. This tasty bread gets a gentle sweetness from brown sugar and dates and a whole-grain boost from whole wheat flour and cornmeal.

PREPARATION: 15 minutes   PROCESSING: 15 seconds   BAKE TIME: 45 to 55 minutes

YIELD: 1 loaf (16 slices)

½ cup (120 ml) plain 0% Greek yogurt, stirred

2 large eggs

½ cup (120 ml) low-fat buttermilk

⅓ cup (73 g) firmly packed light brown sugar

2 pitted dates

1 cup (125 g) unbleached all-purpose flour

½ cup (60 g) whole wheat flour, preferably homemade (page 44)

¾ cup (92 g) whole-grain cornmeal, preferably homemade (page 40)

1 teaspoon baking powder

½ teaspoon baking soda

½ teaspoon sea salt

One 10-ounce (284-g) zucchini, coarsely grated and well drained

1. Preheat the oven to 350°F (180°C). Lightly coat a 9 × 5-inch (33 × 13-cm) loaf pan with cooking spray.

2. Place the yogurt, eggs, buttermilk, brown sugar, and dates into the Vitamix container in the order listed and secure the lid. Select Variable 1. Turn the machine on and slowly increase the speed to Variable 10. Blend for 15 seconds, or until well blended and creamy.

3. Combine the flours, cornmeal, baking powder, baking soda, and salt in a medium bowl.

4. Stir the zucchini into the flour mixture. Pour the yogurt mixture into the bowl and fold by hand just until blended.

5. Scrape the batter into the pan and gently smooth the top. Bake for 45 to 55 minutes, until golden and a toothpick inserted into the center comes out clean.

6. Cool in the pan for 15 minutes, then turn out of the pan onto a wire rack to cool completely.

AMOUNT PER SLICE: calories 110, total fat 1 g, saturated fat 0 g, cholesterol 25 mg, sodium 70 mg, total carbohydrate 21 g, dietary fiber 1 g, sugars 8 g, protein 4 g

The Vitamix Cookbook

Cornmeal Pumpkin Spice Loaf

Pumpkin, spices, whole-grain flours, and chocolate chips too? This tasty loaf is equally at home at breakfast, tucked in a briefcase for an on-the-go snack, or alongside a cup of tea in the afternoon.

PREPARATION: **15 minutes**   PROCESSING: **20 seconds**   BAKE TIME: **35 to 40 minutes**
YIELD: **1 loaf (16 slices)**

½ cup (61 g) whole-grain cornmeal, preferably homemade (page 40)

1¼ cups (150 g) whole wheat flour, preferably homemade (page 44)

2½ teaspoons baking powder

½ teaspoon baking soda

¼ teaspoon salt

½ teaspoon ground cinnamon

½ teaspoon ground nutmeg

½ teaspoon ground ginger

⅓ teaspoon ground allspice

⅓ teaspoon ground black pepper

¾ cup (180 ml) low-fat buttermilk

⅓ cup (80 ml) light olive oil

2 large eggs

1 large egg white

⅓ cup firmly packed (73 g) light brown sugar

1 cup (240 ml) unsweetened pumpkin puree, preferably homemade (page 55)

¼ cup (60 g) dark chocolate chips

1. Preheat the oven to 350°F (180°C). Lightly coat an 8 × 4½-inch (22 × 11-cm) loaf pan with cooking spray.

2. Combine the cornmeal, flour, baking powder, baking soda, salt, cinnamon, nutmeg, ginger, allspice, and pepper in a medium bowl. Set aside.

3. Place the buttermilk, olive oil, whole eggs, egg white, brown sugar, and pumpkin puree into the Vitamix container in the order listed and secure the lid. Select Variable 1. Turn the machine on and slowly increase the speed to Variable 10, then to High. Blend for 20 seconds, or until the mixture has a creamy consistency.

4. Pour the pumpkin mixture into the flour mixture. Add the chocolate chips and fold by hand just until combined.

5. Scrape the batter into the loaf pan and bake for 35 to 40 minutes, until a toothpick inserted into the center comes out clean.

6. Cool for 15 minutes on a wire rack, then remove from the pan to cool completely before cutting.

AMOUNT PER SLICE: calories 140, total fat 7 g, saturated fat 2 g, cholesterol 25 mg, sodium 140 mg, total carbohydrate 18 g, dietary fiber 2 g, sugars 7 g, protein 3 g

Shauna Ahern

When expecting a first baby, many people expect to get baby clothes or perhaps a car seat. But a Vitamix blender? That's just what Shauna and Danny Ahern received when they were expecting their daughter back in 2008. Shauna, a writer, and Danny, a chef, collaborate on the award-winning blog *Gluten-Free Girl and the Chef* (www .glutenfreegirl.com). After the couple announced their news on their site, a generous reader sent the couple a Vitamix machine to celebrate all of the changes that a new baby would bring.

Shauna and Danny began using it immediately, and like many Vitamix users, they use their machine almost daily. Their daughter, Lucy, is six now, and both she and the machine are going strong. The Aherns appreciate their Vitamix blender's ability to produce delightfully smooth soups and perfectly emulsified smoothies. Shauna also loves to make whole-grain crepe batter. Says Shauna, "If I want to make buckwheat crepes in the morning, I mix whole buckwheat groats with a bit of yogurt and water and let it sit all night. In the morning I add a bit of baking powder, a touch of sugar, and some salt, and whirl it up with eggs. Perfect crepe batter, every time."

Shauna has celiac disease—hence the gluten-free focus of their blog—so the Aherns also like being able to grind their own flours. Shauna says that there are many good sources of reliable gluten-free whole grains and that, in her experience, grinding her own flours is generally cheaper than buying them. The Aherns grind teff, millet, oat, sorghum, and buckwheat flours, usually just grinding enough for the particular recipe. (Since 100 grams of teff equals 100 grams of teff flour, it is simple to just grind what you need. As with much of baking, and particularly gluten-free baking, using a digital scale and measuring ingredients by weight will give you the best, most consistent product.) "Fresh flours taste the best in baked goods," Shauna tells us.

To make flour, Shauna says, "I put a bit of grain in the blender, grind it on low speed. Turn off the blender and scrape down the sides with a rubber spatula. And then I turn the Vitamix on High. Afterward, I sift the flour through a fine-mesh sieve to catch any parts of the bran or hull that wasn't fully ground. The whole thing takes about 10 minutes." By using gluten-free grains and grinding them herself, Shauna can fully enjoy her baked goods without any fear of cross-contamination. Thanks to their homemade flours, the bread she is able to make is delicious and reliably gluten-free too.

Oat Porridge (page 22)

Muhammara (page 83)

Edamame Dip
(page 73)

Mango Salsa
(page 79)

Avocado Tahini Dip
(page 66)

Roasted
Red Pepper
Hummus
(page 71)

Chapter 3

Appetizers

My grandma embraced healthy eating as passionately as Grandpa and Papa did. After all, it was her father's health that inspired our family to explore health through whole foods in the first place! She, like many of us, loved to entertain, and she struggled with having enough nutritious recipes that tasted fantastic in order to keep her guests coming back. She was on a mission. Over the years, Grandma worked tirelessly to develop ever more delicious and diverse recipes and techniques for the Vitamix, so she and others would have lots of tasty options to choose from when cooking at home.

Flash-forward to today. My grandma would certainly not have to wonder what to offer her guests now. The delicious recipes in this chapter would have given her lots of good choices. These recipes are quick to assemble, delicious, and—of course—nutritious. Many of the recipes use staples you may already have in your pantry or refrigerator, such as canned beans, lemons, and herbs. By making your own appetizers instead of buying prepared items from a store, you can control the amount of added salt and fat in your offerings—not to mention eliminating preservatives and other hidden additives. You can easily accommodate a vegan, vegetarian, or gluten-free guest as well.

You can serve these delicious dips and spreads with accompaniments as diverse as the recipes themselves. Baked tortilla chips or bell pepper strips are delicious with the bean dip, the bean and cheese dip, the guacamole, or any of the salsas. Scoop up Avocado Tahini Dip (page 66), Cannellini Bean Hummus (page 70), or

Two-Cheese Spread with Spinach (page 90) with whole-grain crackers or steamed asparagus and green beans. Goat Cheese Crostini with Roasted Red Pepper Spread (page 87) and Edamame Dip or Pâté (page 73) spread on homemade crostini are both elegant passed appetizers.

Buy at the Store or DIY

Many of the dips and snacks in this chapter include foods such as salsa and tahini. To control the amount of added salt or fat in these foods, we recommend making them at home.

Homemade roasted red peppers: Use the recipe included in Roasted Red Pepper Hummus (page 71).

Homemade salsa: Our California Salsa (page 80) is so fresh, fast, simple, and delicious, you'll think twice before buying another jar at the store. The cheese and bean dip in this chapter calls for ½ cup salsa, so simply whip up the full recipe of salsa, use what you need for the cheese dip, and serve the remainder alongside the bean dip.

Homemade tahini: Tahini, a sesame seed paste, is a common ingredient in hummus, and we use it in several of the bean dips in this chapter. To make your own, use the recipe on page 67.

Homemade pita chips or crostini: You can buy pita chips and crackers, of course, but you can easily make your own. Both DIY pita chips and crostini are a great way to use up slightly stale bread. Plus, you can add your favorite spices and herbs while also controlling the amount of salt and fat that is added. Win-win!

TO MAKE PITA CHIPS OR CROSTINI: Preheat the oven to 375°F (190°C). Slice 6 pitas into eighths or cut one whole-grain baguette crosswise into ¼-inch-thick slices. Toss with 2 tablespoons olive oil or coat with olive oil cooking spray. Sprinkle with ¼ teaspoon sea salt. (You can also add a pinch of chili powder or a teaspoon of your favorite minced fresh herb.) Spread the pita wedges or bread slices in an even layer on a foil-lined baking sheet. Bake until golden brown and crisp, turning occasionally, 8 to 10 minutes. Store the cooled chips in a container with a tight-fitting lid.

Great at a Party, Delicious in a Brown-Bag Lunch

These dips, spreads, and nibbles will all be so delicious that you will hope for leftovers. Bringing your own lunch to school or work can be healthier and cheaper than buying it, and many of these tasty dips are delicious additions to your brown-bag lunch. As a kid, my dad, John, may have felt a bit self-conscious about the healthy lunch his mother packed, but times have changed. You will feel glad to have your own nutritious meal on hand. Spread leftover Black Bean Hummus (page 69) or Edamame Chickpea Dip (page 74) on whole-grain bread and top with fresh veggies for a delicious sandwich. The bean spread would also be delicious in a quesadilla with a little shredded cheddar, spinach, and a spoonful of salsa. Pack a small container of leftover Avocado Tahini Dip (page 66) or Hummus (page 68) with cut veggies, pretzels, or pita bread for a tasty lunch or snack. If you have access to a microwave, treat yourself to a little Hot Crab and Artichoke Dip (page 85) with crostini for dipping and perhaps a small salad on the side. Enjoy a lunch to rival the best takeout!

Avocado Tahini Dip

This vibrantly green dip will be the star of your next party! This dip is creamy with avocado, a little nutty from the tahini, bursting with herby flavor, and beautifully green, thanks to the herbs and a little steamed spinach or arugula. Great as a sandwich spread too.

PREPARATION: 10 minutes   PROCESSING: 35 to 40 seconds   YIELD: 2¼ cups (540 ml)

⅓ cup (80 ml) tahini, prefererably homemade (page 67)

Juice of 1 lemon (about 3 tablespoons / 45 ml)

1 large avocado, halved, pitted, and peeled

½ teaspoon ground cumin

1 tablespoon fresh flat-leaf parsley leaves

1 tablespoon fresh dill leaves

¼ teaspoon ground black pepper

4 ounces (114 g) baby spinach or arugula, steamed for 20 minutes, then cooled

¼ cup (60 ml) water

Place all the ingredients into the Vitamix container in the order listed and secure the lid. Select Variable 1. Turn the machine on and slowly increase the speed to Variable 10, then to High. Blend for 35 to 40 seconds, using the tamper to press the ingredients into the blades if necessary.

AMOUNT PER 2 TABLESPOON (30 ML) SERVING: calories 50, total fat 4 g, saturated fat 0.5 g, cholesterol 0 mg, sodium 10 mg, total carbohydrate 3 g, dietary fiber 1 g, sugars 0 g, protein 1 g

Tahini

When buying sesame seeds, you can often find larger containers of them at discounted prices in the Asian food section of the grocery store. Toasting the seeds at home gives the tahini a more intense flavor. To toast, bake the seeds at 350°F (180°C) for about 5 minutes or until light brown. Do not overcook.

PREP TIME: **10 minutes**   PROCESSING: **1 to 2 minutes**   YIELD: **2 ½ cups (600 g)**

5 cups (640 g) sesame seeds, lightly toasted

Place the sesame seeds into the Vitamix container and secure the lid. Select Variable 1. Turn the machine on and quickly increase the speed to Variable 10, then to High. Blend for 1 to 2 minutes, using the tamper to press the mixture into the blades. Blend until the tahini has the consistency of peanut butter and all the seeds are completely ground.

AMOUNT PER 2 TABLESPOON (30 G) SERVING: calories 170, total fat 15 g, saturated fat 2 g, cholesterol 0 g, sodium 0 mg, total carbohydrate 7 g, dietary fiber 4 g, sugars 0 g, protein 5 g

Hummus

Many hummus recipes call for tahini (including several in this book), but we also like the fresh, nutty flavor that comes from using raw sesame seeds. Thanks to the Vitamix's unparalleled blending power, the texture of this classic hummus is still silky smooth.

PREPARATION: **10 minutes**   PROCESSING: **1 minute**   YIELD: **3½ cups (840 ml)**

Two 15-ounce (425-g) cans chickpeas

¼ cup (35 g) raw sesame seeds

1 tablespoon olive oil

¼ cup (60 ml) fresh lemon juice

1 garlic clove, peeled

1 teaspoon ground cumin

1 teaspoon kosher salt

1. Rinse and drain one can of the chickpeas. Leave the second can undrained.

2. Place the chickpeas (and the liquid from the second can) into the Vitamix container along with the other ingredients in the order listed and secure the lid. Select Variable 1. Turn the machine on and slowly increase the speed to Variable 10, then to High. Blend for 1 minute, using the tamper to press the ingredients into the blades.

AMOUNT PER 2 TABLESPOON (30 ML) SERVING: calories 35, total fat 1.5 g, saturated fat 0 g, cholesterol 0 mg, sodium 125 mg, total carbohydrate 5 g, dietary fiber 1 g, sugars 0 g, protein 1 g

Black Bean Hummus

Out of chickpeas? Whip up this tasty black bean hummus instead. You can use it as a spread in a sandwich or with crunchy vegetables for dipping.

PREPARATION: **10 minutes**   PROCESSING: **30 seconds**   YIELD: **3 cups (720 ml)**

Two 15-ounce (425-g) cans no-salt-added black beans

¼ teaspoon sea salt

¼ teaspoon ground black pepper

2 garlic cloves, peeled

¼ cup (60 ml) tahini, preferably homemade (page 67)

½ teaspoon grated lemon zest

2 tablespoons (30 ml) fresh lemon juice

1 tablespoon olive oil

1. Rinse and drain one can of the black beans. Leave the second can undrained.

2. Place the beans (including the liquid from the undrained can) and all the remaining ingredients into the Vitamix container in the order listed and secure the lid. Select Variable 1. Turn the machine on and slowly increase the speed to Variable 10, then to High. Blend for 30 seconds, using the tamper to press the ingredients into the blades.

Change the flavor profile by using roasted or sautéed garlic instead of raw, or add cumin or chili powder.

AMOUNT PER 2 TABLESPOON (30 ML) SERVING: calories 40, total fat 2 g, saturated fat 0 g, cholesterol 0 mg, sodium 30 mg, total carbohydrate 4 g, dietary fiber 1 g, sugars 0 g, protein 2 g

Cannellini Bean Hummus

Canned beans should be a pantry staple, and this delicious cannellini bean hummus may very well persuade you to always keep them in stock. This dip is packed with flavor from ingredients you may already have on hand. It has the brightness of lemon and a little hot sauce, the herbiness of thyme, a gentle heat from the garlic, and the creamy goodness of cannellini beans all in a single dip! Spread it on crudités for a snack or in a pita for a quick sandwich.

PREPARATION: **10 minutes**   PROCESSING: **45 seconds**   YIELD: **3½ cups (840 ml)**

Two 15-ounce (425-g) cans no-salt-added cannellini beans

1 teaspoon grated lemon zest

½ lemon, peeled

¼ cup (60 ml) tahini, preferably homemade (page 67)

3 garlic cloves, roasted and peeled

½ teaspoon chili powder

1 tablespoon fresh thyme leaves

½ teaspoon sea salt

2 dashes of hot sauce

1. Rinse and drain one can of the cannellini beans. Leave the second can undrained.

2. Place the beans (including the liquid from the undrained can) and all the remaining ingredients into the Vitamix container in the order listed and secure the lid. Select Variable 1. Turn the machine on and slowly increase the speed to Variable 5. Blend for 15 seconds.

3. Slowly increase the speed to Variable 10, then to High. Blend for 30 seconds, using the tamper to push the ingredients into the blades.

AMOUNT PER 2 TABLESPOON (30 ML) SERVING: calories 30, total fat 1.5 g, saturated fat 0 g, cholesterol 0 mg, sodium 50 mg, total carbohydrate 4 g, dietary fiber 1 g, sugars 0 g, protein 1 g

Roasted Red Pepper Hummus

Red peppers, botanically a fruit, are bursting with vitamins A, C, and B6 as well as a number of phytochemicals. You can buy roasted red peppers or roast your own. If you want to make them yourself, here's how: Place whole bell peppers on a foil-lined baking sheet. Roast them at 375°F (190°C), turning them carefully with tongs every 20 minutes or so for 1 hour, or until they are soft and have begun to brown. Cool for 20 to 30 minutes. Peel and seed the peppers over a bowl or the sink (cooked peppers will contain a few tablespoons of liquid, and peeling them can be a messy job). Cut into strips or slices if desired.

PREPARATION: **10 minutes**   PROCESSING: **1 minute**   YIELD: **3 cups (720 ml)**

Two 15-ounce (425-g) cans chickpeas, rinsed and drained

6 ounces (170 g) roasted red peppers, in water, or homemade roasted peppers (see headnote)

¼ cup (60 ml) fresh lemon juice

1 garlic clove, peeled

1 teaspoon salt (or to taste)

Place all the ingredients into the Vitamix container in the order listed and secure the lid. Select Variable 1. Turn the machine on and slowly increase the speed to Variable 10, then to High. Blend for 1 minute, using the tamper to press the ingredients into the blades.

AMOUNT PER 2 TABLESPOON (30 ML) SERVING: calories 50, total fat 0.5 g, saturated fat 0 g, cholesterol 0 mg, sodium 330 mg, total carbohydrate 8 g, dietary fiber 1 g, protein 2 g

Edamame Dip or Pâté

Sometimes a bowl of bean dip and pita chips is the perfect snack at a party, but sometimes you want something a bit more elegant. At those times, this simple, flavorful edamame pâté is the perfect appetizer. Spread the pâté on thin slices of toasted whole wheat baguette and garnish with a little extra mint or a drizzle of Garlic-Parsley Crème Sauce (page 241).

PREPARATION: **10 minutes**   PROCESSING: **30 seconds**   YIELD: **1¼ cups (300 ml)**

3 tablespoons (45 ml) low-sodium vegetable broth

3 tablespoons (45 ml) fresh lemon juice

1¼ cups (188 g) frozen shelled edamame, thawed

2 tablespoons (12 g) chopped scallions

½ teaspoon sea salt

½ cup (58 g) walnut pieces

⅓ cup (8 g) packed fresh mint leaves

Place all the ingredients into the Vitamix container in the order listed and secure the lid. Select Variable 1. Turn the machine on and slowly increase the speed to Variable 8. Blend for 30 seconds, using the tamper to press the ingredients into the blades, until the desired consistency is reached. (For a thinner consistency, add more vegetable broth.)

AMOUNT PER 2 TABLESPOON (30 ML) SERVING: calories 70, total fat 4.5 g, saturated fat 0 g, cholesterol 0 mg, sodium 130 mg, total carbohydrate 4 g, dietary fiber 1 g, sugars 1 g, protein 3 g

Edamame Chickpea Dip

Edamame (green soybeans) are flavorful as a snack, simply boiled and sprinkled with sea salt. But if you are looking for a different way to serve them, whip up this delightful dip. A tasty spin on hummus, it is creamy with Greek yogurt and tahini; bright with lemon, garlic, and a little cayenne; gently green from the parsley and the edamame. Serve it as a dip with pita chips or spread it in celery sticks for a gloriously green and grown-up spin on ants-on-a-log.

PREPARATION: **15 minutes**   PROCESSING: **35 to 40 seconds**   YIELD: **2 cups (480 ml)**

¼ cup (60 ml) plus
2 tablespoons (30 ml) plain
0% Greek yogurt, stirred

2 tablespoons (30 ml) tahini,
preferably homemade
(page 67)

3 tablespoons (45 ml) fresh
lemon juice

1 cup (150 g) fresh or
frozen shelled edamame,
steamed until tender and
cooled

2 garlic cloves, peeled

¼ teaspoon sea salt

½ cup (12 g) fresh flat-leaf
parsley leaves

¾ cup (114 g) drained
canned chickpeas

Pinch of cayenne pepper

1 teaspoon ground cumin

Place all the ingredients into the Vitamix container in the order listed and secure the lid. Select Variable 1. Turn the machine on and slowly increase the speed to Variable 10, then to High. Blend for 35 to 40 seconds, using the tamper to press the ingredients into the blades, adding ¼ to ½ cup (60 to 120 ml) water if needed, until the desired consistency is reached.

AMOUNT PER 2 TABLESPOON (30 ML) SERVING: calories 40, total fat 1.5 g, saturated fat 0 g, cholesterol 0 mg, sodium 60 mg, total carbohydrate 4 g, dietary fiber 1 g, sugars 0 g, protein 2 g

Bean Spread

Beans may be small in size but they pack an outsized nutritional punch. An excellent source of protein and fiber, beans also have iron, zinc, folate, and potassium. They are tasty and usually inexpensive to boot. Make this delicious bean spread for your next burrito or quesadilla, or enjoy it at your next party, with crunchy vegetables or baked tortilla chips for dipping.

PREPARATION: **15 minutes**   PROCESSING: **1 minute**   YIELD: **3½ cups (840 ml)**

2 tablespoons (30 ml) olive oil

2 cups (320 g) chopped yellow onion

2 garlic cloves, peeled

1 jalapeño pepper, halved and seeded

1 teaspoon ground cumin

½ teaspoon chili powder

½ teaspoon sea salt

¼ teaspoon ground black pepper

½ cup (120 ml) California Salsa (page 80)

Two 15-ounce (425-g) cans red kidney beans, rinsed and drained

1. Heat the oil in a large skillet over medium-high heat. Add the onion, garlic, and jalapeño and cook until the onion is translucent. Stir in the cumin, chili powder, salt, and black pepper and cook for 1 minute. Remove from the heat and cool slightly.

2. Place the onion mixture, salsa, and beans into the Vitamix container in the order listed and secure the lid. Select Variable 1. Turn the machine on and slowly increase the speed to Variable 10, then to High. Blend for 1 minute, using the tamper to press the ingredients into the blades.

AMOUNT PER ¼ CUP (60 ML) SERVING: calories 80, total fat 2.5 g, saturated fat 0 g, cholesterol 0 mg, sodium 220 mg, total carbohydrate 11 g, dietary fiber 3 g, sugars 2 g, protein 4 g

Cheese and Bean Dip

Warm and hearty, this cheese and bean dip served with unsalted blue corn tortilla chips will be the hit of your next Sunday football party. Spread any left-over dip in a tortilla for a quick, delicious snack.

PREPARATION: **10 minutes**   PROCESSING: **30 seconds**   YIELD: **2 cups (480 ml)**

½ cup (120 ml) California Salsa (page 80)

One 4-ounce (114-g) can chopped green chilies, undrained

One 15-ounce (440-g) can red kidney beans, rinsed and drained

¼ teaspoon chili powder

⅛ teaspoon ground cumin

¼ cup (30 g) shredded reduced-fat Cheddar

1 tablespoon fresh cilantro leaves, for garnish (optional)

1. Place the salsa, chilies (and their liquid), beans, chili powder, and cumin into the Vitamix container in the order listed and secure the lid. Select Variable 1. Turn the machine on and slowly increase the speed to Variable 10, then to High. Blend for 30 seconds, using the tamper to press the ingredients into the blades.

2. Transfer to a saucepan and cook over medium heat, stirring frequently, until hot, about 4 minutes.

3. Place in a serving bowl and stir in the Cheddar. If desired, garnish with cilantro.

AMOUNT PER 2 TABLESPOON (30 ML) SERVING: calories 45, total fat 1 g, saturated fat 0 g, cholesterol 0 mg, sodium 125 mg, total carbohydrate 7 g, dietary fiber 2 g, sugars 0 g, protein 3 g

Guacamole

Nutrient-dense avocados contain fiber, potassium, vitamin K, folate, vitamin B6, and more. They do have more fat than most vegetables, but 75 percent of the fat in avocados is unsaturated, making it a sensible choice in place of foods higher in saturated fat. Whip all of this nutritional goodness and a mellow, creamy flavor into this satisfying guacamole. Try it with tortilla chips or strips of red, yellow, and green bell peppers for dipping.

PREPARATION: **20 minutes**   PROCESSING: **35 to 50 seconds**   YIELD: **3¾ cups (900 ml)**

1 Roma (plum) tomato, quartered

4 ripe avocados, halved, pitted, and peeled

½ cup (10 g) fresh cilantro leaves

½ cup (40 g) chopped red onion

2 tablespoons (30 ml) fresh lemon juice

1 teaspoon salt

1. Place 1 tomato quarter, 1 avocado half, the cilantro, onion, lemon juice, and salt into the Vitamix container in the order listed and secure the lid. Select Variable 3. Turn the machine on and blend for 15 to 20 seconds, until the ingredients are mixed, using the tamper to press the ingredients into the blades.

2. Stop the machine and remove the lid. Add the remaining 3 tomato quarters and 7 avocado halves to the Vitamix container and secure the lid. Select Variable 5. Turn the machine on and blend for 20 to 30 seconds, using the tamper to press the ingredients into the blades. Leave chunky. Do not overmix.

AMOUNT PER 2 TABLESPOON (30 ML) SERVING: calories 30, total fat 3 g, saturated fat 0 g, cholesterol 0 mg, sodium 0 mg, total carbohydrate 2 g, dietary fiber 1 g, sugars 0 g, protein 0 g

Mango Salsa

A fruity twist on the classic salsa, this recipe is delicious with chips or spooned over baked fish or chicken.

PREPARATION: **10 minutes**   PROCESSING: **15 seconds**   YIELD: **3 cups (720 ml)**

2 semi-ripe mangoes, pitted and peeled, chunked

1 cup (16 g) fresh cilantro leaves

½ medium red onion, peeled and chopped (about ¾ cup / 120 g)

1 jalapeño pepper, halved and seeded

1 tablespoon fresh lime or lemon juice

Place all the ingredients into the Vitamix container in the order listed and secure the lid. Select Variable 1. Turn the machine on and slowly increase the speed to Variable 4. Blend for 15 seconds, or until the desired consistency is reached, using the tamper to press the ingredients into the blades.

AMOUNT PER 2 TABLESPOON (30 ML) SERVING: calories 20, total fat 0 g, saturated fat 0 g, cholesterol 0 mg, sodium 0 mg, total carbohydrate 5 g, dietary fiber 1 g, sugars 4 g, protein 0 g

California Salsa

Once you have made this fresh, bright salsa, you may hesitate to buy a jar at the store. This salsa is simple and bursting with flavor. Delicious with tortilla chips or spooned over a burrito.

PREPARATION: **15 minutes**   PROCESSING: **10 to 30 seconds**   YIELD: **3 cups (720 ml)**

½ medium onion (2 oz / 56 g), peeled

1 jalapeño pepper, halved and seeded

¼ cup (5 g) fresh cilantro leaves

1 teaspoon fresh lemon juice

½ teaspoon salt

6 Roma (plum) tomatoes, quartered (24 quarters)

1. Place the onion, jalapeño, cilantro, lemon juice, salt, and 6 of the tomato quarters into the Vitamix container in the order listed and secure the lid. Select Variable 1. Turn the machine on and blend for 10 to 15 seconds, using the tamper to press the ingredients into the blades.

2. Stop the machine. Add the remaining tomato quarters. Select Variable 1. Blend until the desired consistency is reached, a few seconds for chunky and up to 20 for smooth, using the tamper to press the ingredients into the blades. Increase the speed as necessary to attain the desired consistency.

AMOUNT PER 2 TABLESPOON (30 ML) SERVING: calories 5, total fat 0 g, saturated fat 0 g, cholesterol 0 mg, sodium 50 mg, total carbohydrate 1 g, dietary fiber 0 g, sugars 1 g, protein 0 g

Pineapple Salsa

Pineapple, while available to most of us all year, is at its best in season from March to July. Luckily for salsa lovers, you can enjoy this vibrant pineapple salsa when you need a different dip for your tortilla chips, especially when good tomatoes are not in season.

PREPARATION: **20 minutes**   PROCESSING: **10 seconds plus pulsing**   YIELD: **2¼ cups (540 ml)**

2 tablespoons (30 ml) olive oil

½ lime, peeled

3 cups (500 g) large pieces peeled pineapple

½ teaspoon kosher salt

¼ cup (40 g) chopped onion

½ cup (75 g) red bell pepper pieces (1 inch / 2.5 cm square)

2 tablespoons (5 g) chopped fresh cilantro leaves

¼ jalapeño pepper

1. Place the olive oil, lime, 1½ cups of the pineapple, and the salt into the Vitamix container in the order listed and secure the lid. Select Variable 1. Turn the machine on and slowly increase the speed to Variable 4. Blend for 10 seconds, using the tamper to press the ingredients into the blades.

2. Stop the machine and remove the lid. Add the remaining pineapple, the onion, bell pepper, cilantro, and jalapeño to the Vitamix container in the order listed and secure the lid. Select Variable 7. Use the On/Off switch to quickly pulse 7 to 10 times, until the desired consistency is reached.

Don't worry about getting all the pineapple peel off. The Vitamix will break it down so you'll never know it's there, yet you'll benefit from the extra nutrition.

AMOUNT PER 2 TABLESPOON (30 ML) SERVING: calories 30, total fat 1.5 g, saturated fat 0 g, cholesterol 0 mg, sodium 55 mg, total carbohydrate 4 g, dietary fiber 0 g, sugars 3 g, protein 0 g

Muhammara
(Red Pepper and Walnut Dip)

This bright, tangy Middle Eastern dip hails from Syria. Pomegranate molasses, which is simply pomegranate juice that has been reduced to a thick syrup, has a deep, tart flavor. It can be found at Middle Eastern markets and now, more frequently, at your local grocery or health food store.

PREPARATION: **15 minutes**   PROCESSING: **20 seconds**   YIELD: **2 cups (480 ml)**

2 tablespoons (30 ml) olive oil

1 slice whole wheat bread, preferably homemade (page 47)

1½ cups (313 g) roasted red peppers (see page 71)

½ lemon, peeled and seeded

2 teaspoons sweet paprika

¼ teaspoon cayenne pepper

2 teaspoons pomegranate molasses

1 garlic clove, peeled

½ teaspoon sea salt

¼ teaspoon ground black pepper

1. Heat the olive oil in a nonstick skillet over medium heat. Add the bread and toast both sides. Remove from the heat.

2. Place the toasted bread and oil from the skillet into the Vitamix container, then add all the remaining ingredients in the order listed and secure the lid. Select Variable 1. Turn the machine on and slowly increase the speed to Variable 8. Blend for 20 seconds, using the tamper to press the ingredients into the blades.

AMOUNT PER 2 TABLESPOON (30 ML) SERVING: calories 50, total fat 2 g, saturated fat 0 g, cholesterol 0 mg, sodium 280 mg, total carbohydrate 6 g, dietary fiber 0 g, sugars 1 g, protein 1 g

Eggplant Onion Dip

Garam masala is a spice blend used in Indian cooking that usually includes turmeric, black and white peppercorns, cumin seeds, cloves, and cardamom seeds. The spice blend's gentle warmth is the perfect complement to the mellowness of roasted eggplant. Serve this delicious dip with toasted pita chips.

PREPARATION: **10 minutes**   PROCESSING: **40 seconds**   BAKE TIME: **30 minutes**   YIELD: **2 cups (480 ml)**

1 medium eggplant (about 1¼ pounds / 568 g), quartered lengthwise

3 tablespoons (45 ml) olive oil

2½ cups (270 g) chopped yellow onion

2 garlic cloves, peeled

2 tablespoons (3 g) fresh mint leaves

2 tablespoons (3 g) fresh cilantro leaves

½ teaspoon garam masala

1. Preheat the oven to 475°F (240°C). Line a baking sheet with foil or a silicone baking mat.

2. Place the eggplant quarters, skin side down, on the baking sheet and brush with 2 tablespoons of the olive oil.

3. Toss the onion, garlic, and remaining 1 tablespoon olive oil and place on the baking sheet.

4. Roast for 15 minutes. Rotate the baking sheet front to back and continue roasting until browned and tender, about 15 minutes longer. When cool enough to handle, carefully peel the skin off the eggplant.

5. Transfer all the roasted vegetables to the Vitamix container and secure the lid. Select Variable 1. Turn the machine on and slowly increase the speed to Variable 8. Blend for 30 seconds, using the tamper to press the ingredients into the blades.

6. Stop the machine and remove the lid plug. Add the mint, cilantro, and garam masala to the Vitamix container and secure the lid. Select Variable 1. Turn the machine on and slowly increase the speed to Variable 8. Blend for 10 seconds, using the tamper to press the ingredients into the blades.

AMOUNT PER 2 TABLESPOON (30 ML) SERVING: calories 40, total fat 2.5 g, saturated fat 0 g, cholesterol 0 mg, sodium 0 mg, total carbohydrate 4 g, dietary fiber 2 g, sugars 2 g, protein 1 g

Hot Crab and Artichoke Dip

Hot, creamy, and just plain delicious, this dip is sure to become a tradition at your winter holiday parties. Serve with pita chips or toast points for dipping.

PREPARATION: **15 minutes**   PROCESSING: **30 seconds**   BAKE TIME: **25 to 30 minutes**
YIELD: **1½ cups (360 ml)**

⅓ cup (80 ml) plain 0% Greek yogurt, stirred

3 tablespoons (45 ml) fat-free mayonnaise

¼ cup (32 g) grated Parmesan

2 garlic cloves, cut into pieces

6 ounces (170 g) imitation crabmeat, chopped

One 14-ounce (398-g) can artichoke hearts, drained and coarsely chopped

⅓ teaspoon sweet paprika

One 4-ounce (114-g) can chopped green chilies, drained

1. Preheat the oven to 350°F (180°C). Coat a 1-quart baking dish with cooking spray.

2. Place the yogurt, mayo, Parmesan, and garlic into the Vitamix container in the order listed and secure the lid. Select Variable 1. Turn the machine on and slowly increase the speed to Variable 4. Blend for 20 seconds.

3. Stop the machine, remove the lid, and scrape the sides of the container. Secure the lid. Select Variable 1. Turn the machine on and slowly increase the speed to Variable 3. Blend for 10 seconds.

4. Combine the crabmeat, artichoke hearts, paprika, and chilies in the baking dish. Scrape the yogurt mixture on top and stir gently to combine. Bake, uncovered, for 25 to 30 minutes, until light golden brown and bubbling.

AMOUNT PER 2 TABLESPOON (30 ML) SERVING: calories 40, total fat 1 g, saturated fat 0.5 g, cholesterol 5 mg, sodium 320 mg, total carbohydrate 5 g, dietary fiber 1 g, sugars 2 g, protein 3 g

Goat Cheese Crostini with Roasted Red Pepper Spread

An elegant appetizer for your next gathering. Both the toasts and the red pepper spread can be made a day in advance so these tasty snacks will come together in a snap! This spread is also wonderful on a sandwich with whole-grain bread, sharp Cheddar, and spinach.

PREPARATION: **15 minutes**   PROCESSING: **30 seconds**

YIELD: **10 servings (2 crostini each); 1½ cups (360 ml) spread**

1 baguette (long enough for twenty 1-inch slices)

2 tablespoons (30 ml) olive oil

4 ounces (114 g) roasted red peppers (see page 71)

1 scallion, halved

1 garlic clove, peeled and roasted

¼ teaspoon grated lemon zest

¼ teaspoon ground black pepper

¼ teaspoon sea salt

4 ounces (114 g) Neufchâtel cheese (⅓-less-fat cream cheese)

4 ounces (114 g) goat cheese, crumbled

OPTIONAL GARNISH:

Chopped scallions

1. Preheat the over to 325°F (170°C). Slice the baguette diagonally into slices ¾ to 1 inch thick. Brush both sides of the bread with olive oil and toast them for 15 to 20 minutes, turning until golden brown.

2. Place the roasted peppers, scallion, garlic, lemon zest, black pepper, salt, and Neufchâtel into the Vitamix container in the order listed and secure the lid. Select Variable 1. Turn the machine on and slowly increase the speed to Variable 6. Blend for 30 seconds, using the tamper to press the ingredients into the blades.

3. Spread the roasted pepper spread evenly on the baguette toasts. Top with the goat cheese and scallions (if using) and serve immediately.

AMOUNT PER SERVING: calories 280, total fat 8 g, saturated fat 3.5 g, cholesterol 15 mg, sodium 670 mg, total carbohydrate 41 g, dietary fiber 2 g, sugars 1 g, protein 12 g

Yogurt, Spinach, and Artichoke Dip

Warm and hearty, this savory spinach and artichoke dip will be a welcome addition to your next winter gathering. Serve it with pita chips or toasts.

PREPARATION: **20 minutes**   PROCESSING: **20 seconds**   BAKE TIME: **15 minutes**   YIELD: **6 cups (1.4 liters)**

1 ounce (**28 g**) whole-grain crackers, crushed into crumbs

¼ teaspoon garlic powder

¼ teaspoon onion powder

2 tablespoons (**16 g**) finely grated Parmesan

6 ounces (**170 g**) plain 0% Greek yogurt, stirred

4 ounces (**114 g**) Neufchâtel cheese (⅓-less-fat cream cheese)

1 teaspoon grated lemon zest

2 teaspoons minced fresh oregano

2 teaspoons minced fresh mint leaves

½ teaspoon sea salt

½ teaspoon ground black pepper

1 tablespoon olive oil

1 large yellow onion (6 oz / 170 g), cut into pieces

1 garlic clove, minced

5 ounces (**142 g**) fresh spinach

One 14-ounce (**398-g**) can water-packed artichoke hearts, rinsed, drained, and cut into pieces

1. Preheat the oven to 400°F (200°C).

2. Combine the cracker crumbs, garlic powder, onion powder, and Parmesan in a small bowl. Set aside.

3. Place the yogurt, Neufchâtel, lemon zest, oregano, mint, salt, and pepper into the Vitamix container in the order listed and secure the lid. Select Variable 1. Turn the machine on and slowly increase the speed to Variable 4. Blend for 20 seconds, using the tamper to press the ingredients into the blades.

4. Heat the oil in a skillet over medium heat. Add the onion and garlic and cook until soft, 4 to 6 minutes. Add the spinach and cook until soft and the liquid has evaporated, 4 to 6 minutes.

5. Remove from the heat and scrape in the artichokes and the yogurt mixture, stirring to combine. Spoon into an 8-inch (20-cm) square baking dish.

6. Sprinkle with the cracker crumb mixture and bake for 15 minutes, or until hot and bubbling. Serve hot.

AMOUNT PER 2 TABLESPOON (30 ML) SERVING: calories 20, total fat 1 g, saturated fat 0 g, cholesterol 0 mg, sodium 100 mg, total carbohydrate 2 g, dietary fiber 1 g, sugars 0 g, protein 1 g

Two-Cheese Spread with Spinach

Bright and creamy and full of fresh spinach, this isn't your standard spinach dip. Feta, goat cheese, and 0% Greek yogurt give this spread a decadent, smooth texture. Serve with crackers or pita chips for an appetizer, or along with cut veggies and pita wedges for a healthy lunch.

PREPARATION: **15 minutes**   PROCESSING: **1 minute**   YIELD: **2 cups (480 ml)**

2 ounces (56 g) feta, at room temperature, crumbled

4 ounces (114 g) goat cheese, at room temperature, crumbled

¾ cup (180 ml) plain 0% Greek yogurt, stirred

2 cups (75 g) fresh spinach

1 garlic clove, peeled

2 teaspoons fresh mint leaves

1 teaspoon grated lemon zest

1 teaspoon fresh lemon juice

⅛ teaspoon sea salt

⅛ teaspoon ground black pepper

1. Place all the ingredients into the Vitamix container in the order listed and secure the lid. Select Variable 1. Turn the machine on and slowly increase the speed to Variable 10, then to High. Blend for 45 seconds.

2. Stop the machine, remove the lid, and scrape the mixture into the blades. Secure the lid. Select Variable 1. Turn the machine on and slowly increase the speed to Variable 10, then to High. Blend for 15 seconds.

AMOUNT PER 2 TABLESPOON (30 ML) SERVING: calories 35, total fat 2.5 g, saturated fat 1.5 g, cholesterol 5 mg, sodium 95 mg, total carbohydrate 1 g, dietary fiber 0 g, sugars 1 g, protein 3 g

WHOLE FOODS SUCCESS STORY

Mary Lou Bukar

As you read the nearly 250 recipes in this book, you will learn about all the different jobs a Vitamix can do. Sure, smoothies, but did you know your machine could make hot soup, no stove required? That it can chop? That it can grind both fresh flours and meat? Or that it can make frozen treats that taste better than ice cream? The possibilities are endless, and once you know the ins and outs of your Vitamix, you can get creative. Make up your own family recipe for a smoothie or a whole-fruit margarita. Make a crisper-cleansing soup or juice. With your Vitamix and your imagination, you can make any number of delicious meals and snacks.

Mary Lou Bukar, an Illinois-based salesperson and product rep for a national kitchenware retailer, purchased her first Vitamix in 2009. Like many a fan, Mary Lou uses her machine a lot, taking advantage of multiple Vitamix techniques. Mary Lou loves using her Vitamix to "think outside the box" when she tackles meal preparation. Some days she uses her machine to grate cheese, whip up a quick dressing, or chop veggies. Other times, Mary Lou will make a fresh pesto or nut butter. All very fast to make, each finished dish is delicious. And she really appreciates being able to make different dishes at home using whole foods instead of having to buy processed products at the store. "It's not surprising to me how easy it is to substitute whole, raw foods for processed food products when you use a Vitamix in meal preparation," remarks Mary Lou.

Using the machine's diverse capacities has allowed Mary Lou to bring more whole foods into her daily diet in a number of different forms. Her favorite thing to make is whole food juices, using a variety of vegetables, fruits, and spices to craft drinks "brightly colored by nature, not by chemicals." Later she might make fresh salsa or peanut butter for a healthy snack. When it comes to dinner, Mary Lou uses her Vitamix to create a fresh, nutritious sauce or dressing. A delicious dessert often rounds out the day, whether she whips cream, mixes a cake batter, or makes a quick frozen yogurt. In a day, she might very well make a recipe from every category in this book! And in the process, she is eating lots of scrumptious, nutritious food too. A whole food success story for sure!

Pear and Apple Salad
with Flax-Crusted
Goat Cheese
(page 152)

Chapter 4

Soups, Salads, and Sides

Soups, salads, and side dishes are a wonderful way to get more fruits, vegetables, and whole grains into your diet. In this chapter, you will find recipes for fresh and crunchy vegetable salads, hearty grain salads, gluten-free rolls, and cooked vegetable dishes. And the soups! Hearty, chunky soups perfect for the coldest winter days, soothing pureed soups bursting with flavor, and refreshing cold soups for the most sweltering summer days. There are even soups that are made completely in the Vitamix, without using the stove.

Any of these soups and sides would be a wonderful addition to a meal or a great light lunch or dinner in and of themselves.

Soups

Restaurants value our products because they can create silky smooth sauces, soups, and vinaigrettes, among other things. In this chapter, you'll find recipes that allow you to achieve similarly sumptuous results at home. Recipes such as Beet Soup with Goat Cheese and Almonds (page 101), Carrot with Fennel Soup (page 109), and Garden-Fresh Tomato Soup (page 132) allow you to enjoy lusciously smooth and just plain delightful soup.

Here are a few tips to keep in mind when you are pureeing hot soups.

- When blending hot ingredients, start your Vitamix on a low speed.

- Be careful! The very act of transferring hot soup to a blender can be tricky for some, and there is no harm in letting the soup cool for a few minutes before beginning to puree it!
- Position the lid with the flaps on the container with the flaps midway between the spout and the handle. Push the lid onto the container until it locks in place. (Make sure the vented lid plug is secured.) The lid must always be secured, especially when processing hot liquids that may scald.
- Don't overfill the container. Hot liquids expand. It is usually safer to fill the canister a little over half full, so that the hot liquid doesn't overflow while you are blending it.

My husband, Frank, learned about checking the lid and the speed the hard way. We were hosting our first Thanksgiving dinner. The table was set, the turkey was cooked, and all the side dishes were prepared and ready to go. We called everyone to dinner as Frank started to make his famous gravy by putting the pan drippings and vegetables in the Vitamix with his secret ingredient—fresh apple. So as we were all gathering around the table, which was right next to the counter, which abutted the gas stove—it was a very tiny kitchen—he turned the Vitamix on without the lid. And on top of the fact that there was no lid, the speed was on High. Hot grease went straight up in the air, coated the ceiling, and splashed down on the stove, bursting into flames. No one was hurt and everyone jumped in to put out the fire and clean up the walls, ceiling, and counter. It managed to completely miss the table and all the guests. Thirty minutes later we sat down with one more thing to be thankful for. And of course, he has never forgotten to put the lid on again!

Silky smooth soups are wonderful, but sometimes we crave something more substantial. No problem. After blending your soup until it is steamy and hot, simply add more ingredients and pulse the blades several times to give it a chunkier, heartier texture. This is the technique used in some soups, like Tuscan Bean Soup with Whole Grains (page 139). In others, such as Garden-Fresh Minestrone (page 136), broth, tomatoes, and beans are pureed to make a lovely, nutrient-rich stock, and this stock is used, in turn, to simmer the vegetables. Pureeing a portion of a cooked soup, as you do in Barley and Vegetable Soup with Chicken and Pesto (page 128), makes a slightly heartier, less brothy soup without making it entirely smooth.

One of the most amazing features of the Vitamix machine is its ability to make a soup ready to serve directly from the blender—no stovetop required. The fact that you can make a cold soup in the Vitamix will be less of a revelation, although you will appreciate Chilled Cucumber and Avocado Soup (page 130) and Avocado Soup with Chipotle Yogurt (page 97) on a hot day just the same. Still, on that crazy-busy day when you come through the door and just want to eat *right now— yes, this very minute,* the fact that you can put raw vegetables in the Vitamix and make hot soup so quickly is something pretty special. You can toss the ingredients for Easy "Cheesy" Vegan Broccoli Soup (page 114), Tortilla Soup (page 127), or Chicken Potato Soup (page 124)—my family's favorite (we serve it in a bread bowl)—into the Vitamix blender and make hot soup in the time it takes to unload the dishwasher . . . maybe even a little faster. Not only will you be able to get a meal on the table quickly, but your food will contain whole foods and less sodium than many other convenience foods. Fast, healthy, and delicious food! A truly winning combination.

Salads and Sides

Fresh, crunchy salads, gluten-free rolls, hearty grain salads, and cooked vegetable sides abound in this chapter, too. Any of these would be a perfect accompaniment to a main dish, or you could build a whole meal out of one or two of these recipes.

You may enjoy a nice bowl of simply dressed leafy greens, but it may be easier to eat more veggies if you expand your salad repertoire with the recipes found in this chapter. There are lots of kale salads on restaurant menus these days, but we would challenge any of them to hold a candle to our nutrient-packed Kale Salad with Avocado Tahini Dressing (page 149). This salad is full of veggies and has a dressing that contains the healthy fats found in avocado and sesame seeds plus a handful of kale. Both Fiesta Salad (page 154) and Lime-Dressed Ginger Carrot Slaw (page 151) use whole fruits to bring flavor and nutrients to salads with lots of different crunchy vegetables. Pear and Apple Salad (page 152) pairs greens and lightly poached fruit with a maple and flax seed oil vinaigrette and goat cheese encrusted with flax seeds and fresh thyme. This composed salad would make an elegant first course for your next dinner party or a lovely light lunch.

Salads can be made from more than just vegetables, of course; this chapter contains a number of grain- and seed-based salads. These hearty sides are perfect as part of a meal or as a substantial lunch or entrée. Chewy barley is featured in two delightful salads. The first, our Barley and Corn Salad (page 144), dresses barley, corn, cucumbers, and tomatoes with a yogurt and chive dressing. The second, our Festive Barley Salad (page 147), has both raw and steamed vegetables tossed with a red wine vinaigrette with fresh herbs. In our Southwestern Quinoa Salad (page 156), quinoa, technically a seed, shines in a hearty salad with a slightly spicy dressing, black beans, corn, bell peppers, chiles, and red onion. This salad travels well and would be an excellent addition to a potluck or brown-bag lunch. Try bulgur, a quick-cooking whole wheat similar to couscous, in the herb-packed Lebanese Tabbouleh (page 155).

There are just a handful of cooked vegetable sides in this chapter, but all are worthy of a place on your table. In our Bulgur-Stuffed Baby Potatoes (page 160), cooked and cooled red potatoes are stuffed with a delicious mixture of bulgur, leeks, corn, and parsley-pecan pesto. These flavor-packed potatoes are the perfect appetizer or side dish. They can also be made ahead of time and served at room temperature. Wild Rice Stuffing (page 161) pairs cooked seeds (that's the wild rice) with a few veggies, lots of dried fruit, and crunchy pumpkin seeds. The perfect, naturally gluten-free stuffing for your holiday meal.

With so many ways to create variety, nutrition, and amazing flavor, getting more whole foods into your diet will be a snap!

Avocado Soup with Chipotle Yogurt

This creamy-without-cream soup with smoky chipotle yogurt is delicious with Southwestern Quinoa Salad (page 156) on the side.

PREPARATION: 15 minutes   PROCESSING: 2 minutes 30 seconds   COOK TIME: 5 minutes
YIELD: 8½ cups (2 liters)

CHIPOTLE YOGURT:

½ cup (240 ml) plain 0% Greek yogurt, stirred

1 teaspoon chipotle peppers in adobo sauce, coarsely chopped

SOUP:

2 tablespoons (30 ml) olive oil

1 cup (160 g) chopped yellow onion

1 garlic clove, peeled

6 cups (1.4 liters) fat-free low-sodium chicken broth

1 teaspoon grated lime zest

2 tablespoons (30 ml) fresh lime juice

2 tablespoons (2 g) fresh cilantro leaves

1 teaspoon sea salt

4 avocados, halved, pitted, and peeled

1. For the chipotle yogurt: Place the yogurt and chipotle pepper into the Vitamix container and secure the lid. Select Variable 1. Turn the machine on and slowly increase to Variable 4. Blend for 10 seconds. Stop the machine, scrape the sides, and repeat 2 times. Spoon into a bowl and chill until serving time.

2. For the soup: Heat the olive oil in a skillet over medium-high heat. Add the onion and garlic and cook until translucent, about 5 minutes. Do not brown. Let cool.

3. Place 3 cups of the chicken broth, half of the onion and garlic mixture, ½ teaspoon of the lime zest, 1 tablespoon of the lime juice, 1 tablespoon of the cilantro, ½ teaspoon of the sea salt, and 4 avocado halves in the Vitamix container in the order listed and secure the lid. Select Variable 1. Turn the machine on and slowly increase the speed to Variable 10, then to High. Blend for 1 minute.

4. Pour the pureed soup into a large bowl. Repeat with the remaining ingredients. Stir together both batches to combine. Refrigerate to chill slightly before serving. Store leftovers in a covered container in the refrigerator for up to 2 days. Use leftover yogurt as a salad dressing or a dip.

AMOUNT PER 1 CUP (240 ML) SOUP (WITH 1 TABLESPOON CHIPOTLE YOGURT): calories 160, total fat 13 g, saturated fat 2 g, cholesterol 0 mg, sodium 340 mg, total carbohydrate 9 g, dietary fiber 5 g, sugars 2 g, protein 5 g

Potato and Cauliflower Bisque

This thick, richly flavored soup with fresh herbs has a pop of freshness from the bright essential oils from the lemon zest. The bisque is delicious on a cold fall or winter afternoon or for a light dinner with fresh baked bread and a green salad.

PREPARATION: **15 minutes**   `PROCESSING: **6 minutes 40 seconds**   COOK TIME: **4 to 6 minutes**
YIELD: **6½ cups (1.5 liters)**

1 tablespoon olive oil

½ cup (60 g) chopped white onion

½ cup (50 g) diced celery

2 small garlic cloves, peeled

½ teaspoon fresh thyme leaves

½ teaspoon fresh rosemary leaves

1 cup (240 ml) low-fat (1%) milk

2½ cups (600 ml) low-sodium chicken broth

2 cups (365 g) quartered Yukon Gold potatoes, parboiled (see note)

1 cup (107 g) cauliflower florets, blanched (see note)

1 teaspoon sea salt

¼ teaspoon ground black pepper

¼ teaspoon grated lemon zest

OPTIONAL GARNISHES:

Minced chives (or other herbs)

Cracked black pepper

Chile oil

1. Heat the olive oil in a skillet over medium heat. Add the onion, celery, and garlic and cook until the onion is translucent, about 5 minutes. Do not brown. Add the thyme and rosemary and stir to coat.

2. Place the milk, broth, potatoes, cauliflower, sautéed vegetable mixture, salt, and pepper into the Vitamix container in that order and secure the lid. Select Variable 1. Turn the machine on and slowly increase the speed to Variable 10, then to High. Blend for 6 minutes 30 seconds, or until steam escapes from the vented lid.

3. Reduce the speed to Variable 2 and remove the lid plug. Through the lid plug opening, add the lemon zest and blend for an additional 10 seconds.

4. Serve hot. If desired, garnish with minced chives (or other herbs), cracked pepper, or chile oil.

To parboil the potatoes and blanch the cauliflower, place the potatoes in a medium pot and add cold water to cover by about 2 inches. Add a pinch of sea salt, cover, and bring to a boil over high heat. When the water comes to a boil, add the cauliflower and continue cooking until both are just tender, about 4 minutes longer, then drain.

AMOUNT PER 1 CUP (240 ML) SERVING (WITHOUT GARNISHES): calories 100, total fat 2.5 g, saturated fat 0.5 g, cholesterol 0 mg, sodium 450 mg, total carbohydrate 14 g, dietary fiber 1 g, sugars 3 g, protein 5 g

Bean and Squash Soup

This soup is the perfect last-minute meal, composed almost entirely of pantry staples. The ginger, Tabasco sauce, and lemon juice balance out the natural sweetness of the squash. The chickpeas add fiber and protein, making the soup more filling. Vegetarian and vegan as is. Make extra to freeze!

PREPARATION: **15 minutes**   PROCESSING: **30 seconds**   COOK TIME: **30 to 35 minutes**
YIELD: **7¼ cups (1.7 liters)**

2 tablespoons (30 ml) olive oil

1 medium yellow onion (6 oz / 170 g), peeled, cut into small pieces

2 garlic cloves, peeled

½ teaspoon ground cinnamon

½ teaspoon ground cumin

½ teaspoon ground ginger

¼ teaspoon ground cloves

1 tablespoon light brown sugar

2 pounds (908 g) butternut squash, peeled, seeded, and cut into small pieces

3 cups (720 ml) low-sodium vegetable broth

One 15.5-ounce (440-g) can chickpeas, rinsed and drained

Dash of Tabasco sauce

1 teaspoon fresh lemon juice

1. Heat the olive oil in a large saucepan over medium heat. Add the onion and garlic and cook until the onion is translucent. Stir in the cinnamon, cumin, ginger, cloves, brown sugar, and squash. Cook, stirring frequently, until the squash is fragrant and just beginning to soften, about 5 minutes.

2. Add the broth and bring to a boil. Reduce to a simmer, cover, and cook until the squash is tender, 20 to 25 minutes. Add the chickpeas, Tabasco, and lemon juice.

3. Ladle the hot soup into the Vitamix container and secure the lid. Select Variable 1. Turn the machine on and slowly increase the speed to Variable 10, then to High. Blend for 30 seconds.

4. Serve hot.

AMOUNT PER 1 CUP (240 ML) SERVING: calories 160, total fat 5 g, saturated fat 0.5 g, cholesterol 0 mg, sodium 140 mg, total carbohydrate 27 g, dietary fiber 3 g, sugars 7 g, protein 4 g

Beet Soup with Goat Cheese and Almonds

In season through the fall, beets add a wonderful splash of color when our plates begin to lose the brilliant hues of summer. You won't be able to taste the roasted Roma tomatoes in the final product, but their acidity will keep the beet flavor from being too sweet.

PREPARATION: **45 minutes**   PROCESSING: **1 minute**   COOK TIME: **30 minutes**
YIELD: **7 cups (1.7 liters)**

2 tablespoons (30 ml) olive oil

2 cups (8 oz / 227 g) yellow onion chunks

1 garlic clove, halved

4 medium beets (20 oz / 568 g total), roasted, cooled, peeled, and diced

4 Roma (plum) tomatoes (about 18 oz / 510 g total), halved, roasted, and cooled

½ teaspoon sea salt

¼ teaspoon ground black pepper

3 cups (720 ml) low-sodium chicken broth

4 ounces (114 g) goat cheese, crumbled, for garnish

1 cup (100 g) sliced almonds, lightly toasted, for garnish

1. Heat the olive oil in a large saucepan over medium heat. Add the onion and garlic and cook until the onion is translucent, about 5 minutes.

2. Add the beets, tomatoes, salt, and pepper and cook for 4 minutes, until the tomatoes have released most of their liquid.

3. Add the broth and bring to a boil. Reduce to a simmer, cover, and cook for 15 minutes.

4. Ladle the hot soup into the Vitamix container and secure the lid. Select Variable 1. Turn the machine on and slowly increase the speed to Variable 10, then to High. Blend for 1 minute.

5. Serve the soup hot. Garnish with the goat cheese and almonds.

AMOUNT PER 1 CUP (240 ML) SERVING: calories 220, total fat 14 g, saturated fat 3.5 g, cholesterol 5 mg, sodium 360 mg, total carbohydrate 17 g, dietary fiber 5 g, sugars 9 g, protein 10 g

Broccoli Cheese Soup

One of the wonders of the Vitamix is the machine's ability to take raw ingredients and transform them into steaming hot soup. Imagine taking the pantry staples for this soup, putting them in your Vitamix, and having dinner in the time it takes to set the table! The rest of our busy lives should be so easy. And because you are making the soup yourself, you can avoid the extra fat and sodium that would likely be in a canned soup.

PREPARATION: **10 minutes**   PROCESSING: **5 to 6 minutes**   YIELD: **2½ cups (600 ml)**

1 cup (240 ml) skim milk

½ cup (60 g) shredded Cheddar

1½ cups (150 g) fresh or frozen broccoli or cauliflower florets, steamed

1 teaspoon diced onion

½ cup (80 ml) low-sodium vegetable broth

Place all the ingredients into the Vitamix container in the order listed and secure the lid. Select Variable 1. Turn the machine on and slowly increase the speed to Variable 10, then to High. Blend for 5 to 6 minutes, until heavy steam escapes from the vented lid.

AMOUNT PER 1 CUP (240 ML) SERVING: calories 110, total fat 2 g, saturated fat 1 g, cholesterol 5 mg, sodium 250 mg, total carbohydrate 13 g, dietary fiber 3 g, sugars 7 g, protein 11 g

Sassy Sweet Potato Soup

Because sweet potatoes are bursting with beta-carotene, vitamin B6, and potassium, and because this soup is simple and quick to assemble, you may reach for this recipe instead of chicken soup the next time you are feeling under the weather. And it is so delicious, you will enjoy it in times of sickness *and* health!

PREPARATION 15 MINUTES   PROCESSING: **45 seconds**   COOK TIME: **25 minutes**
YIELD: **3½ cups (840 ml)**

1 tablespoon olive oil

1 teaspoon toasted sesame oil

¼ cup (17 g) chopped fresh gingerroot

3 cups (720 ml) water

3 cups (421 g) cubed peeled sweet potato

1 tablespoon honey

½ teaspoon sea salt

1. Heat both oils in a medium skillet over medium-high heat. Add the ginger and cook until fragrant and lightly golden. Remove the skillet from the heat.

2. Bring the water to a boil in a medium saucepan. Add the sweet potato, honey, and salt. Reduce to a simmer and cook until the sweet potato is very tender, 15 to 20 minutes.

3. Scrape the sautéed ginger into the Vitamix container. Pour in the hot sweet potato mixture and secure the lid. Select Variable 1. Turn the machine on and slowly increase the speed to Variable 10, then to High. Blend for 45 seconds.

4. Serve hot.

AMOUNT PER 1 CUP (240 ML) SERVING: calories 170, total fat 5 g, saturated fat 1 g, cholesterol 0 mg, sodium 400 mg, total carbohydrate 30 g, dietary fiber 4 g, sugars 10 g, protein 2 g

Soups, Salads, and Sides

Autumn Flavors Bisque

This mellow bisque is like fall in a bowl. Pumpkin puree, a little apple juice and maple syrup, cinnamon, thyme, and cloves. And vanilla? And white balsamic vinegar? Yes and yes! The vanilla adds a wonderful aroma while the vinegar brightens up the otherwise mellow soup.

PREPARATION: **20 minutes**   PROCESSING: **40 seconds**   COOK TIME: **22 minutes**

YIELD: **5 cups (1.2 liters)**

1 tablespoon olive oil

¼ cup (36 g) coarsely chopped yellow onion

¼ cup (35 g) chopped shallots

One ¼-inch-thick (0.6-cm) slice peeled gingerroot

2 tablespoons (15 g) all-purpose flour

3 cups (720 ml) fat-free low-sodium chicken broth

¼ cup (60 ml) apple juice

1¼ cups (284 g) pumpkin puree, preferably homemade (page 55)

1 tablespoon pure maple syrup

¼ teaspoon ground cinnamon

¼ teaspoon ground thyme

¼ teaspoon sea salt

⅛ teaspoon ground black pepper

Pinch of ground cloves

½ cup (120 ml) unsweetened almond milk

¼ teaspoon vanilla extract

1 teaspoon white balsamic vinegar

1. Heat the olive oil in a soup pot over medium-high heat. Add the onion, shallots, and ginger. Cook, stirring, until the shallots and onion are tender, about 2 minutes. Do not brown.

2. Add the flour, stir to coat all the vegetables, then add the broth and apple juice. Bring to a boil, then reduce to a simmer and cook until slightly thickened, about 5 minutes.

3. Whisk in the pumpkin, maple syrup, cinnamon, thyme, salt, pepper, and cloves. Bring to a boil, then reduce the heat to low and simmer for 15 minutes, until the flavors are blended.

4. Ladle the hot mixture into the Vitamix container. Add the almond milk, vanilla, and vinegar and secure the lid. Select Variable 1. Turn the machine on and slowly increase the speed to Variable 10, then to High. Blend for 40 seconds.

5. Serve hot.

AMOUNT PER 1 CUP (240 ML) SERVING: calories 90, total fat 3.5 g, saturated fat 0 g, cholesterol 0 mg, sodium 410 mg, total carbohydrate 14 g, dietary fiber 3 g, sugars 7 g, protein 2 g

Coconut Green Curry Soup

The depth of flavor from the green curry paste and other fresh ingredients in this soup will transport you to the beaches of Thailand upon your first taste.

PREPARATION: **20 minutes**   PROCESSING: **1 minute**   COOK TIME: **38 to 42 minutes**
YIELD: **6¼ cups (1.5 liters)**

2 tablespoons (30 ml) sesame oil

2 garlic cloves, chopped

½ cup (57 g) chopped scallion whites, plus ½ cup (28 g) thinly sliced scallion greens (cut on an angle)

¼ cup (21 g) thinly sliced lemongrass (cut on an angle)

1 tablespoon chopped fresh gingerroot

4 cups (214 g) julienned shiitake mushroom caps

4 cups (960 ml) white miso broth

1¾ cups (420 ml) canned light coconut milk

2 tablespoons (30 ml) green curry paste

¼ cup (35 g) diced red bell pepper

¼ cup (38 g) corn kernels

Lime wedges, for serving

OPTIONAL GARNISHES:

Thinly sliced chile peppers

Fresh cilantro leaves

Bean sprouts

1. Heat 1 tablespoon of the sesame oil in a large saucepan. Add the garlic, scallion whites, lemongrass, and ginger and cook until aromatic, 2 to 3 minutes. Add 2 cups of the shiitakes and cook until soft and wilted, 4 to 6 minutes.

2. Add the broth, coconut milk, and green curry paste and bring to a boil. Reduce to a simmer, cover, and cook for 15 minutes, until the flavors are blended.

3. Ladle the hot soup into the Vitamix container and secure the lid. Select Variable 1. Turn the machine on and slowly increase the speed to Variable 10, then to High. Blend for 1 minute.

4. Wipe out the saucepan and return to medium-high heat. Add the remaining 1 tablespoon oil, bell pepper, scallion greens, corn, and remaining shiitakes. Cook just until soft, 2 to 3 minutes.

5. Add the pureed broth and bring to a simmer. Cover and cook for 15 minutes to blend the flavors.

6. Serve hot, with lime wedges for squeezing. If desired, garnish with chile peppers, a little cilantro, or bean sprouts.

AMOUNT PER 1 CUP (240 ML) SERVING (WITHOUT GARNISHES): calories 100, total fat 7 g, saturated fat 2.5 g, cholesterol 0 mg, sodium 300 mg, total carbohydrate 7 g, dietary fiber 2 g, sugars 2 g, protein 2 g

Soups, Salads, and Sides

Corn, Pepper, and Tomato Soup

Roasting the corn, tomatoes, and red bell peppers concentrates their flavors and gives them a slight smokiness, providing wonderful depth.

PREPARATION: **20 minutes plus roasting time**   PROCESSING: **3 minutes**

COOK TIME: **35 minutes**   YIELD: **8¼ cups (1.9 liters)**

1½ pounds (680 g) tomatoes, halved

3 red bell peppers (22 oz / 625 g), halved and roasted

3 tablespoons (45 ml) extra virgin olive oil

2 cups (296 g) corn kernels

1½ cups (200 g) chopped yellow onion

2 garlic cloves, minced

¼ teaspoon chipotle powder

¼ teaspoon sea salt

¼ teaspoon ground black pepper

3 cups (720 ml) fat-free low-sodium chicken broth

2 cups (282 g) cooked brown rice

¼ cup (38 g) diced avocado, for garnish

2 tablespoons (8 g) minced fresh herbs or scallions, for garnish

1. Position an oven rack in the top position and preheat the broiler. Line a baking sheet with foil.

2. Toss the tomato and pepper halves with 1 tablespoon of the olive oil in a large bowl. Place cut side down on the baking sheet. Broil for 12 minutes, or until charred.

3. Toss the corn kernels with 1 tablespoon of the olive oil in a large bowl. Spread on a baking sheet and broil for 8 minutes, or until charred. Transfer to a large bowl.

4. Once cooled, peel the tomatoes and peppers and cut them into large pieces. Add to the bowl with the corn.

5. Heat the remaining 1 tablespoon olive oil in a large saucepan over medium-high heat. Add the onion and garlic and cook for 3 minutes. Add the chipotle powder, roasted vegetables, salt, black pepper, and broth. Bring to a boil, then reduce to a simmer and cook for 10 minutes, until the flavors are blended.

6. Ladle one-third of the hot soup into the Vitamix container and secure the lid. Turn the machine on and slowly increase the speed to Variable 10, then to High. Blend for 1 minute.

7. Pour the hot soup into a clean pot. Repeat for 2 more batches. Add the rice to the soup and mix thoroughly.

8. Serve hot with garnishes.

AMOUNT PER 1 CUP (240 ML) SERVING: calories 190, total fat 7 g, saturated fat 1 g, cholesterol 0 mg, sodium 270 mg, total carbohydrate 29g, dietary fiber 5 g, sugars 9 g, protein 5 g

Curried Corn and Coconut Soup

Sweet from corn and apple, creamy from low-fat coconut milk, and gently spicy from curry powder, Madras curry paste, and cayenne, this brilliantly yellow soup is sure to please. Garnish with a little cilantro or cooked corn. Add sautéed shrimp to turn this into a main-dish soup. Serve it with lime wedges, as the acidity from the lime brightens the soup up.

PREPARATION: **15 minutes**   PROCESSING: **2 minutes**   COOK TIME: **25 minutes**

YIELD: **12 cups (2.8 liters)**

1 tablespoon olive oil

1 cup (136 g) chopped yellow onion

1 medium apple, seeded and cut into pieces

1 teaspoon curry powder

¼ cup (60 ml) red curry paste

½ teaspoon sea salt

¼ teaspoon ground black pepper

Pinch of cayenne pepper

2 pounds (908 g) frozen corn kernels

4 cups (960 ml) low-sodium vegetable broth

1 cup (240 ml) canned lite coconut milk

Lime wedges, for serving

OPTIONAL GARNISHES:

Corn kernels

Fresh cilantro leaves

1. Heat the olive oil in a large saucepot. Add the onion and apple and cook until they just begin to soften, 2 to 3 minutes. Add the curry powder, curry paste, salt, black pepper, and cayenne and stir to coat.

2. Add the corn and cook for 2 to 3 minutes, stirring frequently. Add the broth and coconut milk and bring to a boil. Reduce to a simmer, cover, and cook for 15 minutes, or until slightly softened.

3. Ladle half of the hot soup into the Vitamix container and secure the lid. Select Variable 1. Turn the machine on and slowly increase the speed to Variable 10, then to High. Blend for 1 minute.

4. Pour the pureed soup into a clean pot. Repeat with the remaining soup. Stir together both batches until combined.

5. Serve hot, with lime wedges for squeezing. If desired, garnish with corn and cilantro.

This recipe may easily be halved.

AMOUNT PER 1 CUP (240 ML) SERVING (WITHOUT GARNISHES): calories 120, total fat 3.5 g, saturated fat 1.5 g, cholesterol 0 mg, sodium 170 mg, total carbohydrate 29 g, dietary fiber 5 g, sugars 9 g, protein 5 g

Earthy, Smoky Grilled Asparagus Soup

Lightly smoky and a little garlicky, this soup is the perfect dish to serve when spring has officially arrived, but the nights are still chilly. Garnish with a little non-fat Greek yogurt and thin slices of the reserved asparagus spears.

PREPARATION: **15 minutes**   PROCESSING: **40 seconds**   COOK TIME: **30 minutes**   YIELD: **7 cups (1.6 liters)**

1½ pounds (680 g) asparagus spears, trimmed

3 tablespoons (45 ml) olive oil

¼ teaspoon ground black pepper

2 cups (254 g) diced red onion

2 garlic cloves, halved

2 teaspoons chopped fresh rosemary

4 cups (960 ml) low-sodium vegetable broth

½ teaspoon sea salt

1 tablespoon fresh lemon juice

½ cup (120 ml) plain 0% Greek yogurt, stirred

1. Preheat a grill or grill pan to medium-high heat.

2. Toss the asparagus with 1½ tablespoons of the olive oil and the pepper to coat in a large bowl.

3. Grill the asparagus, working in small batches, until lightly charred but not burned, 5 to 7 minutes.

4. Cut one-third of the asparagus into small pieces on an angle and set aside for garnish. Cut the remaining asparagus into 1-inch (2.5-cm) pieces.

5. Heat the remaining 1½ tablespoons oil in a large saucepan. Add the onion and garlic and cook until the onion is translucent, about 5 minutes. Add the rosemary and cook for 1 minute. Add the broth and salt and bring to a boil. Reduce to a simmer and cook for 10 minutes. Add the asparagus pieces and lemon juice and cook for 5 minutes longer.

6. Ladle the mixture into the Vitamix container and secure the lid. Select Variable 1. Turn the machine on and slowly increase the speed to Variable 10, then to High. Blend for 40 seconds.

7. Serve the soup hot, garnished with a spoonful of yogurt and the reserved asparagus.

AMOUNT PER 1 CUP (240 ML) SERVING: calories 110, total fat 6 g, saturated fat 1 g, cholesterol 0 mg, sodium 260 mg, total carbohydrate 11 g, dietary fiber 3 g, sugars 5 g, protein 4 g

Carrot with Fennel Soup

More than a few of us have been told, "Eat your carrots! They are good for your eyes!" This popular advice is actually the by-product, in part, of some clever British propaganda during World War II. During the war, the Royal Air Force ran an ad campaign that claimed that their pilots' accuracy was the result of the pilots' eating lots of carrots. A new radar system was responsible for the RAF's success, but they wanted to hide this from the German government. There is truth in the advertisement, though. The lutein and beta-carotene in carrots are known to be beneficial for eye health, particularly in preventing glaucoma. This flavorful soup, with its beautiful and bright orange color, will be a feast for your eyes, and it may help keep them healthy, too!

PREPARATION: **20 minutes**   PROCESSING: **2 minutes**   COOK TIME: **20 to 25 minutes**
YIELD: **9½ cups (2.2 liters)**

1 tablespoon olive oil

1½ cups (170 g) coarsely chopped yellow onion

1 fennel bulb (11 oz / 312 g), cut into pieces (about 3 cups)

1½ pounds (680 g) carrots, cut into pieces

1 teaspoon sea salt

½ teaspoon ground fennel, lightly toasted

1 teaspoon ground coriander

6 cups (1.4 liters) low-sodium vegetable broth

½ teaspoon grated orange zest

OPTIONAL GARNISHES:

Cardamom-spiced Greek yogurt

Chopped toasted pistachios

Ground fennel

1. Heat the olive oil in a large saucepot. Add the onion and fresh fennel and cook until the onion just begins to soften, 4 to 6 minutes.

2. Add the carrots, salt, ground fennel, and coriander and cook for 1 minute. Add the broth, bring to a boil, then reduce to a simmer, cover, and cook until the carrots are tender, 15 to 20 minutes. Remove from the heat and stir in the orange zest.

3. Ladle half of the hot mixture into the Vitamix container and secure the lid. Select Variable 1. Turn the machine on and slowly increase the speed to Variable 10, then to High. Blend for 1 minute.

4. Pour the pureed soup into a clean pot. Repeat with the remaining soup. Stir together both batches of soup.

5. Serve hot. If desired, garnish with the yogurt, pistachios, and/or fennel.

AMOUNT PER 1 CUP (240 ML) SERVING (WITHOUT GARNISHES): calories 70, total fat 2 g, saturated fat 0 g, cholesterol 0 mg, sodium 400 mg, total carbohydrate 12 g, dietary fiber 4 g, sugars 5 g, protein 1 g

Carrot-Ginger Soup

This marigold-orange soup will brighten even the dreariest of days. The mellow sweetness of the carrots and parsnips is brightened by the warm spice of the fresh ginger. With the aid of your Vitamix blender, the soup will have the silky smooth texture of a restaurant-made soup too!

PREPARATION: **10 minutes**   PROCESSING: **8 minutes**   YIELD: **5 cups (1.2 liters)**

3 tablespoons (45 ml) olive oil

3 cups (380 g) chopped carrots

1 tablespoon chopped yellow onion

⅓ cup (50 g) chopped parsnips

3 cups (720 ml) low-sodium vegetable broth

1 thin slice (5 g) fresh gingerroot

½ teaspoon sea salt

¼ teaspoon ground black pepper

1 tablespoon snipped fresh chives

Place the olive oil, carrots, onion, parsnips, broth, ginger, salt, and pepper into the Vitamix container in the order listed and secure the lid. Select Variable 1. Turn the machine on and slowly increase the speed to Variable 10, then to High. Blend for 8 minutes, or until heavy steam escapes from the vented lid. Serve garnished with the chives.

AMOUNT PER 1 CUP (240 ML) SERVING: calories 120, total fat 9 g, saturated fat 1 g, cholesterol 0 mg, sodium 370 mg, total carbohydrate 11 g, dietary fiber 3 g, sugars 5 g, protein 1 g

Black Bean Tortilla Soup

Most Americans aren't eating nearly enough fiber (just 15 grams per day, when we should get closer to 25 grams for women, 30 to 38 grams for men), and eating beans is a great way to close the gap. One cup of black beans contains 12 grams of fiber, and a serving of this soup contains 6 grams of fiber (24% of the recommended daily allowance for women).

PREPARATION: **10 minutes**   PROCESSING: **7 minutes 20 seconds**   YIELD: **6 cups (1.4 liters)**

3 tablespoons (45 ml) olive oil

1 garlic clove, peeled

½ cup (60 g) chopped red onion

1 cup (125 g) chopped red bell pepper

One 15.5-ounce (440-g) can no-salt-added black beans, rinsed and drained

1½ teaspoons ground cumin

½ teaspoon dried oregano

¼ teaspoon chipotle powder

⅓ teaspoon ground cinnamon

½ teaspoon sea salt

¼ teaspoon ground black pepper

3 cups (1.2 liters) low-sodium chicken broth

½ cup (80 g) shelled edamame

1 cup (134 g) diced seeded Roma (plum) tomatoes

OPTIONAL GARNISHES:

Diced avocado • Fresh cilantro leaves • Tortilla chips (regular or blue corn)

1. Place the olive oil, garlic, 1 tablespoon of the onion, ½ cup of the bell pepper, half of the black beans, all the spices, and the broth into the Vitamix container in the order listed and secure the lid. Select Variable 1. Turn the machine on and slowly increase the speed to Variable 10, then to High. Blend for 7 minutes, or until heavy steam escapes from the vented lid.

2. Reduce the speed to Variable 5 and remove the lid plug. Through the lid plug opening, add the edamame, tomatoes, and the remaining red onion, bell pepper, and black beans and blend for an additional 20 seconds.

3. Serve hot. If desired, garnish with avocado, cilantro, and/or tortilla chips.

AMOUNT PER 1 CUP (240 ML) SERVING (WITHOUT GARNISHES): calories 160, total fat 8 g, saturated fat 1 g, cholesterol 0 mg, sodium 290 mg, total carbohydrate 16 g, dietary fiber 5 g, sugars 2 g, protein 9 g

Tastes-Like-Spring Pea Soup

The naturally occurring sugars in peas turn to starch as soon as the peas are picked. Peas that you buy frozen have been picked and frozen when they are very ripe, so they are often sweeter than the fresh peas you can buy. And frozen peas allow you to make this vibrantly green soup and dream of spring, even when snow still covers the ground!

PREPARATION: **15 minutes**   PROCESSING: **1 minute**   COOK TIME: **20 minutes**   YIELD: **7 cups (1.6 liters)**

2 tablespoons olive oil

1 cup (141 g) chopped fennel

¾ cup (95 g) chopped white onion

¼ cup (25 g) chopped celery

4 cups (960 ml) fat-free low-sodium chicken broth

One 1-pound (454-g) bag frozen peas, thawed slightly

3 tablespoons (18 g) fresh tarragon leaves

1 tablespoon fresh lemon juice

¾ teaspoon sea salt

2 cups loosely packed (75 g) spinach

Greek yogurt mixed with grated lemon zest or fresh herbs, for garnish (optional)

1. Heat the olive oil in a large saucepan over medium heat. Add the fennel, onion, and celery and cook just until soft, 4 to 6 minutes.

2. Add the broth and bring to a boil. Reduce to a simmer and cook for 10 minutes. Stir in the peas.

3. Ladle the hot mixture into the Vitamix container. Add the tarragon, lemon juice, salt, and spinach and secure the lid. Select Variable 1. Turn the machine on and slowly increase the speed to Variable 10, then to High. Blend for 1 minute.

4. Wipe out the inside of the saucepan and pour the pureed soup back into the pan.

5. Serve hot. If desired, garnish with a dollop of Greek yogurt infused with lemon or herbs.

AMOUNT PER 1 CUP (240 ML) SERVING (WITHOUT GARNISH): calories 80, total fat 0 g, saturated fat 0 g, cholesterol 0 mg, sodium 440 mg, total carbohydrate 13 g, dietary fiber 4 g, sugars 4 g, protein 7 g

Easy "Cheesy" Vegan Broccoli Soup

This simple vegan soup comes together in a flash with just the Vitamix, no stove required! Using cashews, you can create a creamy texture without adding any dairy. And the nutritional yeast has a nutty, cheese-like flavor and is a good source of vitamin B12.

PREPARATION: **15 minutes**   PROCESSING: **8 minutes**   YIELD: **6 cups (1.4 liters)**

2½ cups (600 ml) water

¼ cup (50 g) roasted red pepper (see page 71)

1 teaspoon sea salt

½ cup (35 g) nutritional yeast

½ teaspoon onion powder

½ teaspoon garlic powder

½ teaspoon dried dill

1¼ cups (178 g) unsalted roasted cashew pieces

1 pound (454 g) broccoli florets, steamed and cooled (or use thawed frozen)

Place all the ingredients into the Vitamix container in the order listed and secure the lid. Select Variable 1. Turn the machine on and slowly increase the speed to Variable 10, then to High. Blend for 8 minutes, or until heavy steam escapes from the vented lid. Serve hot.

AMOUNT PER 1 CUP (240 ML) SERVING: calories 220, total fat 14 g, saturated fat 2.5 g, cholesterol 0 mg, sodium 500 mg, total carbohydrate 17 g, dietary fiber 5 g, sugars 1 g, protein 12 g

Fennel Spinach Soup

You will need three or four fennel bulbs for this recipe. If you buy fennel with the feathery green fronds still attached, consider reserving them and adding a cup to the soup when you add the spinach. The fronds have a lovely fennel flavor all their own and will add a little more green to the soup.

PREPARATION: **15 minutes**   PROCESSING: **1 minute 15 seconds**   COOK TIME: **25 to 30 minutes**
YIELD: **5¼ cups (1.2 liters)**

GARNISH:

½ cup (120 ml) plain 0% Greek yogurt, stirred

½ lemon (with peel), halved

Dash of cayenne pepper

2 red bell peppers, roasted (see page 71)

SOUP:

2 tablespoons (30 ml) extra virgin olive oil

4 cups (484 g) chopped fennel

2 cups (164 g) chopped leeks

1 cup (132 g) chopped shallots

1 tablespoon fresh thyme leaves

¼ teaspoon sea salt

2 cups (480 ml) fat-free low-sodium chicken broth

1 cup (240 ml) water

1 bay leaf

4 cups (114 g) spinach leaves

¼ teaspoon ground black pepper

1. For the garnish: Place the garnish ingredients into the Vitamix container in the order listed and secure the lid. Select Variable 1. Turn the machine on and slowly increase the speed to Variable 10, then to High. Blend for 15 seconds. Transfer to a bowl, cover, and refrigerate until ready to serve.

2. For the soup: Heat the olive oil in a large saucepan over medium heat. Add the fennel, leek, shallots, thyme, and salt. Cover and cook, stirring occasionally, for 10 minutes, or until slightly softened. Add the broth, water, and bay leaf and bring to a boil. Reduce to a simmer, cover, and cook for 10 minutes, or until the flavors are blended. Discard the bay leaf. Stir in the spinach and pepper and remove from the heat.

3. Ladle the hot mixture into the Vitamix container and secure the lid. Select Variable 1. Turn the machine on and slowly increase the speed to Variable 10, then to High. Blend for 1 minute.

4. Serve the soup hot topped with 2 tablespoons (30 ml) of the garnish.

AMOUNT PER 1 CUP (240 ML) SERVING (WITH GARNISH): calories 130, total fat 6 g, saturated fat 1 g, cholesterol 0 mg, sodium 360 mg, total carbohydrate 19 g, dietary fiber 5 g, sugars 5 g, protein 4 g

Garlicky Leek and Artichoke Soup

Chefs love Vitamix blenders, in part because of their ability to make silky, smooth purees and soups. Making this pale green soup gives you a chance to get restaurant-quality results at home! Vitamix chef Bev Shaffer loves this soup for its clean, vibrant artichoke flavor with hints of thyme. Garnish with pesto or some chopped fresh herbs.

PREPARATION: **10 minutes**   PROCESSING: **1 minute**   COOK TIME: **25 to 30 minutes**

YIELD: **7½ cups (1.8 liters)**

2 tablespoons (30 ml) olive oil

3 medium leeks, white parts only, chopped

9 garlic cloves, peeled

10 thyme sprigs

2 medium russet (baking) potatoes (18 oz / 511 g), peeled and cut into 1-inch (2.5-cm) pieces

One 14-ounce (396-g) can water-packed artichoke hearts, rinsed and drained

2 cups (480 ml) low-sodium vegetable broth

½ lemon, peeled

½ teaspoon fine sea salt

OPTIONAL GARNISHES:

Basil pesto, preferably homemade (page 243)

Chopped fresh herbs

1. Heat the olive oil in a large pot over medium-high heat. Add the leeks and garlic. Cook, stirring frequently, until the leeks soften, about 5 minutes. Do not brown. Add the thyme and cook for 1 minute.

2. Add the potatoes, artichokes, and broth and bring to a boil. Reduce the heat to low, cover, and simmer until the potatoes are tender, about 20 minutes.

3. Transfer the mixture to the Vitamix container with the lemon and salt and secure the lid. Select Variable 1. Turn the machine on and slowly increase the speed to Variable 10, then to High. Blend for 1 minute.

4. Serve hot topped with a dollop of pesto or chopped fresh herbs.

AMOUNT PER 1 CUP (240 ML) SERVING: calories 140, total fat 4 g, saturated fat 0.5 g, cholesterol 0 mg, sodium 380 mg, total carbohydrate 23 g, dietary fiber 3 g, sugars 2 g, protein 3 g

Maple Sweet Potato Soup

The next time you find yourself with a couple of leftover baked sweet potatoes, use the leftovers to make this soup, which is perfect for fall. Consider garnishing the soup with a little cranberry sauce or chopped spiced pecans.

PREPARATION: **10 minutes**   PROCESSING: **2 minutes**   COOK TIME: **30 to 35 minutes**
YIELD: **10½ cups (2.4 liters)**

2 tablespoons (30 ml) olive oil

1 cup (125 g) chopped yellow onion

1 cup (139 g) diced celery

6 cups (1.4 liters) fat-free low-sodium chicken broth

1 cup (163 g) chopped red potatoes

⅓ cup (80 ml) maple syrup

¼ teaspoon ground black pepper

2 pounds (908 g) sweet potatoes, baked, cooled, peeled, and quartered

1. Heat the olive oil in a large saucepan over medium heat. Add the onion and celery and cook until just tender, 4 to 6 minutes. Add the broth and red potatoes and bring to a boil. Reduce to a simmer and cook until the potatoes are tender, 15 to 20 minutes.

2. Add the maple syrup, pepper, and sweet potatoes and simmer for 5 minutes longer.

3. Ladle half of the mixture into the Vitamix container and secure the lid. Select Variable 1. Turn the machine on and slowly increase the speed to Variable 10, then to High. Blend for 1 minute.

4. Pour the pureed soup into a clean pot. Repeat with the remaining soup. Stir together both batches to combine.

5. Serve hot (reheat if necessary).

AMOUNT PER 1 CUP (240 ML) SERVING: calories 140, total fat 3 g, saturated fat 0 g, cholesterol 0 mg, sodium 320 mg, total carbohydrate 28 g, dietary fiber 3 g, sugars 11 g, protein 2 g

Lemon Soup with Rice

This soup takes simple ingredients—vegetable broth, brown rice, tofu, turmeric, lemon, and dill—and makes something extraordinary. Silky and filling, yet also bright with lemon and herbs.

PREPARATION: **15 minutes**   PROCESSING: **1 minute**   COOK TIME: **35 to 45 minutes**

YIELD: **6½ cups (1.5 liters)**

4 cups (960 ml) low-sodium vegetable broth

⅓ cup (60 g) uncooked brown rice

1 tablespoon extra virgin olive oil

One 12-ounce (340-g) package soft silken tofu

¼ teaspoon ground turmeric

½ lemon, peeled

2 tablespoons (8 g) fresh dill leaves

¼ teaspoon ground black pepper

OPTIONAL GARNISHES:

Kalamata olives, rinsed to remove excess salt

Chopped fresh flat-leaf parsley

Diced tomato

1. Bring the broth to a boil in a large saucepan. Add the rice, reduce to a simmer, and cover. Cook until the rice is just tender, 30 to 40 minutes.

2. Transfer the rice-broth mixture to the Vitamix container. Add the olive oil, tofu, turmeric, lemon, dill, and pepper and secure the lid. Select Variable 1. Turn the machine on and slowly increase the speed to Variable 10, then to High. Blend for 1 minute.

3. Serve hot. If desired, garnish with olives, parsley, and/or tomato.

AMOUNT PER 1 CUP (240 ML) SERVING (WITHOUT GARNISHES): calories 90, total fat 3.5 g, saturated fat 0 g, cholesterol 0 mg, sodium 85 mg, total carbohydrate 10 g, dietary fiber 1 g, sugars 1 g, protein 3 g

The Vitamix Cookbook

Mushroom Lovers' Soup

Low-fat milk, potatoes, and nonfat Greek yogurt give this mushroom soup a delightfully creamy flavor without adding too many calories or completely masking the mushroom flavor. A little champagne vinegar adds a lovely little punch of acidity, brightening the smooth soup.

PREPARATION: **20 minutes**   PROCESSING: **7 minutes 15 seconds**   YIELD: **6½ cups (1.4 liters)**

1 tablespoon olive oil

12 ounces (400 g) white button mushrooms

1 tablespoon chopped yellow onion

1 garlic clove, peeled

1 tablespoon sweet paprika

¼ cup (15 g) fresh dill

2 cups (480 ml) low-sodium beef broth

2 cups (480 ml) low-fat (1%) milk

1 russet (baking) potato (180 g), baked, peeled, and cut into ½-inch (1.3-cm) pieces

½ teaspoon sea salt

½ teaspoon ground black pepper

½ cup (120 ml) plain 0% Greek yogurt, stirred

1½ tablespoons (22 ml) champagne vinegar

1. Place the olive oil, mushrooms, onion, garlic, paprika, dill, broth, milk, potato, salt, and pepper into the Vitamix container and secure the lid. Select Variable 1. Turn the machine on and slowly increase the speed to Variable 10, then to High. Blend for 7 minutes, or until heavy steam escapes from the vented lid.

2. Reduce the speed to Variable 5 and remove the lid plug. Through the lid plug opening, add the yogurt and vinegar and blend for another 15 seconds.

3. Serve hot.

AMOUNT PER 1 CUP (240 ML) SERVING: calories 180, total fat 3 g, saturated fat 1 g, cholesterol 5 mg, sodium 270 mg, total carbohydrate 29 g, dietary fiber 2 g, sugars 7 g, protein 8 g

Soups, Salads, and Sides

Piquant Peanut Soup

This spicy, stick-to-your-ribs soup may be the best grown-up way to get your peanut butter fix.

PREPARATION: **20 minutes**   PROCESSING: **2 minutes**   COOK TIME: **25 to 35 minutes**
YIELD: **11 cups (2.6 liters)**

1 tablespoon water

1 tablespoon sesame oil

2 cups (240 g) chopped red onion

1 cup (140 g) chopped carrots

1 tablespoon chopped fresh gingerroot

6 cups (1.4 liters) low-sodium chicken broth

4 cups (519 g) diced peeled sweet potatoes

2 teaspoons Sriracha sauce

1 cup (240 ml) peanut butter, preferably home-made (page 250)

2 tablespoons (30 ml) fresh lime juice

⅓ cup (32 g) thinly sliced scallion greens (cut on an angle), for garnish

⅓ cup (48 g) chopped unsalted dry-roasted peanuts, for garnish

1. Heat the water and sesame oil in a large saucepan over medium-high heat. Add the onion, carrots, and ginger and cook until aromatic, 2 to 3 minutes. Add the broth, sweet potatoes, and Sriracha sauce and bring to a boil. Reduce to a simmer, cover, and cook until the potatoes are tender, 20 to 25 minutes. Stir in the peanut butter and lime juice.

2. Ladle half of the hot soup into the Vitamix container and secure the lid. Select Variable 1. Turn the machine on and slowly increase the speed to Variable 10, then to High. Blend for 1 minute.

3. Pour the pureed soup into a clean pot. Repeat with the remaining soup. Stir together both batches to combine.

4. Serve hot, garnished with the scallion greens and peanuts.

AMOUNT PER 1 CUP (240 ML) SERVING: calories 250, total fat 15 g, saturated fat 2 g, cholesterol 0 mg, sodium 410 mg, total carbohydrate 20 g, dietary fiber 4 g, sugars 6 g, protein 8 g

Red Pepper Soup with Hazelnuts

This flavorful red pepper soup is bursting with vitamin C as well as a number of phytochemicals. You will be able to taste the sweet peppers, maybe even get a hint of tomato or Hungarian paprika, but will you guess the secret ingredient? A quarter cup of hazelnuts adds a subtle richness, even a little nuttiness, which rounds out the flavor of this stellar soup.

PREPARATION: **15 minutes**   PROCESSING: **30 seconds**   COOK TIME: **35 to 40 minutes**
YIELD: **5 cups (1.2 liters)**

2 tablespoons (30 ml) extra virgin olive oil

3 large red bell peppers (14 oz / 400 g), cut into pieces

5 tablespoons (50 g) chopped yellow onion

2 medium tomatoes (8 oz / 227 g), quartered

¼ cup (60 ml) dry sherry

2 garlic cloves, peeled

2 tablespoons water

2 cups (480 ml) low-sodium vegetable broth

¼ cup (35 g) skinned hazelnuts

1 teaspoon Hungarian sweet paprika

½ teaspoon sea salt

¼ teaspoon ground black pepper

1. Combine the olive oil, bell peppers, onion, tomatoes, sherry, garlic, and water in a large saucepan. Bring to a simmer and cook, covered, until the tomatoes soften and release their juices, 15 to 20 minutes.

2. Add the broth, hazelnuts, paprika, salt, and black pepper and simmer for 10 minutes longer.

3. Ladle the hot mixture into the Vitamix container and secure the lid. Select Variable 1. Turn the machine on and slowly increase the speed to Variable 10, then to High. Blend for 30 seconds.

4. Serve hot.

AMOUNT PER 1 CUP (240 ML) SERVING: calories 160, total fat 10 g, saturated fat 1 g, cholesterol 0 mg, sodium 300 mg, total carbohydrate 11 g, dietary fiber 3 g, sugars 6 g, protein 3 g

Mushroom Leek Soup

Mushrooms, a solid source of vitamin D and some B vitamins, have a rich, almost meaty taste. This deeply satisfying soup has savory mushroom flavor and lovely notes of rosemary and thyme. The combination of chicken and beef broth gives the soup a rich, silky depth. Consider garnishing the soup with sautéed mushrooms and fresh herbs.

PREPARATION: **20 minutes**   PROCESSING: **1 minute**   COOK TIME: **35 minutes**   YIELD: **9 cups (2.1 liters)**

2 tablespoons (30 ml) olive oil

2 cups (144 g) chopped leeks

1 cup (129 g) chopped celery

2 garlic cloves, peeled

½ cup (66 g) chopped fennel

1 teaspoon fresh thyme leaves

½ teaspoon minced fresh rosemary leaves

1 teaspoon sea salt

½ teaspoon ground black pepper

1 pound (454 g) cremini mushrooms, stemmed and sliced

8 ounces (227 g) white button mushrooms, stemmed and sliced

4 cups (960 ml) fat-free low-sodium chicken broth

1 cup (240 ml) low-sodium beef broth

1. Heat the olive oil in a large saucepan. Add the leeks, celery, garlic, and fennel and cook until the leeks soften, 4 to 6 minutes. Add the thyme, rosemary, salt, and pepper and cook for 1 minute.

2. Add both mushrooms, tossing well to combine. Cover and cook, stirring occasionally, until the mushrooms have released most of their liquid, 8 to 10 minutes.

3. Add both broths and bring to a boil. Reduce to a simmer, cover, and cook for 20 minutes, until the flavors are blended and the vegetables are tender.

4. Ladle the hot mixture into the Vitamix container and secure the lid with the vented lid plug in place. Select Variable 1. Turn the machine on and slowly increase the speed to Variable 10, then to High. Blend for 1 minute.

5. Serve hot.

AMOUNT PER 1 CUP (240 ML) SERVING: calories 60, total fat 3.5 g, saturated fat 0 g, cholesterol 0 mg, sodium 500 mg, total carbohydrate 7 g, dietary fiber 1 g, sugars 2 g, protein 3 g

Summer Squash Soup with Herb Yogurt

This soup, which calls for 10 cups of chopped summer squash, is the perfect solution to a garden overflowing with zucchini the size of baseball bats. Baby spinach, added just before the soup is finished in the Vitamix machine, gives the soup a lovely green hue.

PREPARATION: **15 minutes**   PROCESSING: **2 minutes**   COOK TIME: **35 minutes**   YIELD: **9 cups (2.1 liters)**

½ cup (120 ml) plain 0% Greek yogurt, stirred

Grated zest of 1 lemon

3 teaspoons chopped fresh basil

3 teaspoons chopped fresh oregano

2 tablespoons (30 ml) olive oil

1 cup (142 g) chopped yellow onion

1 garlic clove, halved

2½ pounds (1.1 kg) zucchini, diced

½ teaspoon sea salt

¼ teaspoon ground black pepper

3 cups (720 ml) fat-free low-sodium chicken broth

2 cups loosely packed (64 g) baby spinach

1. Stir together the yogurt, lemon zest, and 1½ teaspoons each of the basil and oregano in a bowl. Set aside for garnish.

2. Heat the olive oil in a large saucepan over medium heat. Add the onion and garlic and cook, stirring frequently, for 4 minutes, or until softened. Do not brown. Add the zucchini, salt, pepper, and remaining 1½ teaspoons each basil and oregano. Cook until the zucchini starts to release its liquid, 10 to 12 minutes.

3. Add the broth and bring to a boil. Reduce to a simmer and cook for 15 minutes, until hot.

4. Ladle half of the hot mixture into the Vitamix container, add 1 cup (32 g) of the spinach, and secure the lid. Select Variable 1. Turn the machine on and slowly increase the speed to Variable 10, then to High. Blend for 1 minute.

5. Pour the pureed soup into a clean pot. Repeat with the remaining soup. Mix together both batches to combine, reheating if necessary.

6. Serve hot with a dollop of the yogurt garnish.

AMOUNT PER 1 CUP (240 ML) SERVING: calories 70, total fat 3.5 g, saturated fat 0.5 g, cholesterol 0 mg, sodium 310 mg, total carbohydrate 8 g, dietary fiber 2 g, sugars 4 g, protein 4 g

Chicken Potato Soup

The next time you roast a chicken and bake potatoes, save extra of both items and whip up this delicious and hearty soup the next day without ever turning on the stove! You will make this deeply comforting and simple-to-assemble soup again and again.

PREPARATION: **15 minutes**   PROCESSING: **5 minutes 15 seconds to 6 minutes 15 seconds**

YIELD: **5¼ cups (1.2 liters)**

1 cup (240 ml) low-sodium or no-salt-added chicken or vegetable broth

1½ cups (360 ml) skim milk

½ small onion, peeled, or ¼ cup (40 g) chopped

3 medium russet (baking) potatoes (14 oz / 400 g), baked or boiled, with skin

⅛ teaspoon dried rosemary

1 tablespoon spinach, cooked or frozen

1 boneless, skinless chicken breast (5 oz / 140 g), cooked and cut up

Salt (optional)

1. Place the broth, milk, onion, 2 of the potatoes, and rosemary into the Vitamix container and secure the lid. Select Variable 1. Turn the machine on and slowly increase the speed to Variable 10, then to High. Blend for 5 to 6 minutes, until heavy steam escapes from the vented lid.

2. Reduce the speed to Variable 3 and remove the lid plug. Through the lid plug opening, add the spinach and remaining potato and blend until the potato is chopped, about 10 seconds.

3. Drop in the chicken and blend for an additional 5 seconds. Season with salt, if desired.

4. Serve hot.

AMOUNT PER 1 CUP (240 ML) SERVING: calories 180, total fat 5 g, saturated fat 1 g, cholesterol 15 mg, sodium 360 mg, total carbohydrate 24 g, dietary fiber 2 g, sugars 5 g, protein 9 g

Roasted Broccoli, Garlic, and Lemon Soup

You may have roasted both broccoli and garlic before, but roasting lemon slices? Yes! The lemon caramelizes, concentrating the juices and adding mellow, sweet notes to balance the sourness of the fruit and the bitterness of the peel. Combined with chicken broth and Greek yogurt, these roasted ingredients create a broccoli soup unlike any you have ever had before.

PREPARATION: **15 minutes**   PROCESSING: **6 minutes 30 seconds**   BAKE TIME: **55 minutes**
YIELD: **5¾ cups (1.4 liters)**

6 garlic cloves, peeled

4 tablespoons (60 ml) olive oil

1¾ pounds (794 g) broccoli florets

1 lemon, sliced

4 cups (960 ml) low-sodium chicken broth

½ cup (120 ml) plain 0% Greek yogurt, stirred

¼ teaspoon ground black pepper

½ teaspoon sea salt

1. Preheat the oven to 400°F (200°C).

2. Wrap the garlic in foil and drizzle with 1 tablespoon of the olive oil. Seal well and roast on a baking sheet for 25 minutes.

3. Meanwhile, toss together the broccoli florets and remaining oil in a large bowl. Spread the broccoli on a foil-lined baking sheet in a single layer. Top with the lemon slices and roast for 30 minutes.

4. Place the broth, yogurt, pepper, salt, roasted garlic, roasted broccoli, and lemon slices into the Vitamix container in the order listed and secure the lid. Select Variable 1. Turn the machine on and slowly increase the speed to Variable 10, then to High. Blend for 6 minutes 30 seconds, or until heavy steam escapes from the vented lid.

5. Serve hot.

AMOUNT PER 1 CUP (240 ML) SERVING: calories 160, total fat 10 g, saturated fat 1.5 g, cholesterol 0 mg, sodium 360 mg, total carbohydrate 11 g, dietary fiber 5 g, sugars 1 g, protein 10 g

Tortilla Soup

Hungry for a healthy meal but short on time? Drop the soup base ingredients into your Vitamix and let it do its magic while you cut up cooked chicken, slice a jalapeño and some olives, and get out tortilla chips. In 15 minutes, you have a steaming hot, vegetable-packed soup, and dinner is served!

PREPARATION: **15 minutes**   PROCESSING: **6 to 7 minutes**   YIELD: **5 cups (1.2 liters)**

SOUP BASE:

3 cups (720 ml) low-sodium chicken, beef, or vegetable broth

1 Roma (plum) tomato, halved

1 medium carrot, halved

1 celery stalk, halved

One ¼- to ½-inch-thick slice onion

1 garlic clove, peeled

One ¼- to ½-inch-thick slice yellow squash

One ¼- to ½-inch-thick slice red bell pepper

One ¼- to ½-inch-thick slice cabbage

1 white button mushroom

Salt and ground black pepper

1 teaspoon taco seasoning

Dash of ground cumin

OPTIONAL INGREDIENTS:

½ cup (70 g) cooked chicken

½ jalapeño pepper

¼ cup (30 g) sliced olives

¼ cup (50 g) no-salt-added canned corn, drained

1 ounce (28 g) tortilla chips

1. For the soup base: Place all the ingredients into the Vitamix container in the order listed and secure the lid. Select Variable 1. Turn the machine on and slowly increase the speed to Variable 10, then to High. Blend for 6 to 7 minutes, until heavy steam escapes from the vented lid.

2. If adding optional ingredients, reduce the speed to Variable 2 and remove the lid plug. Through the lid plug opening, drop in the chicken, jalapeño, olives, corn, and/or chips and blend for an additional 10 seconds.

AMOUNT PER 1 CUP (240 ML) SERVING (WITH OPTIONAL INGREDIENTS): calories 90, total fat 2.5 g, saturated fat 0 g, cholesterol 10 mg, sodium 190 mg, total carbohydrate 10 g, dietary fiber 2 g, sugars 2 g, protein 8 g

Barley and Vegetable Soup with Chicken and Pesto

This hearty soup, almost a stew, is chock-full of whole grains, veggies, and chicken. Instead of flour or another thickener, a portion of the cooked soup base is pureed before the chard leaves, barley, and cooked chicken breast are added. The walnut and garlic pesto, an elegant finishing touch, adds a little richness and a garlicky punch.

PREPARATION: **45 minutes**   PROCESSING: **15 seconds plus pulsing**

COOK TIME: **20 to 25 minutes**   YIELD: **7 cups (1.7 liters) soup; ¾ cup (180 ml) pesto**

PESTO:

2 tablespoons (30 ml) olive oil

1 garlic clove, peeled

½ cup (58 g) walnuts, toasted

½ cup (28 g) freshly grated Parmesan

SOUP:

2 tablespoons (30 ml) olive oil

1½ cups (180 g) chopped yellow onion

2 tablespoons (15 g) minced garlic

Two 4-inch (10-cm) portobello mushroom caps, gills removed, cut into pieces (see note)

1 cup (160 g) cubed peeled butternut squash

½ cup (81 g) chopped carrot

½ cup (69 g) chopped celery

½ cup (44 g) Swiss chard stems thinly sliced on an angle

1 thyme sprig

1 teaspoon minced fresh rosemary

6 cups (1.4 liters) low-sodium chicken broth

¾ teaspoon sea salt

¼ teaspoon ground black pepper

2 boneless, skinless chicken breasts (11 oz), cooked and cut into large pieces

2 cups (325 g) cooked barley

2 cups (72 g) Swiss chard leaves, coarsely chopped

1. For the pesto: Place all the pesto ingredients into the Vitamix container in the order listed and secure the lid. Select Variable 5. Use the On/Off switch to quickly pulse 3 times. Remove the lid, scrape down the sides

and around the blades, secure the lid, and pulse 3 times. Repeat this procedure 3 more times, or until the desired consistency is reached.

2. For the soup: Heat the olive oil in a large saucepan over medium heat. Add the onion and garlic and cook until aromatic and the onion begins to soften, about 2 minutes.

3. Add the mushrooms, squash, carrot, celery, chard stems, thyme, and rosemary. Cook for 2 minutes so the flavors begin to blend. Add the broth, salt, and pepper and bring to a boil. Reduce to a simmer and cook until the vegetables are tender, 15 to 20 minutes.

4. Transfer one-third of the cooked mixture to the Vitamix container and secure the lid. Select Variable 1. Turn the machine on and slowly increase the speed to Variable 10, then to High. Blend for 15 seconds.

5. Stop the machine and remove the lid. Add the chicken to the container and secure the lid. Select Variable 6. Use the On/Off switch to quickly pulse 2 to 3 times to chop.

6. Add the contents of the Vitamix container, the barley, and Swiss chard leaves back to the saucepan. Mix well and heat to warm.

7. Ladle into bowls and garnish with a dollop of the pesto. Store leftover pesto in the refrigerator for up to 1 week, covering the surface with plastic to prevent browning. Stir before using.

To gill the mushrooms: Gently remove the stems from the mushrooms, and using a spoon, go around the underside of the mushroom cap, removing as many of the "gills" as possible by scraping them away. This should result in a smooth underside and create a nice, clean mushroom cap.

AMOUNT PER 1 CUP (240 ML) SERVING WITH 1 TABLESPOON PESTO: calories 290, total fat 14 g, saturated fat 2.5 g, cholesterol 30 mg, sodium 500 mg, total carbohydrate 23 g, dietary fiber 4 g, sugars 3 g, protein 19 g

Chilled Cucumber and Avocado Soup

This light, refreshing soup is the perfect antidote to the hottest summer day. Delicious as an appetizer or a light supper.

PREPARATION: 15 minutes   PROCESSING: 1 minute plus pulsing   YIELD: 7 cups (1.7 liters)

2 cups (240 g) cut-up peeled English cucumber

2 Hass avocados, halved, pitted, and peeled

2 scallions, halved

2 tablespoons (30 ml) fresh lime juice

1 cup (240 ml) plain 0% Greek yogurt, stirred

3 cups (720 ml) cold water

1 teaspoon sea salt

¼ teaspoon cracked black pepper

2 tablespoons (6 g) fresh cilantro leaves

OPTIONAL GARNISHES:

Lump crabmeat

Pico de gallo

Crème fraîche

1. Place the cucumber, avocados, scallions, lime juice, yogurt, water, salt, and pepper into the Vitamix container in the order listed and secure the lid. Select Variable 1. Turn the machine on and slowly increase the speed to Variable 10, then to High. Blend for 1 minute.

2. Stop the machine and remove the lid plug. Add the cilantro through the lid plug opening. Select Variable 8. Use the On/Off switch to quickly pulse 2 times.

3. Chill well before serving. If desired, garnish with crabmeat, pico de gallo, and/or crème fraîche.

AMOUNT PER 1 CUP (240 ML) SERVING (WITHOUT GARNISHES): calories 90, total fat 6 g, saturated fat 1 g, cholesterol 0 mg, sodium 360 mg, total carbohydrate 6 g, dietary fiber 3 g, sugars 2 g, protein 4 g

Roasted Eggplant and Tomato Soup

The mellow roasted eggplant and caramelized roasted tomatoes in this soup are brightened by feta and a generous spoonful of lemon. The half-and-half adds a little richness, and the oregano adds a gentle, herby note.

PREPARATION: **15 minutes**   PROCESSING: **30 seconds**   BAKE TIME: **30 minutes**   YIELD: **8 cups (1.8 liters)**

1½ pounds (680 g) eggplant

¾ teaspoon sea salt

1 pound (454 g) Roma (plum) tomatoes, quartered

1 tablespoon olive oil

2 garlic cloves, halved

4 cups (960 ml) low-sodium vegetable broth

½ cup (96 g) crumbled feta

1 tablespoon fresh lemon juice

2 tablespoons (30 ml) half-and-half

1 tablespoon fresh oregano leaves, for garnish (optional)

1. Peel the eggplant and cut lengthwise into ½-inch (1.3-cm) planks. Salt both sides with the sea salt. Arrange on a wire rack and let drain for 30 minutes to remove the bitterness.

2. Preheat the oven to 425°F (220°C). Line a baking sheet with foil or a silicone baking mat.

3. Wipe the eggplant planks dry. Cut the eggplant into ½-inch (1.3-cm) dice and place in a large bowl. Add the tomatoes, olive oil, and garlic and toss to coat

4. Spread the vegetables on the baking sheet and roast for 30 minutes, or until lightly caramelized.

5. Scrape the roasted vegetable mixture into the Vitamix container. Add 2 cups (480 ml) of the broth and ¼ cup (48 g) of the feta and secure the lid. Select Variable 1. Turn the machine on and slowly increase the speed to Variable 10, then to High. Blend for 30 seconds.

6. Pour the eggplant mixture into a large saucepan. Add the remaining broth, the lemon juice, and half-and-half.

7. Heat over medium-high heat and serve hot. Garnish with the remaining feta and oregano leaves (if using).

AMOUNT PER 1 CUP (240 ML) SERVING: calories 90, total fat 4.5 g, saturated fat 2 g, cholesterol 10 mg, sodium 450 mg, total carbohydrate 10 g, dietary fiber 4 g, sugars 5 g, protein 4 g

Garden-Fresh Tomato Soup

Few soups are as cozy or as nostalgic as good old tomato soup. In our version, you simply put broth, onion, celery, basil, tomato paste, and whole tomatoes in a pot and simmer until the tomatoes are tender. Put the soup—tomato skins, seeds, and all—in the Vitamix and puree to silky, smooth perfection. Garnish with Greek yogurt and basil. This is delicious served with grilled cheese sandwiches.

PREPARATION: **10 minutes**   PROCESSING: **7 minutes**   YIELD: **5 cups (1.2 liters)**

2 cups (480 ml) fat-free low-sodium chicken broth

1 tablespoon chopped yellow onion

2 tablespoons (5 g) fresh basil leaves, plus more for garnish

2 tablespoons (33 g) tomato paste

1 pound (450 g) Roma (plum) tomatoes, quartered

½ teaspoon sea salt

¼ teaspoon ground black pepper

6 tablespoons (90 ml) plain 0% Greek yogurt, stirred

1. Place the broth, onion, basil, tomato paste, tomatoes, salt, and pepper into the Vitamix container in the order listed and secure the lid. Select Variable 1. Turn the machine on and slowly increase the speed to Variable 10, then to High. Blend for 7 minutes, or until heavy steam escapes from the vented lid.

2. Serve hot. Garnish with a dollop of yogurt and basil leaves.

AMOUNT PER 1 CUP (240 ML) SERVING: calories 80, total fat 6 g, saturated fat 1 g, cholesterol 0 mg, sodium 450 mg, total carbohydrate 6 g, dietary fiber 2 g, sugars 4 g, protein 3 g

The Vitamix Cookbook

Spiced Butternut Squash Soup

Lots of people love kale these days, but if you need to sneak some greens to a less enthusiastic kale eater, try this quintessential fall soup. Butternut squash, apple, and carrot juice offer a sweetness that balances the bitterness of the greens. Almond milk and raw almonds give the soup a little creaminess, and the spices make it smell like fall in a bowl.

PREPARATION: **15 minutes**   PROCESSING: **2 minutes**   COOK TIME: **40 minutes**   YIELD: **9 cups (2.1 liters)**

4 cups (471 g) peeled, chunked butternut squash

2 medium Gala apples (11 oz / 317 g), seeded and cut into small pieces

4 cups (89 g) torn kale leaves

1 cup (128 g) diced yellow onion

2 tablespoons (30 ml) apple cider vinegar

5 cups (1.2 liters) carrot juice

½ cup (120 ml) unsweetened almond milk

½ cup (73 g) raw almonds

1 teaspoon ground cinnamon

½ teaspoon ground nutmeg

1. Combine the squash, apples, kale, onion, vinegar, carrot juice, almond milk, almonds, and spices in a large saucepan. Bring to a boil. Reduce to a simmer, cover, and cook until the squash is tender, about 30 minutes.

2. Ladle half of the hot mixture into the Vitamix container and secure the lid. Select Variable 1. Turn the machine on and slowly increase the speed to Variable 10, then to High. Blend for 1 minute.

3. Pour the pureed soup into a clean pot. Repeat with the remaining soup. Stir together both batches to combine.

4. Serve hot.

AMOUNT PER 1 CUP (240 ML) SERVING: calories 160, total fat 4.5 g, saturated fat 0 g, cholesterol 0 mg, sodium 110 mg, total carbohydrate 27 g, dietary fiber 4 g, sugars 6 g, protein 5 g

Thai Tempeh Soup

A popular vegetarian source of protein, tempeh adds heartiness to this full-flavored, veggie-packed, Thai-inspired vegan soup.

PREPARATION: **20 minutes**   PROCESSING: **1 minute**   COOK TIME: **35 minutes**   YIELD: **8 cups (1.9 liters)**

3 tablespoons (90 ml) toasted sesame oil

2 garlic cloves, chopped

1 tablespoon chopped fresh gingerroot

2 tablespoons (11 g) thinly sliced lemongrass

1 jalapeño pepper, thinly sliced

3 cups (170 g) julienned shiitake mushrooms caps

1 teaspoon coriander seeds

1 teaspoon sweet paprika

1 teaspoon ground turmeric

4 cups (960 ml) white miso broth (see note)

One 13.5-ounce (400-ml) can light coconut milk

1 cup (134 g) chopped carrots

½ cup (66 g) thinly sliced scallions

2 cups loosely packed (135 g) thinly sliced napa cabbage

½ pound (227 g) tempeh, steamed and finely diced

¼ cup loosely packed (8 g) chopped fresh cilantro leaves

OPTIONAL GARNISHES:

Bean sprouts • Lime wedges

1. Heat 1½ tablespoons of the sesame oil in a large saucepan over medium heat. Add the garlic, ginger, lemongrass, and jalapeño and cook for 2 minutes. Add half of the shiitake mushrooms and cook until soft, 4 to 6 minutes.

2. Add the coriander seeds, paprika, turmeric, miso broth, and coconut milk and bring to a boil. Reduce to a simmer and cook for 10 minutes.

3. Ladle the hot mixture into the Vitamix container and secure the lid. Select Variable 1. Turn the machine on and slowly increase the speed to Variable 10, then to High. Blend for 1 minute.

4. Heat the remaining 1½ tablespoons oil in a clean saucepan over medium heat. Add the carrots, scallions, cabbage, and remaining shiitakes and cook until the mushrooms are soft, 3 to 4 minutes.

5. Add the pureed broth and tempeh and bring to a boil. Reduce to a simmer and cook for 10 minutes. Stir in the cilantro.

6. Serve hot. If desired, garnish with bean sprouts and serve lime wedges for squeezing.

For miso broth, mix 1 tablespoon shiro miso with 4 cups water.

AMOUNT PER 1 CUP (240 ML) SERVING (WITHOUT GARNISHES): calories 150, total fat 10 g, saturated fat 2.5 g, cholesterol 0 mg, sodium 80 mg, total carbohydrate 10 g, dietary fiber 4 g, sugars 2 g, protein 7 g

Creamy Celery Root Soup

Celery root (or celeriac), beige and knobby looking, is unlikely to win any beauty contests, but this starchy root vegetable has a wonderfully fresh flavor that is very much like parsley and celery. This creamy soup can be simply garnished with a few celery or parsley leaves or dressed up with some wild mushrooms sautéed with fresh herbs. Did your celery root come with stems and leaves attached? These stems have a more bitter flavor than regular celery, so while you can add them to a soup, they are not good for snacking.

PREPARATION: **20 minutes**   PROCESSING: **2 minutes**   COOK TIME: **35 to 40 minutes**

YIELD: **7¾ cups (1.8 liters)**

1 tablespoon olive oil

¼ cup (32 g) chopped white onion

½ cup (61 g) chopped celery, leaves reserved for garnish

½ cup (68 g) chopped parsnips

4 cups (510 g) chopped peeled celery root

3 tablespoons (26 g) chopped shallot

1 garlic clove, peeled

6 cups (1.4 liters) low-sodium chicken broth

1 cup (240 ml) half-and-half

½ teaspoon sea salt

⅓ teaspoon cayenne pepper

OPTIONAL GARNISHES:

Sautéed wild mushrooms with fresh herbs

Parsley leaves

1. Heat the olive oil in a large saucepan over medium heat. Add the onion, celery, parsnips, and celery root. Cook until softened, 4 to 6 minutes. Add the shallot and garlic and cook for 1 minute. Do not brown.

2. Add the broth and bring to a boil. Reduce to a simmer, cover, and cook until the celery root is tender, about 15 minutes.

3. Add the half-and-half, salt, and cayenne and simmer for an additional 5 minutes.

4. Ladle half of the hot mixture into the Vitamix container and secure the lid. Select Variable 1. Turn the machine on and slowly increase the speed to Variable 10, then to High. Blend for 1 minute.

5. Pour the pureed soup into a clean pot. Repeat with the remaining soup. Stir together both batches to combine.

6. Serve hot. If desired, garnish with sautéed mushrooms and parsley or celery leaves.

AMOUNT PER 1 CUP (240 ML) SERVING (WITHOUT GARNISHES): calories 120, total fat 5 g, saturated fat 2.5 g, cholesterol 15 mg, sodium 370 mg, total carbohydrate 12 g, dietary fiber 2 g, sugars 3 g, protein 6 g

Garden-Fresh Minestrone

Here, the vegetable broth, tomatoes, and a little less than half of the kidney beans are pureed to make a thick, flavorful base for the soup. Then nine vegetables (yes, nine!) are cooked until tender, simmered with nutrient-rich broth, and finished with ditalini pasta to make a delicious, stick-to-your-ribs soup.

PREPARATION: **20 minutes** PROCESSING: **7 minutes 20 seconds** YIELD: **8½ cups (2 liters)**

2 cups (8 oz / 227 g) ditalini pasta

4 cups (960 ml) reduced-sodium vegetable broth

½ pound (225 g) Roma (plum) tomatoes, quartered

3 tablespoons (45 ml) extra virgin olive oil

¼ cup (40 g) chopped carrots

¼ cup (40 g) chopped yellow onion

1 garlic clove, peeled

½ teaspoon sea salt

¼ teaspoon ground black pepper

½ teaspoon minced fresh thyme

½ teaspoon minced fresh oregano

One 15-ounce (200-g) can kidney beans, rinsed and drained

¼ cup (40 g) chopped fennel

¼ cup (35 g) chopped red bell pepper

½ cup (71 g) chopped zucchini

½ cup (73 g) chopped yellow squash

1 cup (40 g) thinly sliced escarole (inner leaves only)

OPTIONAL GARNISHES:

Pesto

Shaved Parmesan

1. Cook the pasta in a pot of boiling water according to the package directions. Drain.

2. Meanwhile, place the broth, tomatoes, olive oil, carrots, onion, garlic, salt, pepper, herbs, and ½ cup of the beans into the Vitamix container in the order listed and secure the lid. Select Variable 1. Turn the machine on and slowly increase the speed to Variable 10, then to High. Blend for 7 minutes, or until heavy steam escapes the vented lid.

3. Reduce the speed to Variable 5 and remove the lid plug. Add the fennel, bell pepper, zucchini, yellow squash, escarole, and remaining beans through the lid plug opening and blend for another 20 seconds.

4. Portion into bowls and add the warm pasta. If desired, garnish with pesto and/or Parmesan.

AMOUNT PER 1 CUP (240 ML) SERVING (WITHOUT GARNISHES): calories 150, total fat 6 g, saturated fat 1 g, cholesterol 0 mg, sodium 260 mg, total carbohydrate 20 g, dietary fiber 4 g, sugars 2 g, protein 5 g

Tomato Fennel Soup

Gone are the days of peeling and seeding tomatoes before you make fresh tomato soup! Here, you simply chop whole tomatoes and cook them down with onions, fennel, and herbs. By using low-sodium vegetable broth you control the sodium in your soup too. Easy, healthy, and full of flavor, what soup could be better?

PREPARATION: **10 minutes**   PROCESSING: **35 seconds**   COOK TIME: **25 to 30 minutes**
YIELD: **6¾ cups (1.6 liters)**

2 tablespoons (30 ml) olive oil

1½ cups (193 g) chopped white onion

1 cup (133 g) chopped fennel

2 garlic cloves, peeled

3 cups (500 g) chopped tomatoes

1 tablespoon grated lemon zest

1 tablespoon chopped fresh rosemary

½ teaspoon dried basil

One 6-ounce (170-g) can tomato paste

3 cups (720 ml) low-sodium vegetable broth

1 teaspoon light brown sugar

1 teaspoon sea salt

¼ cup loosely packed (3 g) fresh flat-leaf parsley leaves

1 teaspoon fresh thyme leaves

1. Heat the olive oil in a large saucepan over medium heat. Add the onion and fennel and cook until the onion begins to soften, 4 to 6 minutes. Add the garlic and cook for an additional 2 minutes. Do not brown.

2. Add the tomatoes, lemon zest, rosemary, basil, and tomato paste and cook, stirring occasionally, until the tomatoes have released most of their liquid, about 5 minutes.

3. Stir in the broth, brown sugar, and salt and bring to a boil. Reduce to a simmer, cover, and cook for 15 to 20 minutes.

4. Ladle the hot mixture into the Vitamix container and secure the lid. Select Variable 1. Turn the machine on and slowly increase the speed to Variable 10, then to High. Blend for 30 seconds.

5. Reduce the speed to Variable 6 and remove the lid plug. Through the lid plug opening, add the parsley and thyme and blend for an additional 5 seconds.

6. Serve hot.

AMOUNT PER 1 CUP (240 ML) SERVING: calories 110, total fat 4.5 g, saturated fat 0.5 g, cholesterol 0 mg, sodium 510 mg, total carbohydrate 16 g, dietary fiber 4 g, sugars 8 g, protein 2 g

Tuscan Bean Soup with Whole Grains

Barley, like a number of other whole grains, freezes well. Make this hearty soup—full of beans, vegetables, and nutty barley—and then stash any leftovers in the freezer for a quick lunch or dinner on a busy day.

PREPARATION: **20 minutes**   PROCESSING: **7 minutes 30 seconds**   YIELD: **6½ cups (1.5 liters)**

3 tablespoons (45 ml) olive oil

1 tablespoon chopped onion

¼ cup (40 g) coarsely chopped carrot

1 garlic clove, peeled

1½ cups (225 g) coarsely chopped tomato

10 fresh sage leaves

1 thyme sprig

½ teaspoon sea salt

¼ teaspoon ground black pepper

3 cups (700 ml) fat-free low-sodium chicken broth

2 cups (60 g) spinach leaves

¼ cup loosely packed (4 g) fresh flat-leaf parsley leaves

One 15-ounce (425-g) can no-salt-added white navy beans, rinsed and drained

2 teaspoons grated lemon zest

3 cups (470 g) cooked pearl barley

1. Place the olive oil, onion, carrot, garlic, tomato, sage, thyme, salt, pepper, and broth into the Vitamix container and secure the lid. Select Variable 1. Turn the machine on and slowly increase the speed to Variable 10, then to High. Blend for 7 minutes, or until heavy steam escapes the vented lid.

2. Reduce the speed to Variable 5 and remove the lid plug. Through the lid plug opening, add the spinach, parsley, beans, and lemon zest and blend for an additional 30 seconds.

3. To serve, spoon ½ cup of the cooked barley into soup bowls and top with 1 cup of the hot soup.

AMOUNT PER 1 CUP (240 ML) SERVING: calories 220, total fat 7 g, saturated fat 1 g, cholesterol 0 mg, sodium 420 mg, total carbohydrate 34 g, dietary fiber 8 g, sugars 2 g, protein 6 g

Soups, Salads, and Sides

One Potato, Two Tomato Soup

In this wonderful variation on the classic tomato soup, cinnamon and black pepper add a gentle heat to its flavor, and coconut oil and coconut water complement the spices.

PREPARATION: **20 minutes**   PROCESSING: **30 seconds**   COOK TIME: **30 minutes**   YIELD: **7 cups (1.6 liters)**

1½ teaspoons coconut oil

1 tablespoon whole wheat flour, preferably homemade (page 44)

1 small to medium yellow onion (4½ oz / 128 g), cut into pieces

2 garlic cloves, peeled

2 cups (321 g) cherry tomatoes

One 15-ounce (425-g) can no-salt-added diced tomatoes, with liquid

4 cups (960 ml) low-sodium vegetable broth

1 large russet (baking) potato (9 oz / 255 g), cut into pieces

½ teaspoon ground cinnamon

½ teaspoon sea salt

½ teaspoon ground black pepper

½ lemon, peeled

1 tablespoon agave nectar

¼ cup (60 ml) plain 0% Greek yogurt, stirred

1½ teaspoons chopped fresh basil

1 teaspoon fresh thyme leaves

¼ cup (60 ml) unsweetened coconut water

1. Heat the coconut oil in a large soup pot over medium heat. Stir in the flour and cook just until golden. Add the onion and garlic and cook over medium heat until slightly browned, about 5 minutes. Add the cherry tomatoes and canned tomatoes (with their liquid) and cook for 5 minutes.

2. Add the broth, potato, cinnamon, salt, and pepper and bring to a boil. Reduce to a simmer, partially cover, and cook until the potato is very tender, about 20 minutes. Add the lemon, agave, yogurt, basil, thyme, and coconut water.

3. Ladle half of the soup into the Vitamix container and secure the lid. Select Variable 1. Turn the machine on and slowly increase the speed to Variable 10, then to High. Blend for 30 seconds.

4. Pour the pureed soup into a clean pot. Repeat with the remaining soup. Stir together both batches to combine.

5. Serve hot.

AMOUNT PER 1 CUP (240 ML) SERVING: calories 100, total fat 1 g, saturated fat 1 g, cholesterol 0 mg, sodium 290 mg, total carbohydrate 20 g, dietary fiber 3 g, sugars 8 g, protein 3 g

Roasted Root Vegetable Soup for a Crowd

The perfect soup to start your Thanksgiving dinner or to turn any day into a fall feast! Full of roasted root vegetables, this soup is simple to prepare. It can be made in advance and kept for up to 4 days in the refrigerator or 1 month in the freezer.

PREPARATION: **20 minutes**   PROCESSING: **2 minutes**   BAKE TIME: **35 to 40 minutes**

COOK TIME: **20 to 30 minutes**   YIELD: **12½ cups (3 liters)**

2 pounds (908 g) carrots, diced

½ pound (227 g) parsnips, diced

½ pound (227 g) turnips, diced

½ teaspoon fresh thyme leaves

2 tablespoons (30 ml) olive oil

1 cup (128 g) white onion, cut into pieces

2 garlic cloves, coarsely chopped

10 cups (2.4 liters) low-sodium vegetable broth

1 teaspoon finely minced fresh rosemary leaves

1 teaspoon sea salt

1. Preheat the oven to 400°F (200°C).

2. Combine the carrots, parsnips, turnips, thyme, and 1 tablespoon of the olive oil in a large bowl. Mix thoroughly, divide between 2 foil-lined baking sheets, and roast for 35 to 40 minutes, until the vegetables just begin to brown. Remove from the oven and set aside.

3. Heat the remaining 1 tablespoon oil in a large soup pot over medium heat. Add the onion and cook until just beginning to soften, 4 to 6 minutes. Add the garlic and cook for 2 minutes.

4. Scrape the roasted vegetables into the pot. Add the broth and rosemary and bring to a boil. Reduce to a simmer and cook for 15 minutes more to blend the flavors.

5. Ladle half of the hot soup into the Vitamix container and secure the lid. Select Variable 1. Turn the machine on and slowly increase the speed to Variable 10, then to High. Blend for 1 minute.

6. Pour the pureed soup into a clean pot. Repeat with the remaining soup. Stir together both batches to combine, reheating only if necessary. Season with the salt. Serve hot.

AMOUNT PER 1 CUP (240 ML) SERVING: calories 90, total fat 2.5 g, saturated fat 0 g, cholesterol 0 mg, sodium 370 mg, total carbohydrate 15 g, dietary fiber 4 g, sugars 7 g, protein 1 g

Fennel, Kale, and Portobello Salad

Kale is something of a darling among vegetables at the moment. Nutrient-dense, full of vitamins A, C, and K as well as a number of antioxidants, it is as delicious and nutritious as it is versatile. Here, we toss it with a balsamic vinaigrette, roasted portobello mushrooms, and thinly sliced fennel for a hearty and healthy salad.

PREPARATION: **15 minutes**   PROCESSING: **20 seconds**   BAKE TIME: **20 to 30 minutes**   YIELD: **8 servings**

6 portobello mushrooms

5 or 6 tablespoons (75 to 90 ml) olive oil

3 tablespoons (45 ml) balsamic vinegar

1½ tablespoons (23 ml) water

¼ teaspoon sea salt

⅓ teaspoon ground black pepper

1 garlic clove, peeled

⅓ cup (43 g) finely grated Parmesan

1 fennel bulb, trimmed and thinly sliced

7 ounces (198 g) stemmed, washed, dried, and thinly sliced Tuscan (black/lacinato) kale (about 6 packed cups)

1. Preheat the oven to 375°F (190°C).

2. Gently remove the stems from the mushrooms, and using a spoon, go around the underside of the mushroom cap, removing as many of the "gills" as possible by scraping them away. This should result in a smooth underside and create a nice, clean mushroom cap. Brush the mushrooms with 3 tablespoons of the oil and roast for 20 to 30 minutes, or until tender. When cool enough to handle, slice them.

3. Place the vinegar, water, remaining oil, salt, pepper, garlic, and half of the Parmesan into the Vitamix container in the order listed and secure the lid. Select Variable 1. Turn the machine on and slowly increase the speed to Variable 10, then to High. Blend for 20 seconds.

4. Combine the mushrooms, fennel, and kale in a large bowl. Add the dressing and some of the remaining Parmesan and toss to coat. Top with additional Parmesan as desired.

AMOUNT PER SERVING: calories 150, total fat 13 g, saturated fat 2.5 g, cholesterol 5 mg, sodium 180 mg, total carbohydrate 8 g, dietary fiber 2 g, sugars 2 g, protein 4 g

Barley and Corn Salad with Yogurt Chive Dressing

Toothsome pearl barley and corn are cooked together to form the base of this delicious salad. (You can also use hulled barley, sold at many health food stores. This form of barley has more fiber but also takes longer to cook, closer to 40 to 50 minutes.) This salad is wonderful as a side or as a hearty meatless main dish.

PREPARATION: **10 minutes**   PROCESSING: **20 seconds**   COOK TIME: **35 minutes**   YIELD: **6 servings**

1 cup (240 ml) low-sodium or no-salt-added chicken broth

1¼ cups (300 ml) water

½ cup (100 g) pearl barley

2 cups (290 g) fresh or frozen corn kernels

⅓ cup (80 ml) plain 0% Greek yogurt, stirred

1 tablespoon plus 1 teaspoon red wine vinegar

½ teaspoon sea salt

⅓ teaspoon ground black pepper

2 tablespoons (20 g) chopped shallot

2 tablespoons (6 g) snipped fresh chives

1 medium tomato, halved and thinly sliced

½ medium cucumber, thinly sliced

1. Combine the broth and water in a medium saucepan. Bring to a boil over high heat. Stir in the barley and return to a boil. Reduce the heat to low, cover, and simmer just until the barley is tender but still slightly firm to the bite, about 25 minutes.

2. Stir in the corn, cover, and simmer for 5 minutes longer. Drain off any remaining liquid and transfer the mixture to a large serving bowl. Allow the mixture to cool to room temperature.

3. Place the yogurt, vinegar, salt, pepper, shallot, and chives into the Vitamix container in the order listed and secure the lid. Select Variable 1. Turn the machine on and slowly increase the speed to Variable 6. Blend for 20 seconds, using the tamper to press the ingredients into the blades.

4. Add the dressing, tomato, and cucumber to the barley mixture and stir gently to combine. Serve chilled or at room temperature.

AMOUNT PER SERVING: calories 120, total fat 1 g, saturated fat 0 g, cholesterol 0 mg, sodium 240 mg, total carbohydrate 25 g, dietary fiber 4 g, sugars 4 g, protein 6 g

Kale Chips Salad
with Spicy Dressing

A kale salad unlike any you have ever had before! Tons of herbs, shredded crunchy veggies, greens, and a delightfully spicy dressing are crowned with crispy kale chips. Kale chips made with lacinato kale have a more delicate texture—not unlike that of seaweed chips—than chips made with green curly kale.

PREPARATION: **20 minutes**   PROCESSING: **30 seconds**   BAKE TIME: **30 minutes**   YIELD: **8 servings**

SPICY DRESSING:

2 tablespoons (32 g) dark brown sugar

1 teaspoon grated lime zest

¼ cup (60 ml) fresh lime juice

2 tablespoons (30 ml) fish sauce

2 tablespoons (30 ml) olive oil

2 garlic cloves, peeled

½ red Thai chile or ¼ red jalapeño pepper, seeded and cut into pieces

SALAD:

Thirty 5-inch (12-cm) pieces of Tuscan (black/lacinato) kale leaves (about 4 oz / 114 g)

1 tablespoon olive oil

½ teaspoon coarse sea salt

¼ teaspoon ground black pepper

2 cups loosely packed (46 g) mixed fresh herb leaves, e.g., flat-leaf parsley, mint, basil

3 cups (312 g) mixed shredded veggies, e.g., carrots, red bell pepper, daikon radish

2 cups lightly packed (70 g) arugula or baby spinach

1. For the spicy dressing: Place all the dressing ingredients into the Vitamix container in the order listed and secure the lid. Select Variable 1. Turn the machine on and slowly increase the speed to Variable 10, then to High. Blend for 30 seconds.

2. For the salad: Preheat the oven to 275°F (140°C).

3. Brush the tops of the kale leaves with the oil. Sprinkle with the salt and pepper. Spread the kale on baking sheets. Bake for 30 minutes, or until the kale is crisp, rotating the sheets front to back halfway through the cooking time and watching carefully so the kale doesn't burn. Transfer to a wire rack to cool.

4. Combine the herbs, shredded veggies, and arugula in a large bowl. Toss with half of the dressing (save the remainder, covered and refrigerated, for another use). Serve the salad topped with a generous portion of kale chips. Store leftover kale chips in an airtight container to enjoy later. They will keep for a few days.

AMOUNT PER SERVING: calories 70, total fat 4 g, saturated fat 0.5 g, cholesterol 0 mg, sodium 360 mg, total carbohydrate 9 g, dietary fiber 2 g, sugars 3 g, protein 2 g

Festive Barley Salad

If you want a salad with your lunch or dinner, but want something heartier than a bowl of mixed greens, try this veggie-packed barley salad. Chop the vegetables and whip up the vinaigrette while the barley cooks. Steam the squash, zucchini, and red onion while the barley cools. Toss everything together and enjoy!

PREPARATION: **20 minutes** PROCESSING: **15 seconds** COOK TIME: **45 minutes** YIELD: **4 servings**

6 cups (1.4 L) water

1 cup (200 g) pearl barley

¾ teaspoon sea salt

1 small yellow squash, finely diced (about 1¼ cups / 141 g)

1 medium zucchini, finely diced (about 1½ cups / 210 g)

⅓ cup (40 g) finely diced red onion

½ cup (120 ml) olive oil

2 tablespoons (30 ml) red wine vinegar

½ large lemon, peeled

4 tablespoons (8 g) chopped fresh dill

½ teaspoon ground black pepper

1 English cucumber, finely diced (about 2 cups / 266 g)

1 medium red bell pepper, finely diced (about ¾ cup / 110 g)

2 tablespoons (10 g) thinly sliced scallions

1. Rinse the barley in a fine-mesh sieve until the water runs clear.

2. In a medium saucepan, combine the water with ½ teaspoon of the salt and bring to a boil. Add the barley and bring back to a simmer. Reduce the heat to medium-low, cover, and cook until the barley is tender and all of the water has been absorbed, about 20 minutes.

3. Rinse the cooked barley in a sieve under cool running water to cool completely. Drain well.

4. Set up a large bowl of ice and water. In a steamer basket, combine the yellow squash, zucchini, and red onion. Cover and steam until just tender, 3 to 4 minutes. Cold-shock the vegetables in the bowl of ice water. Drain well.

5. Place the oil, vinegar, lemon, 2 tablespoons of the dill, the black pepper, and remaining ¼ teaspoon salt into the Vitamix container in the order listed and secure the lid. Select Variable 1. Turn the machine on and slowly increase the speed to Variable 10, then to High. Blend for 15 seconds.

6. Combine the barley, steamed vegetables, cucumber, bell pepper, scallions, and the remaining 2 tablespoons dill in a large bowl. Add the dressing and toss to mix well.

AMOUNT PER SERVING: calories 220, total fat 1.5 g, saturated fat 0 g, cholesterol 0 mg, sodium 470 mg, total carbohydrate 47 g, dietary fiber 10 g, sugars 5 g, protein 7 g

Greens and Berries Salad

This fresh, summery salad packs a double punch of strawberry flavor. Some of the strawberries are pureed into the dressing, while the remaining sliced fruit is tossed with greens, blueberries, and toasted nuts.

PREPARATION: **15 minutes**   PROCESSING: **20 seconds**   YIELD: **6 servings**

STRAWBERRY DRESSING:

2 tablespoons (30 ml) fresh lemon juice

1 tablespoon extra virgin olive oil

½ cup (72 g) halved fresh strawberries

SALAD:

7 ounces (200 g) mixed baby spinach, arugula, watercress

1 cup (144 g) fresh strawberries, sliced

½ cup (74 g) fresh blueberries

⅓ cup (40 g) coarsely chopped lightly toasted walnuts or pecans

1. For the strawberry dressing: Place the lemon juice, olive oil, and strawberries into the Vitamix container in the order listed and secure the lid. Select Variable 1. Turn the machine on and slowly increase the speed to Variable 6. Blend for 20 seconds.

2. For the salad: Combine the greens and berries in a large serving bowl. Pour the dressing over the salad mixture and toss gently to combine. Scatter the nuts over the top.

AMOUNT PER SERVING: calories 100, total fat 7 g, saturated fat 0.5 g, cholesterol 0 mg, sodium 55 mg, total carbohydrate 9 g, dietary fiber 3 g, sugars 3 g, protein 2 g

Kale Salad with Avocado Tahini Dressing

Hearty greens like kale pair well with creamy dressings. In this case, our delicious Avocado Tahini Dip (page 66) gets a second, wonderful life as dressing for a kale salad. Packed with veggies and herbs, this salad makes an excellent main dish for lunch or a light supper.

PREPARATION: **10 minutes**   PROCESSING: **35 to 40 seconds**   YIELD: **6 servings**

10 ounces (284 g) kale, torn into bite-size pieces

1 medium cucumber, sliced

1 cup (110 g) grated carrots

½ cup (30 g) minced fresh flat-leaf parsley

2 tablespoons (5 g) chopped fresh basil leaves

2 scallions, thinly sliced

¾ cup Avocado Tahini Dip (page 66)

Combine the kale, cucumber, carrots, parsley, basil, and scallions. Add the Avocado Tahini Dip as a dressing and toss well.

AMOUNT PER SERVING: calories 90, total fat 4 g, saturated fat 0.5 g, cholesterol 0 mg, sodium 50 mg, total carbohydrate 12 g, dietary fiber 3 g, sugars 2 g, protein 4 g

Lime-Dressed Ginger Carrot Slaw

What better way to get a bigger variety of veggies into your next BBQ than to whip up this colorful, vibrant slaw! This salad is a brightly colored tangle of green, red, and orange all tossed in a tangy, slightly spicy dressing. The salad uses about half the vinaigrette, the remainder of which can be used to marinate meat or veggies.

PREPARATION: **20 minutes**   PROCESSING: **30 seconds**   YIELD: **8 servings**

LIME DRESSING:

¼ cup (60 ml) olive oil

1 teaspoon sesame oil

1 lime, peeled

2 tablespoons (30 ml) honey

One 1-inch (2.5-cm) cube fresh gingerroot (0.5 oz / 15 g)

½ orange, peeled

½ teaspoon sea salt

¼ teaspoon red pepper flakes

SALAD:

1 small head cabbage (1½ pounds / 714 g), shredded

1 medium red bell pepper, cut into strips

1 medium green bell pepper, cut into strips

6 medium carrots, shredded

2 oranges, peeled and sectioned

4 scallions, sliced

Grated zest of 1 lime

1. For the lime dressing: Place all the dressing ingredients into the Vitamix container in the order listed and secure the lid. Select Variable 1. Turn the machine on and slowly increase the speed to Variable 10, then to High. Blend for 30 seconds.

2. For the salad: Combine all the salad ingredients in a large bowl. Add half the dressing (refrigerate the remainder for another use) and toss well.

AMOUNT PER SERVING: calories 110, total fat 4 g, saturated fat 0.5 g, cholesterol 0 mg, sodium 125 mg, total carbohydrate 19 g, dietary fiber 5 g, sugars 12 g, protein 2 g

Pear and Apple Salad with Flax-Crusted Goat Cheese

Alice Waters first offered her famous mesclun salad with warm goat cheese in the 1970s at her famed restaurant Chez Panisse. Today, we like to make our own variation with poached fruit, a lightly sweet vinaigrette, and goat cheese rounds encrusted with flax seeds and thyme. This elegant salad makes a lovely first course or light lunch.

PREPARATION: **15 minutes**   PROCESSING: **15 seconds**   COOK TIME: **10 to 12 minutes**   YIELD: **8 servings**

POACHED FRUIT:

2 tablespoons (30 ml) fresh lemon juice

2 tablespoons (27 g) light brown sugar

1 large red pear, sliced

1 large green apple, sliced

VINAIGRETTE:

1 tablespoon maple syrup

1 tablespoon apple cider vinegar

1 tablespoon flax oil

2 tablespoons (30 ml) olive oil

½ teaspoon fresh thyme leaves

¼ teaspoon ground cinnamon

½ teaspoon Dijon mustard

SALAD:

1 tablespoon whole golden flax seeds

1 tablespoon flax meal

1 tablespoon fresh thyme leaves

½ teaspoon ground black pepper

¼ teaspoon sea salt

One 3-ounce (85-g) roll goat cheese

16 cups (24 oz / 680 g) mixed baby salad greens

1. For the poached fruit: Combine 2 cups (480 ml) water, the lemon juice, and brown sugar in a large skillet and bring to a boil. Add the pear and apple slices and gently poach just until soft, about 4 minutes (depending on the thickness of the slices).

2. Carefully lift out the fruit with a slotted spoon and set aside to cool. Reserve the poaching liquid.

3. For the vinaigrette: Measure out ¼ cup (60 ml) of the poaching liquid and place in the Vitamix container,

followed by the maple syrup, vinegar, oils, thyme, cinnamon, and mustard in the order listed and secure the lid. Select Variable 1. Turn the machine on and slowly increase the speed to Variable 10, then to High. Blend for 15 seconds.

4. For the salad: Combine the whole flax seeds, flax meal, thyme, pepper, and salt in a bowl and mix well.

5. Roll the goat cheese in the flax mixture to coat, then slice crosswise into 8 pieces.

6. In a bowl, toss the greens with the dressing. Serve the dressed greens topped with the poached pear and apple slices and goat cheese rounds.

AMOUNT PER SERVING: calories 150, total fat 8 g, saturated fat 2 g, cholesterol 5 mg, sodium 190 mg, total carbohydrate 18 g, dietary fiber 4 g, sugars 11 g, protein 5 g

Fiesta Salad

A little sweet and a little spicy, this fabulously crunchy salad will brighten even the simplest meal. Its flavor would be a perfect complement to tacos or chili, and you are sure to find yourself making it again and again.

PREPARATION: **20 minutes**　　PROCESSING: **30 seconds**　　YIELD: **8 servings**

VINAIGRETTE:

1¾ cups (288 g) diced mango

½ cup (120 ml) grapefruit juice

¼ cup (60 ml) fresh lime juice

½ dried chile pepper, seeded

2 tablespoons (20 g) chopped shallot

1½ tablespoons vegetable oil

½ teaspoon sea salt

⅓ teaspoon ground black pepper

1 garlic clove, peeled

SALAD:

3 cups (210 g) shredded cabbage

3 cups (141 g) thinly sliced romaine lettuce

1½ cups (248 g) diced mango

1 cup (130 g) diced peeled jicama

¾ cup (120 g) red onion pieces

One 7-ounce (200-g) jar roasted red peppers, drained and diced, or use homemade (see page 71)

⅓ cup (40 g) pumpkin seeds, toasted

¼ cup (5 g) fresh cilantro leaves

1. For the vinaigrette: Place all the vinaigrette ingredients into the Vitamix container in the order listed and secure the lid. Select Variable 1. Turn the machine on and slowly increase the speed to Variable 10, then to High. Blend for 30 seconds.

2. For the salad: Combine all the salad ingredients in a very large serving bowl. Add the vinaigrette and toss to coat.

AMOUNT PER SERVING: calories 140, total fat 6 g, saturated fat 1 g, cholesterol 0 mg, sodium 260 mg, total carbohydrate 21 g, dietary fiber 4 g, sugars 12 g, protein 4 g

The Vitamix Cookbook

Lebanese Tabbouleh

In many traditional tabbouleh recipes, the parsley and mint are chopped by hand. Here we whip the herbs with lemon, extra virgin olive oil, and scallions into a fresh, vibrantly green dressing that is tossed with the cooked bulgur. Tomatoes are quickly pulsed in the Vitamix to complete the dish. The presentation may be a little different, but the flavors are true to the original dish.

PREPARATION: **20 minutes**   PROCESSING: **20 seconds plus pulsing**   YIELD: **8 servings**

1²/₃ cups (400 ml) boiling water

1 cup (140 g) bulgur

Grated zest of 1 lemon

¼ cup (60 ml) fresh lemon juice

6 tablespoons (90 ml) extra virgin olive oil

2 cups (120 g) lightly packed fresh flat-leaf parsley leaves

1 cup (110 g) lightly packed fresh mint leaves

2 scallions, cut into pieces

1 medium to large tomato, cut into large pieces

1. Combine the boiling water and the bulgur in a bowl. Cover and soak for 1 hour, then drain. Let stand in a serving bowl until cool.

2. Meanwhile, place the lemon zest, lemon juice, olive oil, parsley, mint, and scallions into the Vitamix container in the order listed and secure the lid. Select Variable 1. Turn the machine on and slowly increase the speed to Variable 5. Blend for 20 seconds, or until the mixture is blended, using the tamper to press the ingredients into the blades.

3. Add the dressing to the bulgur and stir to combine.

4. Rinse out the Vitamix container. Place the tomato pieces into the container and secure the lid. Select Variable 3. Use the On/Off switch to quickly pulse to the desired consistency, using the tamper to press the ingredients into the blades.

5. Gently stir the tomatoes into the bulgur mixture and serve.

AMOUNT PER SERVING: calories 150, total fat 11 g, saturated fat 1.5 g, cholesterol 0 mg, sodium 15 mg, total carbohydrate 11 g, dietary fiber 3 g, sugars 1 g, protein 2 g

Soups, Salads, and Sides

Southwestern Quinoa Salad

Quinoa is a nutritional powerhouse, offering a healthy dose of protein (8 grams), fiber (5 grams), and iron (15% of the recommended daily intake) per cup of cooked. Bring more of this naturally gluten-free seed (yes, a seed) into your diet by making this flavor- and nutrient-packed salad. This salad keeps and travels well and would be a welcome addition to a brown-bag lunch or as a dish to share at a potluck dinner.

PREPARATION: **20 minutes**   PROCESSING: **15 seconds**   COOK TIME: **20 minutes**   YIELD: **6 servings**

3 cups (720 ml) low-sodium vegetable broth

1½ cups (255 g) quinoa, rinsed well and drained

⅓ teaspoon sea salt

⅓ cup (80 ml) fresh lime juice

2 teaspoons ground cumin

½ teaspoon chili powder

⅓ teaspoon chipotle powder

2 tablespoons (30 ml) red wine vinegar

2 tablespoons (30 ml) olive oil

4 garlic cloves, cut into pieces

One 15-ounce (425-g) can black beans, rinsed and well drained

½ cup (73 g) fresh or frozen corn kernels

½ cup (80 g) diced red onion

½ cup (74 g) diced yellow or orange bell pepper

1 tablespoon minced jalapeño pepper

¼ cup (4 g) minced fresh cilantro

1. Bring the broth to a boil in a saucepan. Add the quinoa and salt and simmer, uncovered, until the liquid is almost absorbed, about 15 minutes. Remove from the heat and fluff with a fork. Set aside to cool.

2. Place the lime juice, cumin, chili powder, chipotle powder, vinegar, olive oil, and garlic into the Vitamix container in the order listed and secure the lid. Select Variable 1. Turn the machine on and slowly increase the speed to Variable 5. Blend for 15 seconds.

3. Combine the black beans, corn, onion, bell pepper, jalapeño, and cilantro in a medium bowl.

4. When the quinoa is cooled, add it to the black bean mixture along with the dressing, tossing gently to coat. Serve chilled or at room temperature.

AMOUNT PER SERVING: calories 270, total fat 8 g, saturated fat 1 g, cholesterol 0 mg, sodium 135 mg, total carbohydrate 41 g, dietary fiber 6 g, sugars 2 g, protein 9 g

Gluten-Free Rolls

Few prepackaged gluten-free rolls can rival those that you make yourself. Once you have made your flour mix, these rolls will come together quickly. You don't have to worry about overmixing, as you would bread with gluten; there isn't any gluten to overdevelop here, so you can stir the batter until it is well combined.

PREPARATION: **10 minutes**   PROCESSING: **20 seconds**   BAKE TIME: **15 minutes**   YIELD: **12 rolls**

1 tablespoon quick-rise active yeast

½ cup (120 ml) boiling water

1 tablespoon light brown sugar

1¾ cups (228 g) Gluten-Free Flour Mix (page 36)

¼ cup (30 g) almond meal

1 teaspoon xanthan gum

½ teaspoon salt

1 teaspoon gluten-free baking powder

2 tablespoons (30 ml) olive oil

1 large egg

1. Preheat the oven to 350°F (180°C). Lightly coat 12 cups of a muffin tin with cooking spray.

2. Combine the yeast, boiling water, and brown sugar in a measuring cup. Stir lightly to combine and set aside for 5 minutes to proof.

3. Combine the flour mix, almond meal, xanthan gum, salt, and baking powder in a medium bowl. Set aside.

4. Place the olive oil, ¼ cup (60 ml) water, and the egg into the Vitamix container in that order and secure the lid. Select Variable 1. Turn the machine on and slowly increase the speed to Variable 5. Blend for 20 seconds.

5. Pour the egg mixture into the flour mixture and mix by hand to combine.

6. Fill each muffin cup half full. Cover with lightly sprayed plastic wrap and allow to rise until the dough has doubled in size, about 20 minutes.

7. Bake for 15 minutes, or until golden and puffed. Transfer to cooling racks immediately to prevent moisture from accumulating on the bottom. Serve warm.

AMOUNT PER ROLL: calories 130, total fat 4.5 g, saturated fat 0.5 g, cholesterol 15 mg, sodium 105 mg, total carbohydrate 21 g, dietary fiber 1 g, sugars 1 g, protein 2 g

Bulgur-Stuffed Baby Potatoes

Move over, heavy and unhealthy stuffed baked potatoes, there is a new lighter option. Red potatoes are boiled, cooled, and stuffed with a tempting filling of bulgur, corn, leeks, and a homemade pecan pesto. Delicious as an appetizer or as a side with grilled chicken or fish.

PREPARATION: **15 minutes**   PROCESSING: **2 minutes**   COOK TIME: **50 minutes**
YIELD: **24 stuffed potato halves**

2 pounds (908 g) red potatoes, at least 1½ inches (4 cm) in diameter, boiled whole and cooled

1 tablespoon olive oil

½ cup (45 g) finely diced leeks

½ cup (79 g) fresh corn kernels

2 cups (364 g) cooked bulgur wheat

½ cup (120 ml) Parsley-Pecan Pesto (page 242)

½ teaspoon grated lemon zest

1. Trim a sliver off two opposite sides of each potato, to provide a flat surface on each end.

2. Cut each potato in half and using a 1-inch (2.5-cm) melon baller, scoop out almost the entire potato center to make a hollowed-out potato "cup." Set the potatoes aside, cup side up.

3. Heat the olive oil in a large skillet over medium-high heat. Add the leeks and corn and cook until the leeks are soft, 2 to 4 minutes. Remove from the heat and cool completely.

4. Combine the bulgur, leek and corn mixture, pesto, and lemon zest in a large bowl and mix well.

5. Fill each potato cup with about 1 tablespoon of the bulgur mixture.

AMOUNT PER 2 STUFFED HALVES: calories 180, total fat 8 g, saturated fat 1 g, cholesterol 0 mg, sodium 35 mg, total carbohydrate 25 g, dietary fiber 3 g, sugars 2 g, protein 4 g

Wild Rice Stuffing

Wild rice is not a grain like other rice, but rather is the seed of a long-grain marsh grass native to North America. Wild rice is wonderful plain, of course, but its nutty flavor really shines in this baked stuffing. Vegetables are quickly pulsed in the Vitamix, then sautéed with olive oil. The cooked veggies are folded into the cooked rice with chewy dried fruit and crunchy pumpkin seeds. Full of nutrients and wonderful flavors, this stuffing is the perfect winter side dish.

PREPARATION: **15 minutes**   PROCESSING: **pulsing**   COOK TIME: **45 minutes**

BAKE TIME: **20 minutes**   YIELD: **8 servings**

2 cups (400 g) wild rice blend or wild rice

2 celery stalks, each cut into 4 pieces

1 large yellow onion, peeled and quartered

2 garlic cloves, peeled

1 large jalapeño pepper, halved and seeded

2 tablespoons (30 ml) olive oil

¼ teaspoon sea salt

⅓ teaspoon ground black pepper

½ cup (70 g) roasted pumpkin seeds

¼ cup (40 g) raisins

¼ cup (30 g) unsweetened dried cherries

¼ cup (60 ml) low-sodium vegetable broth

1½ teaspoons ground coriander

1 tablespoon apple cider vinegar

1. Preheat the oven to 375°F (190°C).

2. Cook the wild rice according to the package directions.

3. Fill the Vitamix container to the 3-cup (720-ml) mark with water. Add the celery, onion, garlic, and jalapeño and secure the lid. Select Variable 8. Use the On/Off switch to quickly pulse 4 times. Drain well.

4. Heat the olive oil in a small skillet over medium heat. Add the chopped vegetables and cook until the onion is translucent, about 5 minutes. Season with the salt and black pepper.

5. Toss together the sautéed vegetables, cooked wild rice, pumpkin seeds, raisins, cherries, broth, coriander, and vinegar in a large bowl.

6. Transfer the stuffing to an 8-inch (20-cm) square baking dish and bake for 20 minutes, or until heated through.

AMOUNT PER SERVING: calories 300, total fat 9 g, saturated fat 1.5 g, cholesterol 0 mg, sodium 100 mg, total carbohydrate 50 g, dietary fiber 5 g, sugars 7 g, protein 7 g

Cornbread

We included this simple, delicious cornbread to stuff the Cornbread-Stuffed Roasted Squash (page 187), but you may find yourself making it again to serve along with your favorite soup or chili.

PREPARATION: **10 minutes**   PROCESSING: **20 seconds**   BAKE TIME: **15 to 18 minutes**   YIELD: **8 servings**

½ cup (120 ml) skim milk

3 large egg whites

1 large egg

½ cup (120 ml) plain 0% Greek yogurt, stirred

¼ cup (57 g) best-quality vegan butter spread

3 tablespoons (38 g) sugar

1 cup (125 g) unbleached all-purpose flour

⅓ cup (105 g) cornmeal, preferably homemade (page 40)

1½ teaspoons baking soda

½ teaspoon salt

¼ teaspoon baking powder

1. Preheat the oven to 425°F (220°C). Lightly coat an 8-inch (20-cm) square pan with cooking spray, or a similar-size cast-iron skillet, if you prefer.

2. Place the milk, egg whites, whole egg, yogurt, butter spread, and sugar into the Vitamix container in the order listed and secure the lid. Select Variable 1. Turn the machine on and slowly increase the speed to Variable 8. Blend for 20 seconds.

3. Combine the flour, cornmeal, baking soda, salt, and baking powder in a medium bowl. Mix well.

4. Pour the egg mixture into the flour mixture and mix by hand until well combined.

5. Pour the batter into the pan and bake for 15 to 18 minutes, or until a toothpick inserted into the center comes out with a few moist crumbs attached. Cool in the pan and then slice.

AMOUNT PER SERVING: calories 220, total fat 8 g, saturated fat 2.5 g, cholesterol 25 mg, sodium 440 mg, total carbohydrate 29 g, dietary fiber 1 g, sugars 6 g, protein 6 g

Soups, Salads, and Sides

WHOLE FOODS SUCCESS STORY

Anna Klinger

Vitamix machines appear in professional kitchens around the world. Often a Vitamix blender is the most loved tool in the kitchen. Why? A couple of reasons stand out. First, they are incredibly durable. They can puree, chop, and emulsify day after day, often for long stretches at a time, and still keep working. The purees are silky, the vinaigrettes and sauces are well emulsified. Chefs with diverse culinary interests—ranging from modernist cuisine to raw foods to rustic Italian cooking—have found their Vitamix blenders indispensable.

Anna Klinger, chef and co-owner of al di la Trattoria, Bar Corvo, and Lincoln Station, is one such chef. She first learned about Vitamix about ten years ago. Five years later, she bought two Vitamix machines for her first restaurant, and she has never looked back. In fact, all three of her restaurants are equipped with Vitamix machines. Klinger is impressed with the incredible durability of the machines and with the quality of the food that they produce. She notes that "the Vitamix blender purees much more finely with much less effort than the simple bar blenders I've used in the past. I'm able to produce a silky velouté, for example, with that shiny quality that comes from being pureed very thoroughly, but in a fraction of the time and without the worry that I'm going to exhaust the motor. I have never had to replace mine, and use it daily. I used to buy two little blenders a year."

Most Vitamix machines that are used in restaurant kitchens endure heavy use. Klinger's are no exception. She and her staff use the machines daily. The cooks, and Klinger herself, use Vitamix machines to make a huge range of products. Tangy vinaigrettes, smooth sauces, and delicious aiolis can be made quickly. Ingredients as diverse as sweet corn, peas, and sheep's-milk ricotta are transformed into smooth fillings for ravioli and tortelli. They puree soup, sometimes twenty-two quarts at a time, to a smooth and well-emulsified finish.

The whole foods success story? Klinger's many fans would say it is the exceptionally delicious food created in all three of her kitchens!

Chicken Potato Soup
(page 124)

Roasted Salmon with
Cilantro-Seed Pesto
(page 205)

Chapter 5

Entrées

I f our mornings seem hectic, the nights are often just as busy—or worse. They certainly are in my house! There is dinner to prepare, homework to oversee, sports practice, chores, news to share—you name it—and we are tired and hungry to boot. In the midst of all this chaos, we try to sit down for a family meal as often as possible.

Some nights a soup that you can make right in a Vitamix blender is just perfect for dinner. On other nights, a delicious marinated meat that is ready to grill or a roasted vegetable sauce to toss with pasta will be what you crave. In this chapter, we will explore a whole bunch of healthy entrées that you can make with the help of your Vitamix machine. We will also discuss some of the different ways to chop vegetables in the Vitamix blender and ways you can organize yourself in the kitchen to save precious family time.

Before You Start Cooking

You don't have to be a professional cook to benefit from the habits of one. There are a number of simple steps that most cooks take when they get ready to work, and these habits can be invaluable to a home cook. By organizing yourself before you start cooking and taking regular inventory of your refrigerator and pantry, you will save both time and money.

Before chefs begin a task in the kitchen, they organize their mise en place. *Mise en place*, French for "put in place," simply means getting everything ready before you start cooking: vegetables cut, spices out and measured, all necessary equipment set up. You will notice any missing ingredients and have a calm moment to either make a substitution or dash to the store. Taking time to organize yourself before you start cooking is ultimately a more efficient way to cook and so you will save time in the long run, too.

In a restaurant kitchen, the principle of "first in, first out," or FIFO, helps reduce waste. Simply put, the food that is purchased first is used first. Avoiding food waste helps restaurants and other food businesses save money and time, and this is true for the home cook as well. Once a week, take a quick inventory of what you have on hand. Make a note of everything that needs to be used first. Then think what meals or dishes you can make to use up these foods.

Here is a tip: Having trouble remembering which leftovers were cooked when? Invest in a roll of masking tape and a marker. Label and date containers before you put them in the refrigerator or freezer. You will know exactly what you have and how long you have had it.

Getting Organized

Some people are menu planners. Every week they write up a menu plan for the week and use this plan to write their grocery list. If this doesn't fit with your cooking style, you can still save yourself some time and avoid the temptation of takeout. Anytime you whip up a soup, or make a batch of salad dressing, nut milk, or pasta sauce, make some extra. You can store it in the fridge to be used over the next couple of days or, for some foods, you can freeze it for later. Prepare more pork or fish than you need for dinner, and reinvent the leftovers in a main-dish salad or a wrap.

Look through your crisper drawers and find the things that, as I like to say, "must go!" Then look through the recipes in this book and find a soup, smoothie, or sauce that will use up this produce. You can also go ahead and make a big batch of your favorite smoothie to enjoy over the next few days, or whip up a tasty soup. You will use up all those good veggies and have a ready-to-go meal or snack too!

It will be easier to drive past that drive-through window when you know you have a quick-to-prepare dinner waiting at home. In the long run, cooking more whole foods at home will help you eat better, consume less salt, and possibly save money as well.

Dinner Is Served

The previous chapters have focused on soups, appetizers, and breakfast/brunch recipes. Here, we move on to savory entrées. Some of the dishes are meals in and of themselves. Cheese and Kale Ravioli (page 209), Cornbread-Stuffed Roasted Squash (page 187), Polenta Pizza (page 199), and Fish Tacos with Slaw (page 195) are all great examples.

Some entrées are the beginning of a great meal, but you may want a salad from chapter 4 or a simple sautéed or steamed vegetable to complete the meal. Baked Tofu, Two Ways (page 176), Marinated Sweet and Sour Tempeh (page 184), and Roasted Salmon with Cilantro-Seed Pesto (page 205) are just a few of the dishes you could use to anchor your meal.

We will also show you how to make burgers—yes, burgers! Your Vitamix can help you whip up Turkey Burgers with Cherry Salsa (page 219), Zucchini Burgers (page 223), and Quinoa Black Bean Burgers (page 221) for your next barbecue. Healthy and delicious too!

In this chapter, you will also find recipes that are vegetarian, vegan, gluten-free, and kid-friendly. You will find lots of tasty dishes for every occasion and mood. You might just be amazed at all of the delicious, nutritious, and different ways that a Vitamix blender can help you get dinner on the table!

Techniques Used in This Chapter

If you have read any of the online Vitamix recipes or read one of our other cookbooks, you will be familiar with the two different ways that your machine can chop food. If you are new to Vitamix or just need to refresh your memory, let me just quickly explain dry-chopping and wet-chopping. Both of these techniques will be used in the recipes in this chapter. You can always chop ingredients by hand, of course, but if you are short on time or are not confident in your knife skills, you will find these methods helpful.

- *Dry-chopping.* Dry-chop with the Vitamix when you need to coarsely chop, and even-size pieces are not important. For example, nuts that will be incorporated into a larger recipe do not need to be cut evenly. Place the ingredients in the container and run the machine on a low, variable speed. Or drop them through the lid plug opening while the Vitamix is running on low.

Don't process the food too long! The ingredients will go from big chunks to powder or puree faster than you might think. For instance, boiled eggs can be chopped on a very low speed while carrots are chopped at a higher speed. Also, cheese is much easier to chop in a Vitamix machine if you freeze it first.

- *Wet-chopping.* This technique is used when the ingredients have a lot of moisture in them, e.g., cabbage for slaw. Add enough water to float the ingredients above the blades. The presence of the water will help pull the food down toward the blades, resulting in a more consistent chop. Pulse the Vitamix just a couple of times and chunks of produce will be shredded. Be careful not to pulse it too much or you will have cabbage soup instead of slaw. Drain the ingredients and proceed with the recipe as directed.

LET'S GET COOKING!

Pork Tenderloin in Orange-Ginger Sauce

A zippy orange-ginger sauce brightens up pan-seared pork tenderloin slices. Garnish with sliced scallions and serve with brown rice if desired.

PREPARATION: **15 minutes**   PROCESSING: **15 to 20 seconds**   COOK TIME: **13 to 15 minutes**

YIELD: **6 servings**

1½ pounds (568 to 680 g) pork tenderloin

½ teaspoon salt

¼ teaspoon ground black pepper

1 strip (1 × 2-inch / 2.5 × 5-cm) orange zest

1 orange, peeled and halved

2 thin slices fresh gingerroot

1 teaspoon sesame oil

1 cup (240 ml) low-sodium or no-salt-added chicken broth

½ tablespoon honey

1 tablespoon cornstarch

1 tablespoon vegetable oil

1 small red bell pepper, cut into thin bite-size strips

2 tablespoons (12 g) sliced scallions

1. Cut the tenderloin crosswise into 6 pieces. Place each piece cut side down between pieces of plastic wrap and starting at the center pound to a ¼-inch (0.6-cm) thickness with a meat mallet or rolling pin. Season with the salt and pepper. Set aside.

2. Place the orange zest, orange, ginger, sesame oil, broth, honey, and cornstarch into the Vitamix container and secure the lid. Select Variable 1. Turn the machine on and slowly increase the speed to Variable 10, then to High. Blend for 15 to 20 seconds.

3. Heat the vegetable oil in a 12-inch (30-cm) nonstick skillet over medium-high heat. Add the pork and cook, turning once, until deep golden brown, 8 to 10 minutes. Transfer the pork to a plate.

4. Add the bell pepper to the skillet and cook for 2 minutes. Return the pork to the skillet. Pour the orange mixture into the skillet and cook, stirring occasionally, until the sauce is bubbling and thickened and the pork is no longer pink, about 3 minutes.

5. Serve the pork topped with the sauce and scallions.

AMOUNT PER SERVING: calories 190, total fat 7 g, saturated fat 1.5 g, cholesterol 65 mg, sodium 270 mg, total carbohydrate 7 g, dietary fiber 1 g, sugars 4 g, protein 25 g

Polenta with Flax and Tomato Sauce

Another great, naturally gluten-free dinner! Grind your own cornmeal and then transform it into a tasty polenta with flax, parsley, and Parmesan. A fresh, herby tomato sauce is started on the stove and finished in a Vitamix blender. The polenta slices can be topped with sauce and baked or individually pan-seared in a little olive oil and finished with the warm sauce.

PREPARATION: **20 minutes**   PROCESSING: **1 minute 30 seconds**   COOK TIME: **20 to 25 minutes**

BAKE TIME: **15 minutes**   YIELD: **8 servings**

POLENTA:

2¼ cups (540 ml) water

1¼ cups (7 oz / 200 g) coarse whole-grain cornmeal, preferably homemade (page 40)

⅓ cup (35 g) flax meal

¼ cup (15 g) minced fresh flat-leaf parsley

¼ cup (32 g) finely grated Parmesan

1 teaspoon golden flax seeds

TOMATO SAUCE:

2 tablespoons (30 ml) extra virgin olive oil

2 tablespoons (20 g) chopped yellow onion

1 garlic clove, peeled

1½ pounds (680 g) vine-ripened tomatoes, cut into pieces

1 teaspoon sea salt

¼ teaspoon ground black pepper

½ teaspoon minced fresh basil leaves

¼ teaspoon fresh oregano leaves

¼ teaspoon fresh thyme leaves

1. For the polenta: Bring the water to a boil in a saucepan. Add the cornmeal, whisking constantly. Reduce to a simmer, cover, and cook until thickened, about 5 minutes.

2. Remove from the heat and stir in the flax meal, parsley, Parmesan, and flax seeds. Evenly spread the polenta into a greased 8½ × 4½-inch (22 × 11-cm) loaf pan. Let cool for 30 minutes.

3. For the tomato sauce: Heat the olive oil in a medium

saucepan over medium heat. Add the onion and garlic and cook until the onion is translucent, about 5 minutes. Stir in the tomatoes, salt, pepper, and herbs and cover. Cook, stirring occasionally, until the tomatoes have broken down, 10 to 15 minutes.

4. Ladle the hot tomato mixture into the Vitamix container and secure the lid. Select Variable 1. Turn the machine on and slowly increase the speed to Variable 10, then to High. Blend for 30 seconds.

5. Remove the polenta from the loaf pan and slice into 8 pieces.

6. To bake the polenta: Preheat the oven to 350°F (177°C). Shingle the polenta slices in a baking dish, ladle the sauce over the polenta, and bake for 15 minutes, or until heated through.

7. To pan-sear the polenta: Crisp the polenta slices on a nonstick griddle in a small amount of olive oil.

8. Serve the polenta slices topped with the warm tomato sauce.

AMOUNT PER SERVING: calories 180, total fat 8 g, saturated fat 1.5 g, cholesterol 5 mg, sodium 360 mg, total carbohydrate 22 g, dietary fiber 6 g, sugars 3 g, protein 5 g

Citrus Ginger Marinated Tuna Steaks

A bright, sweet-savory marinade makes simple tuna steaks something even more special. Be careful to marinate 1-inch-thick fish steaks for no longer than 1 hour, and thinner steaks should only be marinated for 30 minutes. Fish is less dense than other proteins, and acidic marinades like this one will penetrate the steaks quickly.

PREPARATION: **1 hour**   PROCESSING: **30 seconds**   YIELD: **4 servings**

2 tablespoons (30 ml) reduced-sodium soy sauce

2 tablespoons (30 ml) olive oil

1 tablespoon sesame oil

1 teaspoon grated orange zest

1 orange, peeled and halved

One 1-inch (2.5-cm) slice of pineapple, peeled, with core intact

2 tablespoons (15 g) chopped fresh gingerroot

1 garlic clove, peeled

2 scallions, cut into pieces

⅓ teaspoon cayenne pepper

Two 1-pound (454-g) tuna steaks, cut 1 inch (2.5 cm) thick

1. Place the soy sauce, olive oil, sesame oil, orange zest, orange, pineapple, ginger, garlic, scallions, and cayenne into the Vitamix container in the order listed and secure the lid. Select Variable 1. Turn the machine on and slowly increase the speed to Variable 10, then to High. Blend for 30 seconds, using the tamper as needed to push the ingredients into the blades.

2. Place the tuna in a shallow baking dish. Pour the marinade over the tuna and refrigerate for 1 hour.

3. Remove the tuna from the marinade and grill over high heat to the desired degree of doneness.

AMOUNT PER SERVING: calories 390, total fat 14 g, saturated fat 3 g, cholesterol 85 mg, sodium 160 mg, total carbohydrate 10 g, dietary fiber 1 g, sugars 7 g, protein 54 g

Baked Tofu, Two Ways

These two baked tofu preparations produce firm, flavorful tofu that can be tucked in a sandwich, served with rice and stir-fried vegetables, or cubed and tossed in a salad. The possibilities are nearly endless!

PREPARATION: **15 minutes per marinade**   PROCESSING: **40 seconds**   BAKE TIME: **45 minutes**

YIELD: **4 servings**

LEMON MARINADE WITH SPICE AND CILANTRO

(recipe follows)

LEMON MARINADE WITH ROSEMARY

(recipe follows)

16 ounces (454 g) firm tofu, drained

1. Make both marinades.

2. Cut the tofu cake into 8 even pieces. Pour half of each marinade into 2 baking dishes. Place 4 tofu slices in a single layer in each baking dish. Pour remaining corresponding marinade over the tofu. Allow the tofu to absorb the flavors and marinate while the oven preheats.

3. Preheat the oven to 400°F (200°C).

4. Bake the tofu for 45 minutes, carefully turning the slices after 25 minutes. The baked tofu will be browned, bubbling, and curling slightly at the edges.

5. Remove from the oven and transfer the slices to a serving platter. Serve the tofu hot, warm, at room temperature, or even chilled. (The tofu will keep in a covered container in the refrigerator for up to 3 days.)

Lemon Marinade with Spice and Cilantro

¼ cup (60 ml) fresh lemon juice

2 tablespoons (30 ml) reduced-sodium soy sauce

3 tablespoons (45 ml) olive oil

½ cup (120 ml) water

¼ cup (5 g) fresh cilantro leaves

1 tablespoon scallion pieces

1 green chile, halved and seeded

¼ teaspoon ground black pepper

Place all the ingredients into the Vitamix container in the order listed and secure the lid. Select Variable 1. Turn the machine on and slowly increase the speed to Variable 7. Blend for 20 seconds, or until well blended.

AMOUNT PER SERVING (MARINADE AND TOFU): calories 50, total fat 3 g, saturated fat 0 g, cholesterol 0 mg, sodium 130 mg, total carbohydrate 3 g, dietary fiber 0 g, sugars 1 g, protein 4 g

Lemon Marinade with Rosemary

¼ cup (60 ml) fresh lemon juice

2 tablespoons (30 ml) reduced-sodium soy sauce

3 tablespoons (45 ml) olive oil

1 tablespoon lightly chopped fresh rosemary

¼ teaspoon ground black pepper

Place all the ingredients into the Vitamix container in the order listed and secure the lid. Select Variable 1. Turn the machine on and slowly increase the speed to Variable 7. Blend for 20 seconds, or until well blended.

AMOUNT PER SERVING (MARINADE AND TOFU): calories 50, total fat 3 g, saturated fat 0 g, cholesterol 0 mg, sodium 200 mg, total carbohydrate 2 g, dietary fiber 0 g, sugars 1 g, protein 4 g

Couscous Chicken Salad

In this colorful main-dish salad, a bright, citrus-filled vinaigrette is tossed with couscous, chicken, red peppers, onions, and parsley. Take it to your next potluck or make on Sunday evening for lunches during the week.

PREPARATION: **20 minutes**   PROCESSING: **10 seconds**   COOK TIME: **30 to 40 minutes**   YIELD: **6 servings**

SALAD:

²/₃ cup (111 g) couscous

¹/₃ cup (54 g) slivered dried apricots

1 cup (240 ml) fat-free low-sodium or no-salt-added chicken broth

8 ounces (227 g) boneless, skinless chicken breast, cut into ½-inch (1.3-cm) chunks

1 medium red bell pepper, diced

¼ cup (40 g) diced red onion

¼ cup (15 g) chopped fresh flat-leaf parsley

DRESSING:

3 tablespoons (45 ml) orange juice

2 tablespoons (30 ml) fresh lemon juice

1½ teaspoons ground cumin

¼ teaspoon granulated sugar

¼ teaspoon sea salt

¼ teaspoon ground black pepper

1 teaspoon grated orange zest

2 tablespoons (30 ml) extra virgin olive oil

1. For the salad: Bring 1¼ cups (300 ml) water to a boil in a medium saucepan. Stir in the couscous and apricots, then cover, remove from the heat, and let stand for 5 minutes. Remove the lid and gently fluff the couscous with a fork. Cover loosely and set aside to cool.

2. Bring the broth to a boil in a medium skillet. Stir in the chicken and simmer, stirring, until the chicken is no longer pink in the center, about 10 minutes. With a slotted spoon, scoop out the chicken and cover to keep moist.

3. Return the skillet to high heat and bring the broth to a boil. Boil rapidly until reduced to about 2 tablespoons (30 ml), 5 to 8 minutes. Strain the liquid and set the reduced chicken broth aside.

4. Combine the chicken, couscous mixture, bell pepper, onion, and parsley in a large salad bowl.

5. For the dressing: Place the reduced chicken broth and all of the dressing ingredients into the Vitamix container in the order listed and secure the lid. Select Variable 1. Turn the machine on and slowly increase the speed to Variable 5. Blend for 10 seconds.

6. Pour the dressing over the salad and toss to combine.

AMOUNT PER SERVING: calories 200, total fat 7 g, saturated fat 1.5 g, cholesterol 20 mg, sodium 190 mg, total carbohydrate 25 g, dietary fiber 4 g, sugars 5 g, protein 12 g

Greek Chicken Pockets

Another great use for leftover rotisserie chicken! These tasty pita pockets pair chicken with a cucumber yogurt sauce, lettuce, cucumber, red onion, and Kalamata olives. If you are packing these sandwiches for a picnic or brown-bag lunch, pack the yogurt sauce separately so the pita doesn't get soggy.

PREPARATION: **20 minutes**   PROCESSING: **3 seconds plus pulsing**   YIELD: **4 sandwiches**

One 12-inch (30-cm) cucumber, halved lengthwise, seeds scooped out, cut into 1½-inch (4-cm) chunks

1½ cups (300 g) plain 0% Greek yogurt, stirred

2 garlic cloves, peeled

1 teaspoon dried dill

Salt and ground black pepper

½ cup (85 g) red onion chunks

¼ cup (33 g) pitted Kalamata olives

2 cooked chicken breast halves (4½ oz / 128 g), skin and bones removed, each cut into 3 pieces

Two 6- or 8-inch (15- to 20-cm) multigrain pita breads, halved crosswise

4 large lettuce leaves

1. Place half of the cucumber chunks into the Vitamix container and secure the lid. Select Variable 2. Use the On/Off switch to pulse 3 times. Use the tamper to press the cucumber into the blades if necessary.

2. Add the yogurt, garlic, dill, and salt and pepper to taste to the Vitamix container and secure the lid. Select Variable 1. Turn the machine on and slowly increase the speed to Variable 3. Blend for 3 seconds. Scoop the mixture into a medium bowl and set aside.

3. Rinse the container. Place the remaining cucumber into the Vitamix container and secure the lid. Select Variable 2. Use the On/Off switch to pulse. If necessary, use a scraper to move larger pieces to the top. Cover and repeat. Drain and pour into another medium bowl.

4. Add red onion to the Vitamix container and secure the lid. Select Variable 4. Use the On/Off switch to quickly pulse 3 times. Use a scraper to move larger pieces to the top and add the olives. Secure the lid and repeat the process 2 times. Scrape into the bowl with the cucumber.

5. Add the chicken to the Vitamix container and secure the lid. Select Variable 4. Use the On/Off switch to quickly pulse 3 times. Add to the vegetables in the bowl.

Entrées

6. Line each pita half with a lettuce leaf. Spoon the chicken mixture into the pita and drizzle the yogurt mixture over the top. Serve additional sauce on the side. (Store any leftover sauce, covered, in the refrigerator.)

AMOUNT PER SANDWICH: calories 270, total fat 5 g, saturated fat 1 g, cholesterol 55 mg, sodium 340 mg, total carbohydrate 25 g, dietary fiber 3 g, sugars 6 g, protein 31 g

Mediterranean Tofu

Consider adding tofu to your diet, even if you are not a vegetarian. Tofu has more than 8 grams of protein per 100-gram serving and contains all eight essential amino acids. Use this tasty baked tofu in place of feta cheese on a vegan Greek salad or slipped into a pita with crunchy vegetables. This recipe can be served either hot or cold.

PREPARATION: **15 minutes**   PROCESSING: **30 seconds**   BAKE TIME: **35 to 45 minutes**
YIELD: **4 servings**

1 pound (454 g) firm tofu

¼ cup (60 ml) olive oil

¼ cup (60 ml) red wine vinegar

½ lemon, peeled

1 garlic clove, halved

2 teaspoons fresh thyme leaves

1 teaspoon sea salt

Pinch of red pepper flakes

1. Drain the excess moisture from the tofu by wrapping it in two layers of paper towels and pressing it between two plates. Let stand overnight in the refrigerator, with a bowl or dish underneath the plates to catch any overflowing liquid.

2. The next day, pat the tofu dry and slice it into ½-inch-(1.25-cm)-thick slices. Preheat the oven to 350°F (180°C).

3. Place the olive oil, vinegar, lemon, garlic, thyme, salt, and red pepper flakes into the Vitamix container in the order listed and secure the lid. Select Variable 1. Turn the machine on and slowly increase the speed to Variable 10, then to High. Blend for 30 seconds.

4. Lay the tofu slices in a baking dish in a single snug layer. Pour the marinade over the tofu.

5. Bake for 35 to 45 minutes, until the tofu is nearly dry and well browned.

AMOUNT PER SERVING: calories 130, total fat 9 g, saturated fat 1 g, cholesterol 0 mg, sodium 50 mg, total carbohydrate 4 g, dietary fiber 1 g, sugars

Entrées

Edamame and Corn Pot Pies

These delicious pot pies will take a little more time than some of the other dishes, but they are worth every minute. You start by making your own cornmeal—easy to do with the dry grains container of your Vitamix—and then cooking it with hot water and fresh thyme. This polenta, in turn, becomes the crust for a hearty pot pie with a corn and edamame filling. Enjoy!

PREPARATION: **15 minutes**   PROCESSING: **30 seconds**

BAKE TIME: **20 to 25 minutes**   YIELD: **4 servings**

POLENTA CRUST:

2½ cups (600 ml) water

1½ teaspoons fresh thyme leaves, minced

1¼ cups (152 g) whole-grain cornmeal, preferably homemade (page 40)

FILLING:

¾ cup (180 ml) low-fat (1%) milk

3 cups (435 g) fresh or thawed frozen corn kernels

2 teaspoons potato starch

½ teaspoon sea salt

⅓ teaspoon ground black pepper

1 teaspoon minced fresh basil

¼ teaspoon minced fresh rosemary

1 cup (150 g) shelled edamame

1. For the polenta crust: Preheat the oven to 375°F (190°C).

2. Bring the water and the thyme to a boil in a 3-quart saucepan. Slowly whisk in the cornmeal, reduce the heat, and simmer, covered, until thickened, about 5 minutes. Remove the polenta from the heat.

3. Divide three-fourths of the polenta among 4 soup crocks, ramekins, or ovenproof bowls that measure 4½ inches (11 cm) across and 2½ inches (6 cm) deep. Using damp hands, lightly press the polenta against the bottom and sides to form a crust.

4. Press or roll the remaining polenta between sheets of parchment paper to a ½-inch (1.25-cm) thickness. Cool completely.

5. Place the crocks on a baking sheet and bake for 6 minutes to set the crust. Leave the oven on.

6. Meanwhile, for the filling: Place the milk and half of the corn into the Vitamix container and secure the lid. Select Variable 1. Turn the machine on and slowly increase the speed to Variable 10, then to High. Blend for 30 seconds.

7. Pour the corn puree into a 3-quart saucepan, place over medium-high heat, and heat to a gentle simmer.

Stir together the potato starch and 2 tablespoons (30 ml) water in a small bowl to make a slurry. Whisk the slurry into the corn puree and cook until thickened, 2 to 3 minutes.

8. Remove the corn puree from the heat and stir in the salt, pepper, basil, rosemary, edamame, and the remaining corn. Mix well.

9. To assemble the pot pies: Divide the filling among the crocks.

10. Cut the remaining polenta sheet into ½-inch-wide (1.3-cm) strips. Carefully lay the strips in a crosshatch pattern across the top of each pot pie.

11. Return the crocks to the oven to bake for 15 to 20 minutes, until heated thoroughly.

AMOUNT PER SERVING: calories 340, total fat 5 g, saturated fat 1 g, cholesterol 0 mg, sodium 360 mg, total carbohydrate 63 g, dietary fiber 10 g, sugars 0 g, protein 14 g

Marinated Sweet and Sour Tempeh

A simple and speedy vegetarian dinner! Protein-packed tempeh simmers in a sweet and sour marinade while you cook brown rice and whip up a gently spicy peanut sauce. Sautéed greens or steamed snap peas would round out the meal.

PREPARATION: **20 minutes**   PROCESSING: **1 minute 20 seconds**   COOK TIME: **15 minutes**
YIELD: **6 servings**

MARINADE:
1½ cups (360 ml) hot water

¼ cup (60 ml) olive oil

1 tablespoon sesame oil

¼ cup (60 ml) reduced-sodium tamari

¼ cup (60 ml) unseasoned rice vinegar

¼ cup (60 ml) mirin

1 tablespoon chopped fresh gingerroot

1 garlic clove, peeled

1 pound (454 g) tempeh, cut into 1-inch (2.5 cm) cubes

PEANUT SAUCE:
1 cup (257 g) unsalted peanut butter, preferably homemade (page 250)

¼ cup (60 ml) honey

3 tablespoons (45 ml) reduced-sodium tamari

3 tablespoons (45 ml) unseasoned rice vinegar

1 tablespoon chopped fresh gingerroot

2 garlic cloves, peeled

½ teaspoon cayenne pepper

2 cups (390 g) cooked brown rice, for serving

1. For the marinade: Place all the marinade ingredients into the Vitamix container in the order listed and secure the lid. Select Variable 1. Turn the machine on and slowly increase the speed to Variable 10, then to High. Blend for 20 seconds.

2. Arrange the tempeh pieces in a single layer in a large skillet. Pour the marinade over them and bring to a boil. Reduce to a simmer, cover, and cook for 10 minutes. Remove from the heat.

3. For the peanut sauce: Place all the sauce ingredients into the Vitamix container in the order listed and secure the lid. Select Variable 1. Turn the machine on and slowly increase the speed to Variable 10, then to High. Blend for 1 minute.

4. Serve the tempeh over the brown rice and top with ¼ cup peanut sauce. Refrigerate the remaining peanut sauce for another use.

AMOUNT PER SERVING: calories 395, total fat 19 g, saturated fat 2.5 g, cholesterol 0 mg, sodium 400 mg, total carbohydrate 38 g, dietary fiber 8 g, sugars 6 g, protein 21 g

Cornbread-Stuffed Roasted Squash

Coming up with a scrumptious, satisfying vegetarian main dish for your Thanksgiving can be tricky. Search no more! This stuffed squash is loaded with classic fall flavors, and thanks in part to the Vitamix wet-chop, the prep for this dish is relatively simple.

PREPARATION: **30 minutes** PROCESSING: **pulsing** BAKE TIME: **1 hour 30 minutes** YIELD: **4 servings**

4 cups (311 g) finely cubed Cornbread (page 163)

½ cup (20 g) unsweetened dried cranberries

2 tablespoons (18 g) dried currants

2 acorn squash (1 pound / 454 g each)

½ medium white onion

2 celery stalks

1 large carrot

2 teaspoons olive oil

1 tablespoon chopped fresh sage leaves

1 garlic clove, peeled

½ cup (120 ml) low-sodium vegetable broth

2 tablespoons (14 g) chopped toasted pecans

1 tablespoon fresh flat-leaf parsley leaves

½ teaspoon sea salt

¼ teaspoon ground black pepper

1. Preheat the oven to 400°F (200°C).

2. Spread the cornbread cubes over a rimmed baking sheet and bake for 30 minutes, stirring halfway through, until golden brown and toasted. Set aside to cool on a wire rack. Leave the oven on but reduce the temperature to 350°F (180°C). Line a baking sheet with foil or a silicone baking mat.

3. Meanwhile, combine the cranberries and currants with 1 cup boiling water in a heatproof bowl and let sit for 30 minutes to rehydrate. Drain well.

4. Halve each squash. Discard the seeds and membranes and place cut side down on the baking sheet. Roast for 30 minutes, or until the squash is just tender. Leave the oven on.

5. Meanwhile, wet-chop the vegetables: Fill the Vitamix container with water up to the 5-cup (1.2-L) mark, add the onion, and secure the lid. Select Variable 8. Use the On/Off switch to quickly pulse 3 times. Drain well and repeat the process with the celery (3 pulses) and carrot (4 pulses), draining throughly in a colander.

6. Heat the olive oil in a large skillet over medium-high heat. Add the onion, celery, carrot, sage, and garlic and

cook until the vegetables are softened and the onion is translucent, 3 to 5 minutes. Remove from the heat.

7. Mix together the toasted cornbread, cranberry-currant mixture, sautéed vegetables, broth, pecans, parsley, salt, and pepper in a large bowl.

8. Divide the stuffing among the squash halves. Place the squash in a large serving/baking dish, stuffing side up, and bake for 30 minutes, or until the squash is tender and the stuffing is golden brown.

AMOUNT PER SERVING: calories 370, total fat 12 g, saturated fat 3 g, cholesterol 20 mg, sodium 740 mg, total carbohydrate 60 g, dietary fiber 7 g, sugars 12g, protein 9 g

Falafel

A fried chickpea patty that is a staple in a number of Middle Eastern countries, falafel may seem like the sort of dish that should be left to restaurants. This flavor-packed falafel recipe comes together quickly in the Vitamix. The balls are then baked, not fried, saving on oil, calories, and mess. Enjoy with Lebanese Tabbouleh (page 155).

PREPARATION: **15 minutes plus overnight soaking**   PROCESSING: **34 seconds**

BAKE TIME: **15 minutes**   YIELD: **12 servings (2 balls per serving)**

2 cups (344 g) dried chickpeas, rinsed and picked over

⅔ cup (105 g) coarsely chopped onion

¼ cup (60 ml) water

¼ cup (15 g) fresh flat-leaf parsley leaves

¼ cup (15 g) fresh cilantro leaves

8 garlic cloves, peeled

2 teaspoons ground cumin

1 teaspoon cayenne pepper

1½ teaspoons baking soda

½ cup (62 g) unbleached all-purpose flour

1. Place the chickpeas in a bowl and cover with cool water by about 1 inch. Cover and refrigerate for 12 to 24 hours.

2. Drain the chickpeas. Place the chickpeas, onion, water, parsley, cilantro, garlic, cumin, and cayenne into the Vitamix container and secure the lid. Select Variable 1. Turn the machine on and slowly increase the speed to Variable 10, then to High. Blend for 30 seconds, using the tamper to press the ingredients into the blades.

3. Sprinkle the baking soda and 1 tablespoon of the flour over the mixture. Select Variable 4. Turn the machine on and blend for 4 seconds, using the tamper to press the ingredients into the blades until evenly combined. Scrape the mixture into a bowl. Add the remaining 7 tablespoons flour and mix by hand to combine. Refrigerate overnight before cooking.

4. Preheat the oven to 400°F (200°C). Coat a large (11 × 17-inch / 28 × 43-cm) baking sheet with cooking spray.

5. Form the mixture into balls using 1½ tablespoons chickpea mixture for each. Place the balls on the baking sheet. Bake for 15 minutes, or until golden. Serve hot.

AMOUNT PER SERVING (2 BALLS): calories 60, total fat 1 g, saturated fat 0 g, cholesterol 0 mg, sodium 70 mg, total carbohydrate 11 g, dietary fiber 3 g, sugars 2 g, protein 3 g

Green Tea and Nut Crusted Salmon

Fatty fish like salmon are "high in two kinds of omega-3 fatty acids: eicosapentaenoic acid (EPA) and docosahexaenoic acid (DHA), which have demonstrated benefits at reducing heart disease." Not only nutritious, this salmon dish, with its crunchy and flavorful topping, is delicious too!

PREPARATION: **10 minutes**   PROCESSING: **15 seconds plus pulsing**

BAKE TIME: **14 to 16 minutes**   YIELD: **4 servings**

1 tablespoon plus 1 teaspoon olive oil

1 tablespoon water

⅓ cup (41 g) unsalted roasted pistachios

1½ teaspoons matcha green tea powder

1 teaspoon light brown sugar

3 tablespoons (21 g) unseasoned fine dried bread crumbs

1 teaspoon finely grated lemon zest

1 pound (454 g) skinless salmon fillet, cut into 4 portions

1. Preheat the oven to 325°F (170°C). Line a rimmed baking sheet with parchment paper.

2. Place the olive oil, water, pistachios, matcha, brown sugar, bread crumbs, and lemon zest into the Vitamix container in the order listed and secure the lid. Select Variable 1. Turn the machine on and slowly increase the speed to Variable 4. Blend for 15 seconds, using the tamper to press the ingredients into the blades.

3. Stop the machine, remove the lid, and scrape the sides of the container to incorporate any unblended ingredients. Replace the lid. Select Variable 6. Use the On/Off switch to quickly pulse 6 times.

4. Place the salmon on the baking sheet and top with the crumb mixture. Bake for 14 to 16 minutes, or to an internal temperature of 140°F (60°C).

AMOUNT PER SERVING: calories 290, total fat 16 g, saturated fat 2.5 g, cholesterol 60 mg, sodium 170 mg, total carbohydrate 8 g, dietary fiber 1 g, sugars 3 g, protein 27 g

Herb-Marinated Pork Tenderloin

Thyme, basil, rosemary, oregano, citrus, and spices make simple pork tenderloin something special. Pair with one or two of the salads in chapter 4 for a satisfying dinner. Leftover pork, cold and thinly sliced, makes wonderful sandwiches.

PREPARATION: **10 minutes plus marinating**   PROCESSING: **10 seconds plus pulsing**
YIELD: **8 servings**

½ cup (120 ml) vegetable oil

¼ cup (60 ml) fresh lime juice

3 tablespoons (18 g) fresh oregano leaves

3 tablespoons (7 g) fresh thyme leaves

2 tablespoons (5 g) fresh basil leaves

1 tablespoon fresh rosemary leaves

1 teaspoon grated lemon zest

1½ teaspoons onion powder

½ teaspoon sea salt

½ teaspoon ground black pepper

2 garlic cloves, peeled

2 pounds (908 g) pork tenderloin, trimmed

1. Place the vegetable oil, lime juice, oregano, thyme, basil, rosemary, lemon zest, onion powder, salt, and pepper into the Vitamix container in the order listed and secure the lid. Select Variable 1. Turn the machine on and slowly increase the speed to Variable 8. Blend for 10 seconds.

2. Stop the machine and scrape the sides of the container with a spatula. Add the garlic to the Vitamix container and secure the lid. Select Variable 6. Use the On/Off switch to quickly pulse 4 to 5 times.

3. Place the pork tenderloin in a large zip-seal plastic bag and pour the marinade into the bag. Refrigerate for 1 hour, but not more than 1 hour 30 minutes.

4. Remove the pork from the marinade (discard the marinade). Grill to the desired level of doneness or to a minimum internal temperature of 145°F (63°C).

AMOUNT PER SERVING: calories 160, total fat 6 g, saturated fat 1 g, cholesterol 75 mg, sodium 100 mg, total carbohydrate 2 g, dietary fiber 0 g, sugars 0 g, protein 24 g

Entrées

Summer Corn Cakes

Few foods are more quintessentially summery than sweet corn. Corn on the cob should be eaten within 24 hours of being picked for the best flavor. If you have two ears that are a bit past their prime, transform them into these corn cakes, a delicious vegetarian main dish or side for your next dinner party.

PREPARATION: **20 minutes**   PROCESSING: **25 seconds**   COOK TIME: **40 minutes**   YIELD: **10 cakes**

½ cup (62 g) whole wheat flour, preferably homemade (page 44)

½ teaspoon baking powder

½ cup (120 ml) whole milk

2 large eggs

2 tablespoons (30 ml) canola oil

½ teaspoon salt

¼ teaspoon ground black pepper

½ cup (12 g) fresh basil leaves

2 cups (308 g) fresh corn kernels (from 2 large ears)

1. Combine the flour and baking powder in a medium bowl. Set aside.

2. Place the milk, eggs, 1 tablespoon of the canola oil, the salt, and pepper into the Vitamix container and secure the lid. Select Variable 1. Turn the machine on and blend for 10 seconds.

3. Remove the lid plug and add the basil through the lid plug opening. Blend for an additional 10 seconds.

4. Stop the machine and remove the lid. Add the corn kernels and secure the lid. Select Variable 2. Turn the machine on and blend for 5 seconds. Pour the corn mixture into the flour mixture and mix by hand to combine.

5. Heat the remaining 1 tablespoon oil in a large nonstick skillet over medium heat. Pour ¼ cup (60 ml) batter for each cake onto the skillet. Cook until the edges are dry, about 2 minutes. Flip and cook for 2 minutes more, until golden brown.

AMOUNT PER CAKE: calories 90, total fat 4.5 g, saturated fat 1 g, cholesterol 40 mg, sodium 160 mg, total carbohydrate 11 g, dietary fiber 1 g, protein 3 g

Fish Tacos with Slaw

Fish is generally a good source of protein and omega-3 fatty acids and is low in saturated fat. Make these tangy, crunchy tacos with cabbage slaw to get one of these servings of the healthy acids. The Vitamix blender will do the bulk of the mixing and chopping for you.

PREPARATION: **20 minutes plus marinating** PROCESSING: **1 minute plus pulsing**

COOK TIME: **15 minutes** YIELD: **8 servings**

MARINADE:

½ cup (120 ml) fresh lime juice

½ cup (120 ml) fresh orange juice (see page 301)

1 cup (240 ml) olive oil

1 teaspoon honey

1½ teaspoons ground cumin

1 teaspoon sea salt

¼ cup tightly packed (7 g) fresh cilantro leaves

2 pounds (908 g) skinless tilapia, walleye, or snapper fillets, cut into eight 4-ounce (114-g) portions

DRESSING:

½ orange, peeled

1 cup (240 ml) plain 0% Greek yogurt, stirred

½ teaspoon ground cumin

½ teaspoon sea salt

⅓ teaspoon chipotle powder

¼ cup tightly packed (7 g) fresh cilantro leaves

SLAW:

1 cup (114 g) large chunks green cabbage

¾ cup (85 g) large chunks red cabbage

1 medium carrot, halved

8 corn tortillas (6 inch / 15 cm)

OPTIONAL GARNISHES:

Lime wedges

Cilantro leaves

Thinly sliced radish and jalapeños

1. For the marinade: Place all the marinade ingredients into the Vitamix container in the order listed and secure the lid. Select Variable 1. Turn the machine on and slowly increase the speed to Variable 10, then to High. Blend for 30 seconds.

2. Place the fish fillets in a shallow pan, pour the marinade over the fish, and marinate in the refrigerator for no longer than 30 to 40 minutes.

3. For the dressing: Place all the dressing ingredients

into the Vitamix container in the order listed and secure the lid. Select Variable 1. Turn the machine on and slowly increase the speed to Variable 6. Blend for 30 seconds. Pour the dressing into a squeeze bottle and set aside until serving.

4. For the slaw: Fill the Vitamix container with water up to the 4-cup (960-ml) mark. Add the green cabbage to the Vitamix container and secure the lid. Select Variable 6. Use the On/Off switch to quickly pulse 4 times. Drain well and transfer to a bowl. Repeat the process with the red cabbage (4 pulses) and the carrot (6 pulses), transferring them to the bowl with the green cabbage.

5. Wrap the tortillas in foil and put them in a warm oven until they're heated through, about 15 minutes.

6. Remove the fillets from the marinade and grill or pan-sear the fish until cooked through.

7. Fill each tortilla with about ¼ cup of the slaw, a portion of the fish, and 2 tablespoons of the dressing. Garnish as desired.

AMOUNT PER SERVING: calories 240, total fat 10 g, saturated fat 1.5 g, cholesterol 55 mg, sodium 310 mg, total carbohydrate 14 g, dietary fiber 2 g, sugars 5 g, protein 26 g

Spicy Jerk Chicken

The wonderfully spicy flavor in this jerk marinade will transport you to the West Indies, brightening even the gloomiest days. Freshly ground spices and ginger really make the flavors pop. Serve with brown rice and garnish with thinly sliced scallions.

PREPARATION: **15 minutes**   PROCESSING: **45 seconds**   BAKE TIME: **12 to 15 minutes**
YIELD: **8 servings**

MARINADE:

6 tablespoons (90 ml) olive oil

¼ cup (60 ml) fresh lime juice

4 scallions, cut into pieces

1 small Scotch Bonnet or jalapeño pepper, halved and seeded

3 garlic cloves, peeled

2 tablespoons fresh thyme leaves

One ½-inch (1.3-cm) piece fresh gingerroot, peeled

1 tablespoon dark brown sugar

2 teaspoons allspice berries

1 teaspoon sea salt

¼ teaspoon ground black pepper

2 tablespoons (30 ml) distilled white vinegar

2 pounds (908 g) skinless, boneless chicken thighs

1. For the marinade: Place all the marinade ingredients into the Vitamix container in the order listed and secure the lid. Select Variable 1. Turn the machine on and slowly increase the speed to Variable 10. Blend for 45 seconds.

2. Place the chicken in a glass dish and toss with the marinade. Cover and refrigerate for 4 hours or up to overnight.

3. Bake or grill until the chicken is cooked through and the juices run clear, 12 to 15 minutes.

AMOUNT PER SERVING: calories 240, total fat 15 g, saturated fat 2.5 g, cholesterol 110 mg, sodium 400 mg, total carbohydrate 4 g, dietary fiber 0 g, sugars 2 g, protein 22 g

Polenta Pizza

A naturally gluten-free entrée to add to your dinner rotation. Grind your own cornmeal and make a quick polenta. Top with a simple pizza sauce, low-fat mozzarella, and veggies, and bake to bubbling perfection. Enjoy!

PREPARATION: **20 minutes**   COOK TIME: **10 minutes**   BAKE TIME: **25 minutes**   YIELD: **8 servings**

1¼ cups (300 ml) low-sodium vegetable broth

1¼ cups (300 ml) low-fat (1%) milk

2 tablespoons (30 ml) plus ½ teaspoon olive oil

¼ teaspoon sea salt

1¼ cups (160 g) coarse whole-grain cornmeal, preferably homemade (page 40)

½ cup (120 ml) Quick and Easy Pizza Sauce (page 239)

½ cup (56 g) shredded part-skim mozzarella

2 tablespoons (20 g) diced red onion

2 tablespoons (19 g) diced orange bell pepper

2 tablespoons (28 g) thinly sliced cremini mushrooms

2 tablespoons (23 g) sautéed spinach

1. Preheat the oven to 400°F (200°C). Lightly coat a 9-inch (23-cm) round springform pan with cooking spray.

2. Combine the broth, milk, 2 tablespoons (30 ml) of the olive oil, and the salt in a medium saucepan and bring to a boil. Reduce to a simmer and add the cornmeal, whisking constantly. Reduce the heat to low, cover, and cook for 5 minutes to thicken.

3. Remove the polenta from the heat and immediately pour into the springform pan. With a lightly greased spatula or spoon, gently push the polenta over the bottom and at least ¼ inch up the sides of the pan to create a raised edge/crust.

4. Brush the remaining ½ teaspoon oil over the crust and bake for 12 to 15 minutes, until the crust is lightly browned. Remove from the oven and let cool for 5 minutes. Leave the oven on.

5. Top the polenta crust with the pizza sauce, mozzarella, and the vegetables (or other toppings of your choice).

6. Return the pizza to the oven and bake for 5 minutes, or until the cheese has melted.

7. Remove the sides of the springform pan, cut the pizza into 8 wedges, and serve hot.

AMOUNT PER SLICE: calories 180, total fat 8 g, saturated fat 2 g, cholesterol 5 mg, sodium 220 mg, total carbohydrate 21 g, dietary fiber 3 g, sugars 3 g, protein 6 g

Herb and Goat Cheese Turkey

You may have made stuffed chicken breasts before, but perhaps you haven't ever thought about turkey. After you make these herb, cheese, and walnut roasted turkey breasts, you will be hooked! Full of flavor and finished with a simple pan sauce, this dish is elegant enough for your next dinner party and quick enough for a weeknight supper.

PREPARATION: **15 minutes**   PROCESSING: **pulsing**   BAKE TIME: **8 to 10 minutes**

COOK TIME: **5 minutes**   YIELD: **6 servings**

⅓ cup (40 g) walnut halves

1 ounce (28 g) goat cheese, softened

1½ ounces (43 g) Neufchâtel cheese (⅓-less-fat cream cheese)

2 teaspoons grated lemon zest

2 garlic cloves, halved

⅓ teaspoon lightly minced fresh rosemary

Sea salt and ground black pepper

Six 4-ounce (114-g) pieces boneless, skinless turkey breast

1 tablespoon olive oil

1 tablespoon fresh lemon juice

¼ cup (60 ml) fat-free low-sodium or no-salt-added chicken broth

1 tablespoon walnut oil

2 tablespoons (8 g) fresh flat-leaf parsley

1. Preheat the oven to 375°F (190°C).

2. Place the walnuts, goat cheese, Neufchâtel, lemon zest, garlic, rosemary, ¼ teaspoon salt, and ⅛ teaspoon pepper into the Vitamix container in the order listed and secure the lid. Select Variable 7. Use the On/Off switch to quickly pulse 3 times, using the tamper to press the ingredients into the blades. Stop the machine, remove the lid, and scrape down the sides of the container. Secure the lid and pulse an additional 3 times. Transfer the goat cheese filling to a small bowl.

3. Cut a small pocket into the side of each turkey breast. Evenly divide and stuff the filling into the turkey breast pockets. Gently press to flatten the turkey, making sure to keep the stuffing in. Lightly season the turkey with salt and pepper.

4. Heat the olive oil in a large ovenproof skillet over medium-high heat. Add the turkey breast and cook until golden brown, then carefully flip the turkey and transfer the pan to the oven. Roast for 8 to 10 minutes, or to an internal temperature of 165°F (74°C).

5. Transfer the turkey to a platter to keep warm.

6. Place the pan back over medium heat. Add the lemon juice and broth to the pan and cook, scraping up the browned bits from the bottom of the pan. Simmer for 4 minutes to slightly reduce. Stir in the walnut oil and parsley.

7. Spoon the sauce over the turkey and serve.

AMOUNT PER SERVING: calories 240, total fat 12 g, saturated fat 2.5 g, cholesterol 80 mg, sodium 210 mg, total carbohydrate 2 g, dietary fiber 1 g, sugars 1 g, protein 30 g

Spaghetti with Roasted Vegetable Sauce

Roasting vegetables for this pasta sauce deepens their flavors and helps to caramelize any naturally occurring sugars. (In addition, the lycopene in tomatoes is more easily absorbed by the body when the tomatoes are cooked.) The finished sauce has a deeply nuanced flavor and, thanks to the Vitamix machine, a silky smooth texture that will coat the spaghetti evenly.

PREPARATION: **20 minutes**   PROCESSING: **1 minute 10 seconds**   BAKE TIME: **20 minutes**   YIELD: **6 servings**

2 pounds (908 g) Roma (plum) tomatoes, halved

3 garlic cloves, peeled

½ large carrot

1½ cups (144 g) white button mushrooms

1 wedge (1½ inches / 4 cm thick) red onion

3 tablespoons (45 ml) extra virgin olive oil

Salt and ground black pepper

12 ounces (340 g) whole wheat spaghetti

4 ounces (113 g) Parmigiano-Reggiano or Pecorino Romano, cut into 1-inch (2.5-cm) chunks

One 6-ounce (170-g) can tomato paste

¼ cup firmly packed (6 g) fresh basil leaves

¼ cup firmly packed (6 g) fresh oregano leaves

1. Preheat the oven to 450°F (230°C).

2. Place the tomatoes, garlic, carrot, mushrooms, and onion on an 11 × 17-inch (28 × 43-cm) baking sheet. Drizzle with the olive oil and season with salt and pepper. Roast for 20 minutes, or until the tomatoes are very tender, stirring once.

3. Meanwhile, cook the pasta according to the package directions. Drain well, reserving ½ cup (120 ml) of the cooking water. Keep warm.

4. Place the cheese into the Vitamix container and secure the lid. Select Variable 1. Turn the machine on and slowly increase the speed to Variable 7. Blend until finely grated. Transfer to a small bowl.

5. Place the roasted vegetables (and any liquid from the pan) and tomato paste into the Vitamix container and secure the lid. Select Variable 1. Turn the machine on and slowly increase the speed to Variable 7. Blend for 1 minute, or until smooth, using the tamper to press the ingredients into the blades.

6. Stop the machine and remove the lid. Add the basil and oregano to the Vitamix container and secure the lid. Select Variable 1. Turn the machine on and slowly

increase the speed to Variable 3. Blend for 5 seconds. If a thinner sauce is desired, add the reserved pasta cooking water 1 tablespoon at a time.

7. Serve the sauce over the pasta. Sprinkle with the cheese.

AMOUNT PER SERVING: calories 400, total fat 14 g, saturated fat 3.5 g, cholesterol 15 mg, sodium 380 mg, total carbohydrate 55 g, dietary fiber 13 g, sugars 10 g, protein 18 g

Roasted Salmon with Cilantro-Seed Pesto

Not only is salmon chock-full of omega-3 fatty acids, but it is quick to cook too. While the salmon is roasting, you will have just enough time to whip up this unique pesto. The pesto, made from cilantro, coriander seeds, pumpkin seeds, garlic, lime, and olive oil, provides a bright, tangy contrast to the rich fish.

PREPARATION: **15 minutes**   PROCESSING: **45 seconds**   BAKE TIME: **12 to 14 minutes**   YIELD: **4 servings**

PESTO:

¼ cup (60 ml) extra virgin olive oil

½ cup (60 g) unsalted roasted pumpkin seeds

½ cup tightly packed (14 g) fresh cilantro leaves

¼ teaspoon coriander seeds

1 small garlic clove, peeled

1 tablespoon fresh lime juice

¼ teaspoon sea salt

⅓ teaspoon ground black pepper

SALMON:

1½ pounds (680 g) skin-on salmon fillet, cut into 6 portions

2 tablespoons (30 ml) olive oil

1 tablespoon fresh thyme leaves

Grated zest of 1 lemon

½ teaspoon ground black pepper

Parsley, for garnish

1. For the pesto: Place all the pesto ingredients into the Vitamix container in the order listed and secure the lid. Select Variable 1. Turn the machine on and slowly increase the speed to Variable 4. Blend for 15 seconds, using the tamper to press the ingredients into the blades. Stop, scrape, and repeat twice.

2. For the salmon: Preheat the oven to 325°F (170°C). Line a baking sheet with foil or a silicone baking mat.

3. Place the salmon skin side down on the baking sheet. Brush with the olive oil and rub with the thyme, lemon zest, and pepper. Roast the salmon for 12 to 14 minutes, or until it is opaque in the center and the internal temperature reaches 140°F (60°C).

4. Serve the pesto atop the roasted salmon, and garnish with a sprig of parsley.

AMOUNT PER SERVING: calories 350, total fat 25 g, saturated fat 4 g, cholesterol 60 mg, sodium 230 mg, total carbohydrate 2 g, dietary fiber 1 g, sugars 0 g, protein 27 g

Yogurt-Marinated Turkey Breast

This flavor-packed marinade gives lean turkey breasts a big boost of flavor. The recipe yields eight servings, and any leftovers will be the beginning of a pretty amazing turkey sandwich or wrap.

PREPARATION: **15 minutes**   PROCESSING: **30 seconds**   YIELD: **8 servings**   BAKE TIME: **15 to 20 minutes**

8 pieces boneless, skinless turkey breast (about 6 oz / 170 g each)

⅓ cup (80 ml) olive oil

2 cups (480 ml) plain 0% Greek yogurt, stirred

½ small lime, peeled

6 garlic cloves, peeled

One 2-inch (5-cm) piece fresh gingerroot, peeled and cut into pieces

1 tablespoon garam masala

1 teaspoon sea salt

1 teaspoon ground black pepper

1 cup (16 g) fresh cilantro leaves

1 medium yellow onion (6 oz / 170 g), cut into pieces

1. Place the turkey between sheets of wax paper and gently pound to a ½-inch (1.3-cm) thickness.

2. Transfer the turkey to a sturdy zip-seal plastic bag.

3. Place the olive oil, yogurt, lime, garlic, ginger, garam masala, salt, pepper, cilantro, and onion into the Vitamix container in the order listed and secure the lid. Select Variable 1. Turn the machine on and slowly increase the speed to Variable 10, then to High. Blend for 30 seconds.

4. Pour the marinade over the turkey, seal the bag, and refrigerate for at least 3 hours and up to overnight.

5. Remove the turkey from the marinade (discard the marinade). Grill (or broil) over medium-high heat until the internal temperature is 170°F (78°C), 15 to 20 minutes.

AMOUNT PER SERVING: calories 260, total fat 3.5 g, saturated fat 0.5 g, cholesterol 105 mg, sodium 180 mg, total carbohydrate 6 g, dietary fiber 1 g, sugars 3 g, protein 47 g

Fall Flavors Ravioli

The only thing better than a ravioli full of the flavors of fall is how easy it can be to make this simple, savory dish yourself.

PREPARATION: **20 minutes**   PROCESSING: **30 seconds plus pulsing**   YIELD: **30 ravioli (6 servings)**

2 cups (280 g) chunked roasted pumpkin or butternut squash

⅓ cup (43 g) grated Parmesan

⅓ teaspoon ground sage

Pinch of ground nutmeg

⅓ teaspoon sea salt

⅓ teaspoon ground black pepper

60 wonton wrappers

1 cup (240 ml) low-sodium vegetable broth

1½ teaspoons minced fresh flat-leaf parsley, plus more for garnish

1. Place the roasted pumpkin into the Vitamix container and secure the lid. Select Variable 1. Turn the machine on and slowly increase the speed to Variable 6. Blend for 15 seconds, using the tamper to press the ingredients into the blades. Stop the machine, remove the lid, and scrape the sides of the container. Repeat the procedure.

2. Remove the lid. Add the Parmesan, sage, nutmeg, salt, and pepper to the Vitamix container and secure the lid. Select Variable 4. Use the On/Off switch to quickly pulse 4 to 5 times, using the tamper to press the ingredients into the blades. Scrape the filling into a bowl.

3. Place half of the wonton wrappers on a lightly floured work surface. Spoon 2 teaspoons of the filling into the center of each wrapper. Dip your finger in water and wet the edges of the wrapper. Place an unfilled wrapper over the filling and press gently to seal the edges and work out any air bubbles.

4. Heat the broth and parsley in a small saucepan to a simmer. Meanwhile, cook the ravioli in a large pot of boiling water. Add them in small batches and cook until they float, about 4 minutes. Scoop out the ravioli with a slotted spoon and drain well, then portion them into wide shallow bowls and top with the broth and parsley.

5. Serve garnished with additional parsley.

AMOUNT PER SERVING: calories 230, total fat 3 g, saturated fat 1 g, cholesterol 15 mg, sodium 510 mg, total carbohydrate 42 g, dietary fiber 2 g, sugars 1 g, protein 8 g

Cheese and Kale Ravioli

The filling for this cheese and kale ravioli comes together quickly in the Vitamix machine. To assemble them, get your kids, friends, or even your dinner guests to help.

PREPARATION: **15 minutes**   PROCESSING: **pulsing**   COOK TIME: **1 hour**   YIELD: **28 ravioli (7 servings)**

1 tablespoon olive oil

3 tablespoons (30 g) chopped shallots

1 bunch Tuscan (black/ lacinato) kale, stemmed and cut into small pieces (about 5½ ounces / 155 g)

½ cup (124 g) part-skim ricotta

2 ounces (57 g) goat cheese

⅓ cup (80 ml) plain 0% Greek yogurt, stirred

½ teaspoon ground black pepper

1 teaspoon dried basil

4½ cups (810 g) coarsely chopped tomatoes

2 tablespoons (5 g) chopped fresh basil

56 wonton wrappers

1. Heat the oil in a large skillet over medium-high heat. Add the shallots and cook until just tender, 5 to 10 minutes. Add the kale and cook until wilted, 3 to 4 minutes. Let cool completely.

2. Place the cheeses, yogurt, pepper, and dried basil into the Vitamix container and secure the lid. Select Variable 6. Use the On/Off switch to quickly pulse 4 to 6 times.

3. Add the kale mixture and secure the lid. Select Variable 1. Use the On/Off switch to pulse 8 times. Remove the lid and scrape the sides of the container. Pulse an additional 8 times while using the tamper in between pulses to press the ingredients into the blades.

4. Combine the tomatoes and basil in a bowl and set aside.

5. Place half of the wonton wrappers on a lightly floured work surface. Spoon 2 teaspoons of the cheese mixture into the center of each wrapper. Dip your finger in water and wet the edges of the wrapper. Place an unfilled wrapper over the filling and press gently to seal the edges and work out any air bubbles.

6. Bring a large pot of water to a boil. Reduce to a simmer and place 6 to 8 of the ravioli at a time into the pot. Cook for 4 to 5 minutes. Remove with a slotted spoon and drain well.

7. Serve the ravioli hot with the tomato mixture.

AMOUNT PER SERVING (4 RAVIOLI): calories 280, total fat 6 g, saturated fat 2.5 g, cholesterol 15 mg, sodium 430 mg, total carbohydrate 45 g, dietary fiber 3 g, sugars 4 g, protein 12 g

Spinach Couscous Patties

These bright spinach patties combine many of the flavors of Greek spinach pie—greens, feta, dill—in a healthier package with fewer calories than most purchased varieties of spinach pie. A great vegetarian dinner or a hot appetizer.

PREPARATION: **10 minutes**   PROCESSING: **15 seconds plus pulsing**   COOK TIME: **30 minutes**
YIELD: **12 patties**

1½ cups (1.6 oz / 46 g) baby spinach

1 cup (167 g) whole wheat couscous

1 cup (240 ml) plain 0% Greek yogurt, stirred

⅓ cup (50 g) crumbled feta

1 garlic clove, peeled

¼ teaspoon sea salt

½ teaspoon ground black pepper

¼ cup (40 g) chopped red onion

¼ cup lightly packed (9 g) fresh dill

1 tablespoon olive oil

1. Heat 1 tablespoon water in a large saucepan, add the spinach, and cook until the spinach wilts and releases its liquid. Remove from the heat and transfer to a fine-mesh sieve. Let cool completely, pressing out any remaining moisture.

2. Bring 1¼ cups (300 ml) water to a boil in a small saucepan. Stir in the couscous, remove from the heat, cover, and set aside for 10 minutes. Uncover, fluff the couscous with a fork, and transfer to a large bowl.

3. Place the yogurt, feta, garlic, salt, and pepper into the Vitamix container in the order listed and secure the lid. Select Variable 1. Turn the machine on and slowly increase the speed to Variable 4. Blend for 15 seconds.

4. Stop the machine, remove the lid, and scrape down the sides of the container. Add the spinach, onion, dill, and olive oil. Secure the lid. Select Variable 6. Use the On/Off switch to quickly pulse 10 times, using the tamper between pulses. You may need to scrape down the sides of the container with a spatula between pulses.

5. Combine the yogurt mixture with the cooked couscous and mix well. Form into 12 patties.

6. Working in batches, cook the patties in a nonstick skillet coated with cooking spray over medium heat until

light golden brown, 3 to 4 minutes per side. Transfer the patties to a baking sheet.

7. Prior to serving, place the patties in a 300°F (150°C) oven for 6 minutes, or until heated through.

AMOUNT PER PATTY: calories 80, total fat 2.5 g, saturated fat 1 g, cholesterol 5 mg, sodium 110 mg, total carbohydrate 13 g, dietary fiber 2 g, sugars 1 g, protein 4 g

Stuffed Chard Leaves with Kalamata Olive Vinaigrette

The next time you need a special entrée for a vegetarian guest or you simply want an elegant meatless meal, reach for this recipe. Swiss chard leaves are blanched and then filled with a satisfying mix of potato, Swiss chard stems, herbs, and goat cheese. The rolls are baked and then topped with flavorful Kalamata olive vinaigrette. Greens have never tasted so good!

PREPARATION: **20 minutes**   PROCESSING: **15 seconds plus pulsing**   COOK TIME: **10 minutes**

BAKE TIME: **15 to 20 minutes**   YIELD: **12 servings**

12 ruby chard leaves, stemmed (about 2 bunches)

FILLING:

1 tablespoon extra virgin olive oil

4 garlic cloves, minced

½ cup (74 g) diced yellow onion

1 cup (90 g) diced chard stems

2 medium russet (baking) potatoes (1¼ pounds / 555 g), baked until tender (45 to 60 minutes at 400°F / 205°C) and peeled

¾ teaspoon sea salt

½ teaspoon ground black pepper

¼ teaspoon ground nutmeg

4 ounces (114 g) goat cheese

2 tablespoons (5 g) chopped fresh basil

2 tablespoons (5 g) snipped fresh chives

VINAIGRETTE:

½ cup (120 ml) olive oil

6 tablespoons (90 ml) red wine vinegar

½ teaspoon sea salt

¼ teaspoon ground black pepper

½ cup (76 g) pitted Kalamata olives, rinsed

¼ cup (35 g) minced shallots

1. Preheat the oven to 375°F (190°C).

2. Bring a large pot of water to a boil. Set up a large bowl of ice and water. Carefully blanch each chard leaf and then cold-shock in the ice water. Drain well and pat dry on paper towels.

3. For the filling: Heat the olive oil in a large skillet over medium-high heat. Add the garlic, onion, and chard stems. Cook until the onion is tender, 4 to 6 minutes. Remove from the heat.

4. Transfer the sautéed vegetables to the Vitamix container and secure the lid. Select Variable 6. Use the On/Off switch to quickly pulse 4 times. Stop, remove the lid, and scrape the sides of the container. Repeat the process 3 more times for a total of 12 pulses.

5. In a large bowl, mash the potatoes with a fork and then add the sautéed onion mixture, salt, pepper, nutmeg, goat cheese, basil, and chives. Mix well.

6. Lay out the blanched chard leaves on a clean work surface. Place about 3 tablespoons (45 ml) of the potato mixture in the center of each leaf. Fold in the sides and starting at the top of the leaf roll up to enclose all the filling. Place in a greased 8-inch (20-cm) square baking dish.

7. Bake the stuffed chard for 15 to 20 minutes, or until heated through.

8. Meanwhile, for the vinaigrette: Place the olive oil, vinegar, salt, and pepper into the Vitamix container in the order listed and secure the lid. Select Variable 1. Turn the machine on and slowly increase the speed to Variable 10, then to High. Blend for 10 seconds.

9. Stop the machine and remove the lid. Add the olives and shallots to the Vitamix container and secure the lid. Select Variable 1. Turn the machine on and slowly increase the speed to Variable 4. Blend for 5 seconds.

10. To serve, top the warmed chard rolls with the vinaigrette.

AMOUNT PER SERVING: calories 200, total fat 14 g, saturated fat 3 g, cholesterol 5 mg, sodium 500 mg, total carbohydrate 14 g, dietary fiber 2 g, sugars 2 g, protein 4 g

Tempeh Teriyaki with Slaw

Cabbage has just 22 calories per cup and tons of crunch. Here, in this refreshing, Asian-influenced slaw, the cabbage provides the perfect complement to the chewy, slightly salty tempeh.

PREPARATION: **15 minutes**   PROCESSING: **pulsing**   COOK TIME: **20 minutes**   YIELD: **4 servings**

SLAW:

3 cups (255 g) napa cabbage chunks

½ medium carrot

¼ small red onion, halved

1 teaspoon hoisin sauce

2 teaspoons unseasoned rice vinegar

⅛ teaspoon sea salt

TEMPEH:

8 ounces (227 g) tempeh, cut into thin strips

1 teaspoon Chinese five-spice powder

1 tablespoon sesame oil

2 tablespoons (30 ml) reduced-sodium soy sauce

2 large whole wheat pita breads, halved crosswise

1. For the slaw: Fill the Vitamix container with 6 cups water. Add the cabbage and secure the lid. Select Variable 8. Use the On/Off switch to quickly pulse 3 times. Drain the cabbage well in a fine-mesh sieve, pressing out as much liquid as possible. Transfer to a large bowl.

2. Place the carrot and onion into the Vitamix container and secure the lid. Select Variable 6. Use the On/Off switch to quickly pulse 6 times. Stop, scrape down the sides of the container, and pulse an additional 6 times.

3. Transfer the carrot-onion mixture to the bowl with the cabbage. Add the hoisin, vinegar, and salt and mix well. Set aside.

4. For the tempeh: Bring 1 cup (240 ml) water to a simmer in a large skillet. Add the tempeh and cook, covered, until plump and just soft, 8 to 10 minutes. Remove the tempeh from the skillet and sprinkle with the five-spice powder.

5. Heat the sesame oil in a large skillet over medium heat. Add the tempeh strips and cook for a few minutes, turning once, until lightly browned, being careful not to burn them. Remove the pan from the heat and sprinkle the tempeh with the soy sauce.

6. To serve, divide the tempeh and slaw among the 4 pita halves.

AMOUNT PER SERVING: calories 250, total fat 9 g, saturated fat 1.5 g, cholesterol 0 mg, sodium 450 mg, total carbohydrate 30 g, dietary fiber 8 g, sugars 2 g, protein 16 g

Whole Wheat Pasta with Sun-Dried Tomato and Caper Vinaigrette Sauce

Perhaps best described as a sun-dried tomato pesto, this delicious sauce will be the perfect finishing touch for your pasta when fresh tomatoes are not in season. Made of pantry staples, this is also a great go-to dinner on nights when the fridge is on the empty side.

PREPARATION: **15 minutes**   PROCESSING: **10 to 15 seconds**   COOK TIME: **15 minutes**

YIELD: **6 servings**

1 pound (454 g) whole wheat pasta

3 tablespoons (45 ml) olive oil

2 tablespoons (30 ml) red wine vinegar

½ cup (55 g) sun-dried tomatoes in olive oil, rinsed, well drained, and chopped into pieces

1 tablespoon small capers, rinsed and well drained

1 tablespoon fresh thyme leaves

1 garlic clove, peeled

¼ teaspoon ground black pepper

1. Cook the pasta according to the package directions. Drain and keep warm.

2. Meanwhile, place the olive oil, vinegar, tomatoes, capers, thyme, garlic, and pepper into the Vitamix container in the order listed and secure the lid. Select Variable 5. Turn the machine on and blend for 10 to 15 seconds.

3. Transfer the hot pasta to a large serving bowl, spoon the sun-dried tomato mixture on top, and generously toss to coat the pasta well. Serve hot.

AMOUNT PER SERVING: calories 350, total fat 10 g, saturated fat 1 g, cholesterol 0 mg, sodium 80 mg, total carbohydrate 55 g, dietary fiber 13 g, sugars 1 g, protein 13 g

Entrées

Quinoa and Barley Sliders

Try these hearty, flavorful vegan burgers for your next barbecue. Cook the barley and quinoa separately and then pulse the grains together in the Vitamix. These burgers are best cooked in a pan with hot oil. Searing creates a golden-brown crust that helps these delicate, grain-filled burgers hold together.

PREPARATION: **10 minutes**   PROCESSING: **45 seconds**   COOK TIME: **1 hour**   YIELD: **14 sliders**

2¾ cups (660 ml) low-sodium vegetable broth

½ cup (85 g) quinoa, rinsed well and drained

½ cup (100 g) pearl barley

7 ounces (200 g) firm tofu

2 garlic cloves, peeled

¼ cup (4 g) fresh cilantro leaves

½ teaspoon chili powder

½ teaspoon ground cumin

1½ cups (120 g) plus 2 tablespoons (10 g) panko bread crumbs

2 tablespoons (60 ml) canola/olive oil blend

14 whole wheat slider buns, split and toasted

OPTIONAL GARNISHES:
Baby spinach
Tomato slices
Red onion slices

1. In a small saucepan, bring 1 cup of the vegetable broth to a boil. Add the quinoa and simmer for 10 minutes, or until the quinoa has puffed and is cooked through. Remove the saucepan from the heat and cool completely.

2. In a small saucepan, cook the barley in the remaining 1¾ cups (420 ml) vegetable broth. Cool completely.

3. Place the tofu, garlic, cilantro, chili powder, cumin, ½ cup of the cooked barley, and 2 tablespoons of the panko into the Vitamix container in the order listed and secure the lid. Select Variable 1. Turn the machine on and slowly increase the speed to Variable 10, then to High. Blend for 45 seconds, using the tamper to press the ingredients into the blades.

4. Pour the tofu mixture into a large bowl. Add the quinoa and remaining barley and stir to combine. Form the mixture into 2-ounce (56-g) slider patties. Coat the patties with the remaining 1½ cups (120 g) panko.

5. Heat the oil in a large skillet over medium heat. Add the patties and cook until golden and heated through, 3 to 4 minutes per side.

6. Serve sliders on toasted slider buns. If desired, garnish with baby spinach, tomato slices, and/or red onion.

AMOUNT PER SLIDER: calories 230, total fat 7 g, saturated fat 0.5 g, cholesterol 0 mg, sodium 270 mg, total carbohydrate 36 g, dietary fiber 5 g, sugars 1 g, protein 8 g

Turkey Burgers with Cherry Salsa

Did you know you could grind meat in your Vitamix? It will be more of a very fine chop, rather than the grind you may be used to from the grocery store. The upside of grinding your own meat is that you know exactly what is in it. No mystery meat! Cutting and partially freezing the meat before you pulse it helps the Vitamix cut the meat instead of tearing or smearing it.

PREPARATION: **20 minutes**   PROCESSING: **pulsing**   YIELD: **4 patties**

SALSA:

1 navel orange, peeled and halved

1 jalapeño pepper, quartered and seeded

1 cup (140 g) pitted fresh or thawed frozen Bing cherries

¼ cup lightly packed (6 g) fresh cilantro leaves

1 tablespoon agave nectar

BURGERS:

½ medium onion, quartered

1 pound (454 g) boneless turkey breast, partially thawed, cut into 1-inch (2.5-cm) cubes

1 large egg

1 tablespoon reduced-sodium soy sauce

¼ teaspoon ground black pepper

¼ cup (30 g) unseasoned fine dried bread crumbs

2 tablespoons (15 g) grated Parmesan

2 garlic cloves, minced

2 whole wheat hamburger buns, split and toasted

1. For the salsa: Place all the salsa ingredients into the Vitamix container in the order listed and secure the lid. Select Variable 6. Use the On/Off switch to quickly pulse 12 to 14 times, using the tamper to press the ingredients into the blades.

2. For the burgers: To wet-chop the onion, fill the Vitamix container with water up to the 4-cup (960-ml) mark. Add the onion and secure the lid. Select Variable 6. Use the On/Off switch to quickly pulse 4 times. Drain well and clean the container.

3. To grind the turkey, work in two batches, ½ pound (227 g) at a time. Add the partially frozen turkey to the

Vitamix container and secure the lid. Select Variable 8. Use the On/Off switch to pulse 8 to 10 times, until the mixture resembles ground meat. Use the tamper while pulsing to press the ingredients into the blades.

4. Place the ground turkey in a large bowl and add the onion, egg, soy sauce, pepper, bread crumbs, Parmesan, and garlic. Mix well.

5. Form into 4 patties and grill over medium-high heat to an internal temperature of 165°F (74°C).

6. Serve the burgers open-face on a toasted bun half. Top with the salsa.

AMOUNT PER PATTY: calories 310, total fat 4.5 g, saturated fat 1.5 g, cholesterol 95 mg, sodium 480 mg, total carbohydrate 33 g, dietary fiber 4 g, sugars 16 g, protein 35 g

Quinoa Black Bean Burgers

This is an amazing vegan burger! Packed with delicious and nutritious ingredients—black beans, quinoa, corn, roasted poblano peppers, and lots of spices—these burgers will be a hit with vegetarians and meat eaters alike. Serve with Guacamole (page 77) or California Salsa (page 80), sliced tomatoes, lettuce, sliced red onion, and pickled jalapeños.

PREPARATION: **15 minutes**   PROCESSING: **30 seconds**   COOK TIME: **12 to 20 minutes**   YIELD: **8 patties**

2 tablespoons (30 ml) water

One 15-ounce (425-g) can no-salt-added black beans, rinsed and drained

½ cup (92 g) cooked quinoa

½ cup (82 g) frozen corn kernels, thawed

1 roasted poblano pepper, peeled, seeded, and chopped (about ¼ cup / 56 g)

½ cup (40 g) panko bread crumbs

¼ cup (4 g) fresh cilantro leaves

4 drops of Tabasco sauce

½ teaspoon chili powder

½ teaspoon ground cumin

½ teaspoon garlic powder

½ teaspoon sea salt

½ teaspoon ground black pepper

4 tablespoons (60 ml) olive oil

1. Place the water and half of the black beans into the Vitamix container and secure the lid. Select Variable 1. Turn the machine on and slowly increase the speed to Variable 4. Blend for 30 seconds, using the tamper to press the ingredients into the blades.

2. Transfer the bean puree to a large bowl and add the quinoa, corn, poblano, panko, cilantro, Tabasco, chili powder, cumin, garlic powder, salt, and black pepper. Mix well to incorporate. Form into 8 small patties and transfer to a baking sheet. Place the baking sheet in the refrigerator for at least 15 to 20 minutes to firm up / set the patties.

3. Heat 2 tablespoons of the olive oil in a large skillet over medium heat. Add 4 of the patties and cook until golden brown and crispy, 3 to 5 minutes per side. Repeat with the remaining oil and patties.

AMOUNT PER PATTY: calories 130, total fat 7 g, saturated fat 1 g, cholesterol 0 mg, sodium 115 mg, total carbohydrate 14 g, dietary fiber 3 g, sugars 0 g, protein 3 g

Zucchini Burgers

When your garden is bursting with zucchini, and you have eaten all of the zucchini bread you can manage, try making these delicious burgers. Packed with zucchini and spices, these burgers are baked instead of pan-seared. Serve on whole-grain buns with lettuce, tomato, and red onion. Instead of ketchup, try the patties with California Salsa (page 80).

PREPARATION: **15 minutes**   PROCESSING: **pulsing**   BAKE TIME: **15 minutes**   YIELD: **8 patties**

1 pound (450 g) zucchini, cut into large chunks

½ large onion (100 g), quartered

¾ cup (90 g) Italian seasoned bread crumbs

1 large egg

1 large egg white

¼ cup (50 g) shredded Pecorino Romano or Parmesan

¼ teaspoon garlic powder

¼ teaspoon onion powder

¼ teaspoon dried parsley

¼ teaspoon dried basil

¼ teaspoon dried oregano

1. Preheat the oven to 450°F (230°C). Coat an 11 × 17-inch (28 × 43-cm) baking sheet with cooking spray.

2. To wet-chop the zucchini, place it into the Vitamix container and add enough water so the zucchini floats off the blades. Secure the lid. Select Variable 4. Use the On/Off switch to quickly pulse. Repeat 4 times. Drain well and pat dry. Transfer to a large bowl. This wet-chop process makes light work of an otherwise time-consuming process.

3. Place the onion into the Vitamix container and secure the lid. Select Variable 3. Use the On/Off switch to quickly pulse 4 times to evenly chop. Add to the zucchini.

4. Add the bread crumbs, eggs, cheese, and seasonings to the bowl and stir until evenly combined. Measure ¼-cup (60-g) portions of the zucchini mixture and place on the baking sheet. Spread gently to form the patties.

5. Bake the patties for 15 minutes, or until heated through.

AMOUNT PER PATTY: calories 80, total fat 2.5 g, saturated fat 1 g, cholesterol 35 mg, sodium 240 mg, total carbohydrate 10 g, dietary fiber 1 g, sugars 2 g, protein 5 g

Entrées

WHOLE FOODS SUCCESS STORY

Susan Amick

Many athletes at all performance levels enjoy smoothies and whole food juices as part of their training diet, while others drink them to aid their after-workout recovery. Susan Amick, her boyfriend, Boris, and her son are a seriously active and athletic family and routinely make smoothies and juices. But prior to buying a Vitamix machine, they couldn't stop breaking blenders.

"We were making lots of smoothies," Susan remembers. "If we wanted to use frozen fruit or ice, anything that was still whole, be it a fruit or vegetable, [the blenders] just couldn't take it!" Susan bought a Vitamix blender in 2003, and she and her family have been using it nonstop ever since. The family is now using a newer Vitamix machine, but their first machine is still going strong with new owners.

Today, Susan, a tai chi instructor, Boris, a triathlete coach and gym owner, and Susan's son, a professional cyclist in Europe, still use their Vitamix blender to power their busy, active lives. Susan says she frequently makes healthy smoothies as well as soups. Susan's son likes to make quick recovery drinks of protein powder and fruit after hard workouts. (He even took a Vitamix machine with him when he went to college.) Susan said the family started using their Vitamix machine the moment it arrived. "Our Vitamix [blender]," Susan laughs, "probably gets used more than in any other household with one. We use it a couple of times a day!" Susan's son misses his Vitamix blender when he is racing in Europe and looks forward to buying one there so he can power his races with his favorite smoothies.

Using whole foods to power a healthy, very active life? A whole foods success story if ever there was one!

Fresh Tomato
Sauce (page 238)

Raisin Almond
Breakfast Spread
(page 245)

Chapter 6

Dressings, Sauces, and Spreads

My grandma Ruth and grandpa Bill were quite a pair! Grandpa was a natural salesman, full of ideas and a genuine love of people, animals, and laughter. Grandma brought order to the pandemonium that his gregarious style often created. My grandfather had a powerful presence but always joked, teased, and made funny faces. He was bigger than life. He had great ideas and the tenacity to pursue them. My grandmother would silently, quietly put things in place. They couldn't do it without each other.

How does this relate to sauces and dressings? Think of it like this. Plain vegetables are good. They are certainly healthy as they are, simple and pretty tasty. But a nutritious vinaigrette can really make a salad sing. And undressed pasta might be the perfect dish for many children, but a hearty tomato sauce makes it a more complete meal. The sauces and dressings, on the other hand, aren't really good to eat on their own. They need something to dress. A good partnership can be a wonderful presence in our lives and on our plates. Grandma and Grandpa worked together like pasta and tomato sauce, like a healthy salad dressing and a bowlful of fresh, crunchy vegetables. A perfect combination, an amazing team.

At Vitamix, we completely understand that we are more likely to want to eat healthy food if it tastes delicious. The sauces and dressings in this chapter add flavor, spice, and sparkle to your food. Intense and rich flavor is achieved using whole foods, healthy fats, and lots of spices and herbs, both dried and fresh. Making these sauces and dressings at home instead of buying them gives you the opportunity to know exactly what you are eating. You can avoid the additives and extra sodium often found in purchased products, and you might just save a little money in the process. Let's take a look at some of the recipes featured in this chapter.

Delectable Sauces

There are two fantastic tomato sauces in this chapter. For Fresh Tomato Sauce (page 238), whole tomatoes, onions, carrots, garlic, spices, a little tomato paste, and brown sugar are combined in the Vitamix and simmered until the juices reduce a little and the flavors come together. This sauce will freeze beautifully once it has cooled. Spicy Tomato Cream Sauce (page 237) combines low-fat milk or soy milk, a cooked sweet potato, fresh tomatoes, garlic, sun-dried tomatoes, and spices. The ingredients for this tasty sauce are cooked in the Vitamix, just like the soups in chapter 4. Sauces containing low-fat dairy should not be frozen, because the dairy can separate when it is reheated. Instead, enjoy this sauce within four days of preparing it.

Not-So Cheese Sauce (page 240) would dress up any vegetable and provides tons of cheesy flavor without any dairy. Parsley-Pecan Pesto (page 242), a delicious riff on the traditional Genovese pesto, would be welcome mixed with cooked grains, tossed with steamed vegetables, or as a spread on a sandwich. Cashew Crema (page 249), a decadent nondairy cream, will transform a bowl of sliced fresh fruit into a simple and delicious dessert.

Flavorful Vinaigrettes

When you have a homemade salad dressing in your refrigerator, getting a healthy salad on the table is a little easier. Three of the vinaigrettes in this chapter—Fresh Apple and Pear Dressing (page 232), Tomato Vinaigrette (page 231), and Balsamic Orange Dressing (page 229)—call for whole fruits along with more traditional ingredients like oil, lemon juice, or vinegar. These whole foods add nutrients as well as a fresh, vibrant flavor not often found in vinaigrettes.

Silky Miso Vinaigrette (page 233) uses tofu along with spices, herbs, and other ingredients to create a creamy, bright salad dressing without any dairy.

LET'S GET SAUCY!

Balsamic Orange Dressing

Once you get the hang of making your own salad dressings, you may never buy a bottle of it again! This fresh, zippy dressing is the perfect finishing touch for a bowl of mixed greens, and it comes together in minutes.

PREPARATION: **10 minutes**   PROCESSING: **20 seconds**   YIELD: **1¼ cups (300 ml)**

2 tablespoons water

¼ cup (60 ml) balsamic vinegar

2 teaspoons grated orange zest

½ orange, peeled

¼ teaspoon sea salt

¼ teaspoon ground black pepper

1 teaspoon Dijon mustard

10 tablespoons (150 ml) extra virgin olive oil

½ teaspoon fresh thyme leaves

1. Place the water, vinegar, orange zest, orange, salt, pepper, and mustard into the Vitamix container in the order listed and secure the lid. Select Variable 1. Turn the machine on and slowly increase the speed to Variable 10, then to High. Blend for 10 seconds.

2. Reduce the speed to Variable 4 and remove the lid plug. Drizzle in the olive oil in a thin steady stream through the lid plug opening. Replace the lid plug and slowly increase the speed to Variable 10. Blend for 5 seconds.

3. Stop the machine, remove the lid, and add the thyme. Select Variable 1. Turn the machine on and slowly increase the speed to Variable 2. Blend for 5 seconds to mix.

AMOUNT PER 2 TABLESPOON (30 ML) SERVING: calories 140, total fat 14 g, saturated fat 2 g, cholesterol 0 mg, sodium 75 mg, total carbohydrate 2 g, dietary fiber 0 g, sugars 2 g, protein 0 g

Dressings, Sauces, and Spreads

Tomato Vinaigrette

Toss this delicious dressing with steamed green beans or cauliflower and a little parsley to make a fantastic vegetable side.

PREPARATION: **10 minutes**   PROCESSING: **30 seconds**   BAKE TIME: **40 minutes**   YIELD: **1 cup (240 ml)**

3 Roma (plum) tomatoes, quartered

2 garlic cloves, halved

1 shallot, quartered

¼ cup (60 ml) plus 1 tablespoon olive oil

½ teaspoon sea salt

¼ teaspoon ground black pepper

2 tablespoons (30 ml) sherry vinegar

1. Preheat the oven to 400°F (200°C). Line a rimmed baking sheet with foil or a silicone baking mat.

2. Toss the tomatoes, garlic, shallot, 1 tablespoon of the olive oil, the salt, and pepper in a large bowl. Evenly spread the vegetables over the baking sheet. Roast for 40 minutes, or until the garlic and shallot are golden. Set the baking sheet on a wire rack to cool completely.

3. Transfer the roasted vegetables to the Vitamix container. Add the remaining ¼ cup (60 ml) oil and the vinegar and secure the lid. Select Variable 1. Turn the machine on and slowly increase the speed to Variable 10, then to High. Blend for 30 seconds.

AMOUNT PER 2 TABLESPOON (30 ML) SERVING: calories 80, total fat 9 g, saturated fat 1.5 g, cholesterol 0 mg, sodium 150 mg, total carbohydrate 2 g, dietary fiber 0 g, sugars 1 g, protein 0 g

Fresh Apple and Pear Dressing

This fresh, lightly sweet dressing is delicious drizzled on salad greens or tossed with shredded cooked chicken, finely chopped celery and red onion, and some fresh parsley for a tasty and slightly unconventional chicken salad.

PREPARATION: **15 minutes**   PROCESSING: **20 seconds plus pulsing**   COOK TIME: **30 minutes**
YIELD: **2¼ cups (540 ml)**

1 pear, cored and chopped

1 apple, cored and chopped

¼ cup (50 g) sugar

1 teaspoon fresh tarragon leaves, or 2 teaspoons dried

⅔ cup (160 ml) water

2 tablespoons (30 ml) apple cider vinegar

2 tablespoons (30 ml) fresh lemon juice

1. Place the pear, apple, sugar, tarragon, and water in a medium saucepan. Cover and bring to a simmer over medium heat. Cook until the fruit is very soft, about 8 minutes. Remove from heat and uncover, allowing the mixture to begin cooling and the water to evaporate. There should be about 1¾ cups (420 ml) fruit and liquid when finished cooking. Let cool for 15 minutes.

2. Ladle the mixture into the Vitamix container and secure the lid. Select Variable 1. Turn the machine on and slowly increase the speed to Variable 10, then to High. Blend for 20 seconds, or until smooth.

3. Add the vinegar and lemon juice to the Vitamix container and secure the lid. Select Variable 1. Use the On/Off switch to quickly pulse 2 to 3 times to combine. Cool to room temperature before serving.

AMOUNT PER 2 TABLESPOON (30 ML) SERVING: calories 30, total fat 0 g, saturated fat 0 g, cholesterol 0 mg, sodium 0 mg, total carbohydrate 8 g, dietary fiber 1 g, protein 0 g

Silky Miso Vinaigrette

Umeboshi paste, made from Japanese salt-pickled plums, adds a sour, briny note to this delicious vinaigrette. Spoon this sauce over steamed vegetables or toss it with crunchy romaine lettuce and thinly sliced radishes, carrots, and scallions.

PREPARATION: **15 minutes**   PROCESSING: **1 minute 15 seconds**   YIELD: **3 cups (720 ml)**

6 ounces (170 g) firm tofu, drained

¼ cup (60 ml) apple cider vinegar

1 lemon, peeled and halved

1 tablespoon plus 1 teaspoon shiro (white) miso paste

1 tablespoon chopped fresh gingerroot

1 garlic clove, peeled

1 tablespoon umeboshi paste

2 teaspoons honey

½ cup (120 ml) extra virgin olive oil

¾ cup (180 ml) olive oil

1. Place the tofu, vinegar, lemon, miso, ginger, garlic, umeboshi paste, and honey into the Vitamix container in the order listed and secure the lid. Select Variable 1. Turn the machine on and slowly increase the speed to Variable 10, then to High. Blend for 15 seconds.

2. Reduce the speed to Variable 4 and remove the lid plug. Slowly drizzle the oils through the lid plug opening in a pencil-thin stream. Once all of the oil has been added, replace the lid plug and slowly increase the speed to Variable 10. Blend for an additional 15 seconds.

AMOUNT PER 2 TABLESPOON (30 ML) SERVING: calories 110, total fat 12 g, saturated fat 1.5 g, cholesterol 0 mg, sodium 70 mg, total carbohydrate 1 g, dietary fiber 0 g, sugars 1 g, protein 1 g

Dressings, Sauces, and Spreads

Farmers' Market Marinara Sauce

Make this simple, flavorful marinara sauce when your garden or the local farmers' market is bursting with red, ripe tomatoes. First, use the wet-chop method to dice the garlic, carrot, and onion, and then use the dry-chop method to chunk up the tomatoes—seeds, skins, and all. Once the sauce is cooked, use the Vitamix to puree it to your desired consistency. Enjoy now or, if you like, freeze for later. For more variety, add sautéed mushrooms or eggplant. Meat lovers can add turkey sausage.

PREPARATION: **15 minutes**   PROCESSING: **30 seconds**   COOK TIME: **1 hour 10 minutes**
YIELD: **4½ cups (1 liter)**

2 garlic cloves, peeled

1 small carrot, cut into big pieces

1 small onion, quartered

3 tablespoons (45 ml) olive oil

⅓ cup (80 ml) dry red wine

5 pounds (2.2 kg) tomatoes, quartered

¼ cup (10 g) fresh basil leaves

1 tablespoon fresh oregano leaves

1 tablespoon fresh thyme leaves

1 teaspoon sea salt

½ teaspoon ground black pepper

1 teaspoon sugar

1. For the wet-chop: Place the garlic, carrot, and onion into the Vitamix container. Add water until the vegetables float above the blades. Secure the lid. Select Variable 1. Turn the machine on and slowly increase the speed to Variable 6. Turn off the machine. Repeat until your desired consistency is reached. Drain well.

2. Heat the olive oil in a large saucepan over medium-low heat. Add the drained onion mixture and cook, stirring often, until soft but not browned, about 15 minutes.

3. Add the wine and stir well, loosening any bits stuck to the bottom of the pan. Simmer and cook until slightly reduced, about 8 minutes.

4. Place one-third of the tomatoes into the Vitamix container and secure the lid. Select Variable 1. Turn the machine on and slowly increase the speed to Variable 4. Blend for 5 to 10 seconds, or until chopped, using the tamper to press the ingredients into the blades. Transfer to a bowl and repeat with the remaining tomatoes.

5. Add the tomatoes and their juices to the saucepan. Add the basil, oregano, and thyme and simmer for 45 minutes. Remove from the heat and let cool for 10 minutes.

6. Ladle the hot tomato mixture into the Vitamix container. Add salt, pepper, and sugar and secure the lid. Select Variable 1. Turn the machine on and slowly increase the speed to Variable 8. Blend for 20 seconds, or until the desired consistency is reached.

7. Use right away or cool completely and refrigerate or freeze.

AMOUNT PER ½ CUP (120 ML) SERVING: calories 100, total fat 5 g, saturated fat 0.5 g, cholesterol 0 mg, sodium 280 mg, total carbohydrate 12 g, dietary fiber 3 g, sugars 8 g, protein 2 g

Spicy Tomato Cream Sauce

Ten ingredients are put into the Vitamix and six minutes later, a creamy, slightly spicy tomato sauce emerges. This sauce is delicious tossed with pasta or spooned over roasted chicken.

PREPARATION: **20 minutes**   PROCESSING: **6 minutes**   YIELD: **4 cups (960 ml)**

2 cups (480 ml) low-fat (1%) milk or soy milk

½ medium sweet potato, baked and quartered

2 Roma (plum) tomatoes, quartered

½ teaspoon salt

1 garlic clove, peeled

1½ teaspoons chopped fresh basil, or ½ teaspoon dried

1½ teaspoons chopped fresh oregano, or ½ teaspoon dried

½ cup (28 g) sun-dried tomatoes

¼ teaspoon red pepper flakes

⅛ teaspoon ground white pepper

Place all the ingredients into the Vitamix container in the order listed and secure the lid. Select Variable 1. Turn the machine on and slowly increase the speed to Variable 10, then to High. Blend for 6 minutes, or until heavy steam escapes from the vented lid.

AMOUNT PER ¼ CUP (60 ML) SERVING: calories 60, total fat 0 g, saturated fat 0 g, cholesterol 0 mg, sodium 210 mg, total carbohydrate 6 g, dietary fiber 1 g, sugars 2 g, protein 2 g

Fresh Tomato Sauce

Instead of peeling, seeding, and chopping the vegetables for this fresh, tasty tomato sauce, you simply pop them in the Vitamix and process them to silky, smooth perfection. Once the sauce has simmered and the flavors have come together, you can toss it over pasta or freeze it in containers with tight-fitting lids for another time.

PREPARATION: **15 minutes**   PROCESSING: **1 minute**   COOK TIME: **35 to 40 minutes**   YIELD: **2 cups (480 ml)**

6 medium Roma (plum) tomatoes, quartered

1 small onion, halved

1 small carrot, halved

2 tablespoons (33 g) tomato paste

1 garlic clove, peeled

½ teaspoon dried basil

½ teaspoon dried oregano

½ teaspoon fresh lemon juice

½ teaspoon light brown sugar

½ teaspoon sea salt

1. Place all the ingredients into the Vitamix container in the order listed and secure the lid. Select Variable 1. Turn the machine on and slowly increase the speed to Variable 10, then to High. Blend for 1 minute, using the tamper to press the ingredients into the blades if necessary.

2. Pour into a saucepan and simmer for 35 to 40 minutes.

AMOUNT PER ¼ CUP (60 ML) SERVING: calories 25, total fat 0 g, saturated fat 0 g, cholesterol 0 mg, sodium 170 mg, total carbohydrate 6 g, dietary fiber 2 g, sugars 4 g, protein 1 g

Quick and Easy Pizza Sauce

This simple pizza sauce, made with onions, garlic, herbs, canned tomatoes, and tomato paste, yields a generous quantity of sauce. Freeze in ½-cup portions so you can whip up a pizza like Polenta Pizza (page 199) anytime.

PREPARATION: **10 minutes**   PROCESSING: **25 to 45 seconds**   COOK TIME: **1 hour**   YIELD: **4 cups (960 ml)**

3 tablespoons (45 ml) olive oil

1¾ cups (230 g) yellow onion chunks

1 tablespoon chopped fresh basil

1 tablespoon fresh oregano leaves

3 large garlic cloves, halved

2 tablespoons (33 g) tomato paste

One 28-ounce (794-g) can crushed tomatoes with added puree

½ teaspoon sea salt

¼ teaspoon ground black pepper

1. Heat the olive oil in a medium saucepan over medium heat. Add the onion, basil, and oregano and cook, stirring occasionally, until the onion softens slightly, about 6 minutes. Stir in the garlic and cook for 2 minutes.

2. Add the tomato paste and cook for 3 minutes, stirring occasionally. Add the crushed tomatoes and bring to a simmer. Simmer until the sauce thickens, about 30 minutes. Season with the salt and pepper and remove from the heat. Let cool for 15 minutes.

3. Ladle the sauce into the Vitamix container and secure the lid. Select Variable 1. Turn the machine on and slowly increase the speed to Variable 4. Blend for 25 to 45 seconds, until the desired consistency is reached.

AMOUNT PER ¼ CUP (60 ML) SERVING: calories 50, total fat 2.5 g, saturated fat 0 g, cholesterol 0 mg, sodium 160 mg, total carbohydrate 4 g, dietary fiber 0 g, sugars 2 g, protein 1 g

Not-So Cheese Sauce

It is really kind of amazing to watch as six ingredients are put into a Vitamix and then, about five minutes later, a warm nondairy cheese sauce emerges. This delicious, tangy sauce will dress up steamed broccoli or cauliflower and would not be out of place drizzled on a burrito or mixed with macaroni to re-create an all-time favorite.

PREPARATION: **15 minutes**   PROCESSING: **3 minutes 15 seconds**   YIELD: **1¾ cups (420 ml)**

1 cup (240 ml) water

2 tablespoons (30 ml) fresh lemon juice

¼ cup (50 g) canned pimientos, or 1 large roasted red pepper (see page 71), peeled

⅔ cup (93 g) cashews or almonds

1¼ teaspoons onion powder

¼ cup (30 g) nutritional yeast

Sea salt (optional)

Place all the ingredients into the Vitamix container in the order listed and secure the lid. Select Variable 1. Turn the machine on and slowly increase the speed to Variable 10, then to High. Blend for 3 minutes 15 seconds, or until heavy steam escapes from the vented lid.

AMOUNT PER ¼ CUP (60 ML) SERVING: calories 100, total fat 7 g, saturated fat 0.5 g, cholesterol 0 mg, sodium 25 mg, total carbohydrate 5 g, dietary fiber 3 g, sugars 1 g, protein 5 g

Garlic-Parsley Crème Sauce

Too long dismissed as merely a garnish, parsley should be enjoyed in its own right. Tangy with garlic, some red pepper flakes, and red wine vinegar, this sauce will liven up grilled seafood or meats, portobello mushrooms, or sautéed tofu.

PREPARATION: **10 minutes**   PROCESSING: **30 seconds**   YIELD: **1 cup (240 ml)**

½ cup (120 ml) olive oil

¼ cup (60 ml) red wine vinegar

½ teaspoon sea salt

⅓ teaspoon red pepper flakes

1 garlic clove, peeled

2 cups lightly packed (56 g) fresh flat-leaf parsley leaves

1. Place all the ingredients into the Vitamix container in the order listed and secure the lid. Select Variable 1. Turn the machine on and slowly increase the speed to Variable 4. Blend for 15 seconds.

2. Stop the machine, remove the lid, and scrape the sides of the container with a spatula. Secure the lid. Select Variable 1. Turn the machine on and slowly increase the speed to Variable 10. Blend for an additional 15 seconds.

AMOUNT PER 2 TABLESPOON (30 ML) SERVING: calories 130, total fat 14 g, saturated fat 2 g, cholesterol 0 mg, sodium 150 mg, total carbohydrate 1 g, dietary fiber 0 g, sugars 0 g, protein 0 g

Parsley-Pecan Pesto

When you think of pesto, the traditional Genovese pesto with basil and pine nuts may be the first thing that comes to mind. But what do you do when basil is out of season and the price of pine nuts goes through the roof? Whip up this delicious pesto made with readily available and often cheaper ingredients. Toss it on pasta and steamed green beans for a simple, tasty dinner.

PREPARATION: **10 minutes**   PROCESSING: **1 minute**   YIELD: **1 cup (240 ml)**

3½ tablespoons (53 g) water

2 tablespoons (30 ml) olive oil

1½ cups (33 g) fresh flat-leaf parsley leaves

1 garlic clove, peeled

¼ cup (29 g) unsalted roasted pecans

2 tablespoons (16 g) shredded Parmesan

1 tablespoon nutritional yeast

1 teaspoon fresh lemon juice

Pinch of sea salt

Pinch of ground black pepper

1. Place all the ingredients into the Vitamix container in the order listed and secure the lid. Select Variable 1. Turn the machine on and slowly increase the speed to Variable 4. Blend for 30 seconds, using the tamper to press the ingredients into the blades.

2. Stop, remove the lid, and scrape down the sides of the container. Secure the lid. Select Variable 1. Turn the machine on and slowly increase the speed to Variable 6. Blend for 30 seconds, using the tamper to press the ingredients into the blades.

AMOUNT PER 2 TABLESPOON (30 ML) SERVING: calories 70, total fat 17 g, saturated fat 1 g, cholesterol 5 mg, sodium 96 mg, total carbohydrate 2 g, dietary fiber 1 g, sugars 0 g, protein 3 g

The Vitamix Cookbook

Pesto

Delicious as a pasta sauce or a great addition to other recipes, this pesto is fresh and easy to make in just a couple of minutes.

PREP TIME: **5 minutes**   PROCESSING: **1 minute**   YIELD: **1½ cups (360 ml)**

½ cup (120 ml) olive oil

½ cup (50 g) grated Parmesan

3 medium garlic cloves, peeled

2 cups (80 g) fresh basil leaves

3 tablespoons (25 g) pine nuts

Salt and ground black pepper

Place the olive oil, Parmesan, garlic, basil, and pine nuts into the Vitamix container in the order listed and secure the lid. Select Variable 1. Turn the machine on and quickly increase the speed to Variable 7. Blend for 1 minute, using the tamper to press the ingredients into the blades. Season with salt and pepper.

AMOUNT PER 2 TABLESPOON (30 ML) SERVING: calories 172, protein 17 g, total fat 3 g, saturated fat 2 g, total carbohydrate 1 g, dietary fiber 0 g, sugars 88 mg

Red Pepper Paste

Once you have made this red pepper paste, bursting with wonderful fragrance and flavor, you will not be able to imagine your life without it. Slather on grilled chicken, meats, or tofu for a guilt-free delight.

PREPARATION: **10 minutes**   PROCESSING: **30 seconds**   COOK TIME: **15 minutes**   YIELD: **½ cup (120 ml)**

¼ cup (60 ml) dry red wine (Cabernet or Merlot)

1 teaspoon cayenne pepper

½ teaspoon sea salt

¼ teaspoon ground ginger

⅓ teaspoon ground cardamom

⅓ teaspoon ground cinnamon

⅓ teaspoon ground coriander

⅓ teaspoon ground cloves

⅓ teaspoon ground nutmeg

⅓ teaspoon ground black pepper

2 tablespoons (20 g) diced yellow onion

1 garlic clove, peeled

¼ cup (28 g) sweet paprika

1. Place the wine, spices, onion, and garlic into the Vitamix container and secure the lid. Select Variable 1. Turn the machine on and slowly increase the speed to Variable 10, then to High. Blend for 15 seconds.

2. Stop the machine, remove the lid, and scrape the sides of the container. Secure the lid. Select Variable 1. Turn the machine on and slowly increase the speed to Variable 10, then to High. Blend for an additional 15 seconds.

3. Heat the paprika in a 1-quart saucepan over medium heat, stirring frequently, for 1 minute. Gradually whisk in the wine mixture. Bring to a simmer and cook until thick and hot, about 4 minutes.

4. Cool completely.

AMOUNT PER 2 TABLESPOON (30 ML) SERVING: calories 40, total fat 1 g, saturated fat 0 g, cholesterol 0 mg, sodium 300 mg, total carbohydrate 5 g, dietary fiber 3 g, sugars 1 g, protein 1 g

Raisin Almond Breakfast Spread

At once a nut butter and a jam, this all-in-one spread is a wonderful toast topping or sandwich filling. A little zing from the ginger balances out the savory nuts and deep sweetness of the honey and dried fruit.

PREPARATION: 10 minutes   PROCESSING: 1 minute 30 seconds   YIELD: 1½ cups (360 ml)

2 tablespoons (42 g) honey or agave nectar

1 cup (145 g) raw almonds

One 2-inch (5-cm) cube of fresh gingerroot

2 tablespoons (20 g) raw sesame seeds

1 cup (145 g) raisins, or ½ cup (70 g) raisins plus 4 pitted dates and 4 dried apricots

1. Place all the ingredients into the Vitamix container in the order listed and secure the lid. Select Variable 1. Turn the machine on and slowly increase the speed to Variable 10, then to High. Blend for 40 seconds, using the tamper to press the ingredients into the blades.

2. Stop the machine and remove the lid. Scrape down the sides of the container with a spatula and secure the lid. Select Variable 1. Turn the machine on and slowly increase the speed to Variable 5. Blend for 50 seconds, using the tamper to press the ingredients into the blades as needed.

AMOUNT PER 2 TABLESPOON (30 ML) SERVING: calories 140, total fat 7 g, saturated fat 0.5 g, cholesterol 0 mg, sodium 0 mg, total carbohydrate 17 g, dietary fiber

Applesauce

After you try this fresh, bright, and completely raw and vegan applesauce, you may never crave cooked or purchased varieties again. Enjoy as a snack or on top of Apple Pancakes (page 28).

PREPARATION: **10 minutes**   PROCESSING: **1 minute 45 seconds**   YIELD: **3¾ cups (900 ml)**

2 pounds (908 g) apples, seeded and cut into large pieces (with or without peel)

2 tablespoons (30 ml) fresh lemon juice

Place all the ingredients into the Vitamix container in the order listed and secure the lid. Select Variable 1. Turn the machine on and slowly increase the speed to Variable 7. Blend for 1 minute 45 seconds, using the tamper to press the ingredients into the blades.

AMOUNT PER ½ CUP (120 ML) SERVING: calories 60, total fat 0 g, saturated fat 0 g, cholesterol 0 mg, sodium 0 mg, total carbohydrate 16 g, dietary fiber 3 g, sugars 12 g, protein 0 g

Berry Applesauce

A small cup of this beautifully pink and flavorful berry applesauce would be a great addition to your child's packed lunch. Full of fruit but without any added sugar or food coloring, it is a tasty and healthy treat.

PREPARATION: **10 minutes**   PROCESSING: **20 seconds**   COOK TIME: **20 minutes**   YIELD: **4¼ cups (1 liter)**

4 medium crisp, sweet-tart apples (about 4 cups / 500 g), seeded and cut into large pieces

1½ cups (360 ml) water

1 tablespoon honey

1 teaspoon fresh lemon juice

1½ cups (188 g) fresh or frozen red raspberries

1. Place the apples and the water in a large nonreactive saucepan and bring to a simmer over high heat. Reduce the heat to medium and simmer for 10 minutes.

2. Add the honey and remove the saucepan from the heat. Let cool for 10 minutes.

3. Ladle the hot apple mixture into the Vitamix container. Add the lemon juice and raspberries and secure the lid. Select Variable 1. Turn the machine on and slowly increase the speed to Variable 10, then to High. Blend for 20 seconds, or until smooth.

AMOUNT PER ½ CUP (120 ML) SERVING: calories 50, total fat 0 g, saturated fat 0 g, cholesterol 0 mg, sodium 0 mg, total carbohydrate 13 g, dietary fiber 3 g, sugars 8 g, protein 0 g

Cashew Crema

This lightly sweet, decadent cashew crema is a vegan's answer to whipped cream. Spoon this crema over fresh fruit or a slice of vegan cake for a delicious after-dinner treat.

PREPARATION: **15 minutes**   PROCESSING: **1 minute**   YIELD: **2 cups (480 ml)**

2 tablespoons (30 ml) fresh lemon juice

1 tablespoon fresh orange juice

1 tablespoon light olive oil

1 teaspoon vanilla extract

8 ounces (227 g) extra-firm tofu, drained

¼ cup (60 ml) agave nectar

¾ cup (114 g) cashew pieces

½ teaspoon sea salt

Place all the ingredients into the Vitamix container in the order listed and secure the lid. Select Variable 1. Turn the machine on and slowly increase the speed to Variable 10, then to High. Blend for 1 minute, using the tamper to press the ingredients into the blades. Refrigerate until well chilled before using.

AMOUNT PER 2 TABLESPOON (30 ML) SERVING: calories 70, total fat 4 g, saturated fat 0.5 g, cholesterol 0 mg, sodium 50 mg, total carbohydrate 6 g, dietary fiber 0 g, sugars 4 g, protein 2 g

Peanut Butter

Once you taste freshly made peanut butter, you may never want to buy it again. As with the Cashew Peanut Butter (page 251), use the tamper to push the nuts toward the blades and don't be afraid to run the Vitamix blender on its top speed. That is how it was designed and engineered to work best, and the results will amaze you!

PREPARATION: **5 minutes**   PROCESSING: **2 minutes**   YIELD: **1½ cups (360 ml)**

3 cups (440 g) unsalted roasted peanuts

1. Place the nuts into the Vitamix container and secure the lid. Select Variable 1. Turn the machine on and slowly increase the speed to Variable 10, then to High. Use the tamper to press the ingredients into the blades.

2. In 1 minute you will hear a high-pitched chugging sound. Once the butter begins to flow freely through the blades, the motor sound will change and become low and laboring. Stop the machine.

3. Refrigerate the butter in an airtight container for up to 1 week. It can also be frozen for longer storage.

AMOUNT PER 2 TABLESPOON (30 ML) SERVING: calories 210, total fat 18 g, saturated fat 2.5 g, cholesterol 0 mg, sodium 0 mg, total carbohydrate 8 g, dietary fiber 3 g, sugars 2 g, protein 7 g

Cashew Peanut Butter

The milder flavor of cashews combined with roasted peanuts creates a delicious nut butter. The flavor is decidedly peanutty and the texture will stay smooth, even when it is refrigerated—unlike natural peanut butters bought in the store.

PREPARATION: **10 minutes**   PROCESSING: **1 minute 30 seconds**   YIELD: **1¾ cups (420 ml)**

2 cups (288 g) salted roasted peanuts

2 cups (274 g) salted roasted cashews

1. Place the nuts into the Vitamix container and secure the lid. Select Variable 1. Turn the machine on and slowly increase the speed to Variable 10, then to High. Use the tamper to press the ingredients into the blades.

2. In 1 minute you will hear a high-pitched chugging sound. Once the butter begins to flow freely through the blades, the motor sound will change and become low and laboring. Stop the machine. Then blend for an additional 30 seconds, or until the butter reaches the desired consistency.

3. Store in an airtight container in the refrigerator for up to 1 week. It can also be frozen for longer storage.

AMOUNT PER 2 TABLESPOON (30 ML) SERVING: calories 180, total fat 15 g, saturated fat 2.5 g, cholesterol 0 mg, sodium 80 mg, total carbohydrate 7 g, dietary fiber 2 g, protein 7 g

Dressings, Sauces, and Spreads

Pecan Peanut Butter

According to the USDA, pecans are the most antioxidant-rich tree nut and rank among the top fifteen foods with the highest levels of antioxidants. Sprinkle toasted pecans on top of your Oat Porridge (page 22), and be sure to make this delicious nut butter, too.

PREPARATION: **10 minutes**   PROCESSING: **1 minute 30 seconds**   YIELD: **1½ cups (360 ml)**

1½ cups (220 g) lightly salted dry-roasted peanuts

1½ cups (175 g) unsalted roasted pecans

1 tablespoon honey

Place all the ingredients into the Vitamix container in the order listed and secure the lid. Select Variable 1. Turn the machine on and slowly increase the speed to Variable 10, then to High, using the tamper to press the ingredients into the blades. In 1 minute you will hear a high-pitched chugging sound. Once the butter begins to flow freely through the blades, the motor sound will become low and laboring. Stop the machine. Then blend for an additional 30 seconds, or until the butter reaches the desired consistency.

AMOUNT PER 2 TABLESPOON (35 G) SERVING: calories 220, total fat 20 g, saturated fat 2 g, cholesterol 0 mg, sodium 60 mg, total carbohydrate 7 g, dietary fiber 3 g, sugars 3 g, protein 7 g

Janice Summers

Janice Summers, like many Vitamix owners, heard about the machine from another satisfied Vitamix owner. In 1981, Janice became interested in milling her own fresh flours. "I wanted to grind my own to have the freshest, and therefore most healthy, grains possible. The taste, smell, and texture are far superior to store-bought flours and meals that have been aging on the shelf." Summers went to bookstores in search of information on the process. While she was doing her research, she met a woman who told her how easily she could make flours, among other things, in her Vitamix blender. "I called Vitamix's 800 number and, as the saying goes, the rest is history."

When asked if using a Vitamix machine makes it easier to eat healthier, Janice says that for her it absolutely does. "This is especially the case with vegetables. If I don't have the time to sit and eat a large salad every day, then I drink them. The Vitamix [blender] doesn't remove the fiber so I know I'm getting whole vegetables. I just wash the vegetables well, peel those that should be peeled, and throw them in. I use water if [I am] adding fruit, but if I'm only making a vegetable drink I add organic chicken broth to further enhance the taste. Sometimes I choose to add a dash of pepper sauce for a little heat. Pour it over ice, toss in a stick of celery, and run out the door."

Janice has also shared her passion for healthy, homemade foods just as the Barnard family has done. Her niece, daughter, and sister all have Vitamix blenders now too, thanks in part to Janice's influence. (And her good cooking too, no doubt!) And when Janice sees a demonstration in progress? If she sees a shopper who seems skeptical that anyone could take whole foods and ice and whip up a delicious drink, she pipes up. "Seeing their doubt, sometimes I'll mention that I do it all the time. Their eyebrows raise as if the person who just blended the drink in front of them might have had magical powers . . . if a common woman shopping in the store can do it, then maybe it's possible. They always ask if I like it. I let them know that it is my singlemost used and valued piece of kitchen equipment, that I use for smoothies, sauces, soups, ice cream, slushies, and so much more."

Creating delicious healthy food and then giving people the tools to follow in your lead? A whole foods–powered legacy to be very proud of!

Applesauce (page 246)

Batter Cake with
Bing Cherries
(page 260)

Chapter 7

Desserts

Into every life, some sweetness must fall. Dessert is as right a part of life as sunshine, laughter, and hugs, all simple things that can bring us great joy. My grandpa brought sweetness to our lives. He loved to laugh. He was a master of funny faces, jokes, and silly stories. Do you remember Mount Tooska-Ooska Wooska-Choo from the introduction? Fun doesn't have to be complicated. It can be simple and delightfully easy. Grandpa also had more ideas than he knew what to do with, many of which he figured out how to make happen. For example, he decided to get a pilot's license in his forties and discovered that he loved to fly. My uncle Grove once said that flying "gave him a freedom that he couldn't justify in his mind otherwise."

I have a great story that involves both flying and his love of a good joke. When I was looking at colleges, Grandpa offered to fly me out west to look at a school. Before we stopped in Lincoln, Nebraska, to refuel, my ever-mischievous grandpa decided to play a practical joke on the airport staff. When he radioed ahead, he announced that he was about to land with a princess—he made up the country I was from—and asked if the airport staff had the red carpet ready. There was much confusion among the ground staff, but Grandpa Bill cheerfully insisted that he *had* called ahead and that not having a red carpet would be a great insult to the princess. A teenager at the time, I cringed and blushed as my grandpa cheerfully chatted on the radio. I wanted to disappear. When we landed, an airport employee rushed to the plane and spread out his coat, the best the staff could come up with on short notice. I emerged, mortified, from the plane, and good old Grandpa had the whole ground crew in stitches, laughing together at his joke.

Just as my grandpa made joy out of the simplest situations, you can use your Vitamix blender to take simple ingredients and transform them into joyfully delicious desserts. The recipes in this chapter will show you twenty-nine different ways to satisfy your sweet tooth. You will learn about desserts that have little added sugar, lots of whole fruits, and other delicious and nutritious ingredients. Some of the treats, particularly the frozen desserts, will come together in minutes. The cakes, cookies, crisps, and truffles will take a little longer, but will be worth the wait. Who knew eating whole foods could be so sweet, so satisfying?

Baked Desserts

In chapter 2, you learned how a Vitamix blender can help you make delicious quick breads, and here we will show you the cakes and cookies that you can whip up just as easily. By mixing up the wet ingredients in the Vitamix machine, you can use fruit in place of some or all of the refined sugar that you might need otherwise. In Batter Cake with Bing Cherries (page 260), you use pitted dates with a little agave nectar for sweetness. The dates give the cake a deep, satisfying flavor. In Carrot Cake (page 261), a combination of canned pineapple in its own juice and raisins are used in lieu of sugar. Banana Drops (page 267), a homey vegan cookie, get delicious fruit flavor and a moist, tender texture from bananas pureed with a little vanilla, oil, and oats.

You can also use the Vitamix to pulse together delicious crisp toppings. In Apple-Ginger Crisp (page 265), cornflakes, whole wheat flour, crystallized ginger, and coconut oil are combined to create a crunchy vegan topping for apples. Top this quintessentially fall dessert with Apple Pie Ice Cream (page 273) or Cashew Crema (page 249) if you like. For Vegan Fruit Crumble (page 266), whole wheat flour, cornmeal, almonds, unsweetened coconut, pitted dates, and coconut oil are pulsed with spices and baking powder to form a biscuit-like topping for peaches and blueberries. This crisp is wonderful on its own, yet heavenly when served with Peach Soy Sorbet (page 282).

Frozen Desserts

One of the wonders of a Vitamix blender is its unique ability to take simple ingredients, some of them frozen, and transform them into delicious, spoonable frozen treats. Eighteen of the desserts in this chapter—including Apple Pie Ice Cream (page 273), Coconut-Pineapple Sherbet (page 277), Pink Grapefruit Granita (page 281), and Strawberry Yogurt Freeze (page 291)—are all examples of this kind of dessert. Any of these would be delicious topped with fresh fruit, scooped into a cone, or capped with Mixed Berry Puree (page 272) or Cashew Crema (page 249) for an over-the-top—no pun intended—treat. These desserts can be enjoyed right away or packed into a freezer-safe container with a tight-fitting lid for later. Remember to follow the blending instructions carefully to ensure delightfully simple, yummy success every time. Keep in mind that the same machine that can make hot soup can quickly transform a creamy, scoopable treat into a cold smoothie in very little time!

A healthy diet need not be all sacrifice. By making your sweet treats at home and using whole fruits and whole grains, you can satisfy your cravings and get a few more servings of whole food at the same time. Delicious food *and* peace of mind: What could be sweeter?

Batter Cake with Bing Cherries

Some days—well, maybe all days—benefit from a slice of cake eaten in the late afternoon. This delicious cake gets its sweetness from light agave nectar, dates, and sweet cherries. Dust with powdered sugar before serving.

PREPARATION: **15 minutes**   PROCESSING: **15 seconds**   BAKE TIME: **35 minutes**   YIELD: **8 servings**

1 tablespoon plain 0% Greek yogurt, stirred

1 cup (240 ml) low-fat (1%) milk

2 tablespoons (30 ml) agave nectar

2 tablespoons (20 g) chopped pitted dates

1 tablespoon vanilla extract

2 large eggs

3 large egg whites

1 cup (120 g) whole wheat flour, preferably homemade (page 44)

⅓ teaspoon sea salt

2 cups (280 g) pitted sweet black cherries, fresh (halved and patted dry) or frozen (thawed and well drained)

Powdered sugar, for dusting

1. Preheat the oven to 425°F (220°C). Lightly grease a 9-inch (23-cm) round cake pan.

2. Place the yogurt, milk, agave, dates, vanilla, whole eggs, and egg whites into the Vitamix container in the order listed and secure the lid. Select Variable 1. Turn the machine on and slowly increase the speed to Variable 10, then to High. Blend for 15 seconds, or until well blended.

3. Combine the flour and salt in a medium bowl. Whisk the yogurt mixture into the flour mixture until smooth. (The batter will be thin.)

4. Pour the batter into the cake pan, then distribute the cherries evenly over the top. Bake for 15 minutes. Reduce the oven temperature to 400°F (200°C). Bake for 20 minutes, or until a toothpick inserted into the center comes out clean and a golden brown crust has formed on top.

5. Serve warm, dusted with powdered sugar.

AMOUNT PER SERVING: calories 140, total fat 2 g, saturated fat 0.5 g, cholesterol 50 mg, sodium 90 mg, total carbohydrate 25 g, dietary fiber 2 g, sugars 11 g, protein 6 g

Carrot Cake

This moist, tender carrot cake gets all of its sweetness from whole foods: pineapple in its own juice, raisins, and grated carrots. Enjoy in the afternoon with a cup of tea or tuck a square in a school lunch box for a healthy dessert.

PREPARATION: **15 minutes**   PROCESSING: **15 seconds**   BAKE TIME: **40 to 50 minutes**
YIELD: **10 servings**

2 large eggs

6 tablespoons (90 ml) canola / olive oil blend

One 8-ounce (227-g) can juice-packed crushed pineapple

1 teaspoon vanilla extract

¾ cup (120 g) raisins

1½ cups (180 g) whole wheat flour, preferably homemade (page 44)

1 teaspoon ground cinnamon

¼ teaspoon ground allspice

¼ teaspoon ground nutmeg

¼ teaspoon sea salt

1½ teaspoons baking powder

1 cup (110 g) grated carrots (about 2 medium)

1. Preheat the oven to 350°F (180°C). Coat an 8-inch (20-cm) square baking pan with cooking spray.

2. Place the eggs, oil, pineapple (with juice), vanilla, and ⅓ cup (45 g) of the raisins into the Vitamix container in the order listed and secure the lid. Select Variable 1. Turn the machine on and slowly increase the speed to Variable 10. Blend for 15 seconds.

3. Combine the flour, cinnamon, allspice, nutmeg, salt, and baking powder in a medium bowl. Fold in the egg mixture, carrots, and remaining 5 tablespoons raisins by hand.

4. Spread the batter in the pan and bake for 40 to 50 minutes, until a toothpick inserted into the center comes out clean. Cool on a wire rack.

AMOUNT PER SERVING: calories 210, total fat 10 g, saturated fat 1 g, cholesterol 35 mg, sodium 160 mg, total carbohydrate 27 g, dietary fiber 3 g, sugars 13 g, protein 4 g

Cornmeal Honey and Date Cake

This homey, cozy cornmeal cake will delight everyone, particularly those who need to avoid gluten. Serve with fresh fruit and whipped cream with Mixed Berry Puree (page 272) or simply dust with a little powdered sugar.

PREPARATION: **15 minutes**   PROCESSING: **15 seconds**   BAKE TIME: **30 to 35 minutes**   YIELD: **10 servings**

1¾ cups (280 g) whole-grain brown rice flour, preferably homemade (page 36)

¼ cup (40 g) coarse cornmeal, preferably homemade (page 40)

¼ cup (30 g) corn flour

1½ teaspoons baking soda

½ teaspoon sea salt

½ cup (120 ml) extra virgin olive oil

2 tablespoons (30 ml) honey

⅓ cup (50 g) pitted dates

½ cup plus 2 tablespoons (150 g) plain 0% Greek yogurt, stirred

2 teaspoons vanilla extract

1 teaspoon lemon extract

Grated zest of 1 lemon

¼ cup (26 g) flax meal

1 cup (240 ml) low-fat (1%) milk

1. Preheat the oven to 375°F (190°C). Lightly coat an 8-inch (20-cm) square baking pan with cooking spray.

2. Combine the brown rice flour, cornmeal, corn flour, baking soda, and salt in a medium bowl.

3. Place the olive oil, honey, dates, yogurt, vanilla, lemon extract, lemon zest, flax meal, and milk into the Vitamix container in the order listed and secure the lid. Select Variable 1. Turn the machine on and slowly increase the speed to Variable 10, then to High. Blend for 15 seconds.

4. Pour the oil-yogurt mixture into the flour mixture and stir lightly by hand to combine.

5. Pour the batter into the pan and bake for 30 to 35 minutes, until a toothpick inserted into the center comes out with a few moist crumbs attached. Cool in the pan on a wire rack.

AMOUNT PER SERVING: calories 260, total fat 13 g, saturated fat 2 g, cholesterol 0 mg, sodium 290 mg, total carbohydrate 30 g, dietary fiber 3 g, sugars 8 g, protein 5 g

Mango Flax Coffee Cake

Delicious for brunch or for dessert, this wholesome cake is a crowd-pleaser. The cake's nutty flavor comes from whole wheat flour and wheat bran, while dates, mango, and just a little brown sugar give it sweetness.

PREPARATION: **20 minutes**   PROCESSING: **15 seconds**   BAKE TIME: **35 to 40 minutes**   YIELD: **9 servings**

¾ cup (45 g) wheat bran

1 cup (240 ml) low-fat (1%) milk

1 large egg

2 tablespoons (30 ml) flax oil

⅓ cup (53 g) pitted dates

1 cup (120 g) whole wheat flour, preferably homemade (page 44)

¼ cup (26 g) flax meal

1 tablespoon baking powder

¼ teaspoon salt

1 teaspoon ground cinnamon

2 mangoes, pitted and sliced

TOPPING:

¼ cup firmly packed (55 g) dark brown sugar

1 tablespoon whole wheat flour, preferably homemade (page 44)

1½ teaspoons ground cinnamon

1 tablespoon flax oil

1. Preheat the oven to 375°F (190°C). Lightly grease an 8-inch (20-cm) square baking pan.

2. Combine the bran and ¾ cup (180 ml) of the milk and let soak for 10 minutes.

3. Place the remaining ¼ cup (60 ml) milk, the egg, flax oil, and dates into the Vitamix container in the order listed and secure the lid. Select Variable 1. Turn the machine on and slowly increase the speed to Variable 10, then to High. Blend for 15 seconds, or until the mixture is creamy.

4. Combine the flour, flax meal, baking powder, salt, and cinnamon in a medium bowl. Add the milk-egg mixture and soaked bran and stir just until blended.

5. Spread the batter in the baking pan. Place the mango slices over the batter.

6. For the topping: Combine the dark brown sugar, flour, cinnamon, and flax oil in a small bowl and mix until the mixture forms crumbs. Sprinkle over the mango slices.

7. Bake for 35 to 40 minutes, until a toothpick inserted into the center comes out clean. Serve warm.

AMOUNT PER SERVING: calories 190, total fat 6 g, saturated fat 1 g, cholesterol 20 mg, sodium 220 mg, total carbohydrate 33 g, dietary fiber 6 g, sugars 18 g, protein 5 g

Apple-Ginger Crisp

The perfect dessert to showcase the first delicious apples of fall, this tasty vegan dessert is made mostly of pantry staples. Should you have any leftovers, consider eating the crisp cold with a little soy yogurt for breakfast.

PREPARATION: **15 minutes**   PROCESSING: **10 seconds**   BAKE TIME: **35 to 40 minutes**   YIELD: **9 servings**

6 small/medium crisp apples (such as McIntosh), thinly sliced and slices halved (no more than 6 cups / 2.2 lb / 1 kg unsliced)

4 tablespoons (55 g) firmly packed light brown sugar

2 teaspoons fresh lemon juice

⅓ cup (30 g) cornflakes

3 tablespoons (22 g) whole wheat flour, preferably homemade (page 44)

2 tablespoons (20 g) crystallized ginger pieces

2 tablespoons (27 g) coconut oil

1. Preheat the oven to 400°F (200°C). Coat an 8-inch (20-cm) square baking dish with cooking spray.

2. Place the apples in the baking dish. Add 1 tablespoon of the brown sugar and the lemon juice and toss gently to coat.

3. Place the cornflakes, remaining 3 tablespoons brown sugar, the flour, ginger, and coconut oil into the Vitamix container in the order listed and secure the lid. Select Variable 1. Turn the machine on and slowly increase the speed to Variable 5, using the tamper as needed to push the ingredients into the blades. Blend for 10 seconds.

4. Sprinkle the crumb mixture over the apples and press gently. Bake for 35 to 40 minutes, until the apples are tender and the mixture is bubbling. Serve warm, at room temperature, or chilled.

AMOUNT PER SERVING: calories 140, total fat 3.5 g, saturated fat 2.5 g, cholesterol 0 mg, sodium 25 mg, total carbohydrate 30 g, dietary fiber 3 g, sugars 20 g, protein 1 g

Vegan Fruit Crumble

Coconut, both unsweetened flakes and the oil, is a delightful presence here. The flavor is subtle, but a delicious pairing with the blueberries and peaches.

PREPARATION: **20 minutes**   PROCESSING: **20 seconds**   BAKE TIME: **35 to 45 minutes**   YIELD: **8 servings**

TOPPING:

1⅓ cups (160 g) whole wheat flour, preferably homemade (page 44)

¼ cup (40 g) cornmeal, preferably homemade (page 40)

1 teaspoon baking powder

½ teaspoon ground cinnamon

½ cup (54 g) slivered almonds

⅓ cup (27 g) unsweetened flaked coconut

½ cup (80 g) pitted dates

2 tablespoons (30 ml) coconut oil, melted and cooled

½ teaspoon almond extract

FRUIT FILLING:

2 tablespoons (30 ml) water

2 tablespoons (16 g) cornstarch

4 cups (592 g) fresh blueberries

3 cups (420 g) unsweetened frozen peach slices, thawed and drained

1 teaspoon honey

1. Preheat the oven to 350°F (180°C).

2. For the topping: Place the flour, cornmeal, baking powder, and cinnamon in a medium bowl and stir by hand to combine.

3. Place the almonds, flaked coconut, and dates into the Vitamix container in the order listed and secure the lid. Select Variable 1. Turn the machine on and slowly increase the speed to Variable 4. Blend for 20 seconds, using the tamper to press the ingredients down. The mixture should form coarse crumbs.

4. Reduce the speed to Variable 1 and remove the lid plug. Drizzle in the coconut oil and almond extract, using the tamper to press the ingredients into the blades. Add the date mixture to the flour mixture and stir well to combine.

5. For the fruit filling: Stir the water into the cornstarch in a small bowl. Combine the blueberries, peach slices, honey, and cornstarch-water mixture in a large bowl.

6. Transfer the fruit mixture to a 3-quart round baking dish with high sides. Crumble the topping mixture evenly over the fruit.

7. Bake for 35 to 45 minutes, until the fruit is bubbling and the crumb topping is golden.

AMOUNT PER SERVING: calories 280, total fat 10 g, saturated fat 5 g, cholesterol 0 mg, sodium 65 mg, total carbohydrate 47 g, dietary fiber 7 g, sugars 20 g, protein 6 g

Banana Drops

The batter for these simple, homey vegan cookies comes together in just 10 minutes. Healthy enough to be eaten for breakfast, these banana drops are wonderful tucked in a lunch box or as an after-school treat, too.

PREPARATION: **10 minutes**   PROCESSING: **30 seconds**   BAKE TIME: **20 to 25 minutes**
YIELD: **12 cookies**

2 ripe bananas
¼ cup (60 ml) vegetable oil
1 teaspoon vanilla extract
2 cups (160 g) rolled oats
1 cup (165 g) raisins

1. Preheat the oven to 350°F (180°C). Line a baking sheet with foil or a silicone baking mat.

2. Place the bananas, vegetable oil, vanilla, and 1 cup (80 g) of the oats into the Vitamix container in the order listed and secure the lid. Select Variable 1. Turn the machine on and slowly increase the speed to Variable 10, then to High. Blend for 30 seconds, using the tamper to press the ingredients into the blades.

3. Pour the batter into a bowl. Stir in the raisins and the remaining 1 cup (80 g) oats.

4. Form into 12 balls and place on the baking sheet. Press to flatten slightly.

5. Bake for 20 to 25 minutes, until firm to the touch. Remove and cool in the pan on a wire rack.

AMOUNT PER COOKIE: calories 150, total fat 6 g, saturated fat 0.5 g, cholesterol 0 mg, sodium 0 mg, total carbohydrate 24 g, dietary fiber 3 g, sugars 12 g, protein 2 g

Chocolate Mousse

Who knew chocolate mousse could be so simple and so fast? Once you have the ingredients on hand, you can put this decadent dessert together in a flash.

PREPARATION: **10 minutes**   PROCESSING: **35 to 40 seconds**   YIELD: **2 cups (480 ml)**

¼ cup (60 ml) whole milk

1½ teaspoons vanilla extract

½ cup (40 g) unsweetened cocoa powder, sifted

½ ounce (14 g) milk chocolate, finely chopped

1½ ounces (43 g) bittersweet chocolate, finely chopped

6 pitted dates

½ cup (120 ml) plain 0% Greek yogurt, stirred

½ cup (124 g) plus 1 tablespoon part-skim ricotta

Fresh seasonal berries or shaved chocolate, for garnish

1. Place all the ingredients except the garnish into the Vitamix container in the order listed and secure the lid. Select Variable 1. Turn the machine on and slowly increase the speed to Variable 10, then to High. Blend for 35 to 40 seconds, using the tamper to press the ingredients into the blades.

2. Serve immediately, garnished with fresh berries, or shaved chocolate for more decadence.

AMOUNT PER ½ CUP (120 ML) SERVING (WITHOUT GARNISH): calories 200, total fat 10 g, saturated fat 5 g, cholesterol 10 mg, sodium 65 mg, total carbohydrate 25 g, dietary fiber 6 g, sugars 15 g, protein 11 g

Vegan Truffles

A decadent, delicious treat for your next gathering! You can use a melon baller or a tablespoon to shape the truffles if you like. If you use the tablespoon, roll the truffle gently between your palms to create a ball. Dust the finished truffles with extra cocoa powder or powdered sugar if desired.

PREPARATION: **15 minutes**   PROCESSING: **1 minute**   YIELD: **24 truffles**

⅓ cup (80 ml) soy milk, preferably homemade (page 353)

1 cup (140 g) raw almonds

¾ cup (130 g) large pitted dates

2 tablespoons (30 ml) agave nectar

1 tablespoon unsweetened cocoa powder

¼ cup (40 g) Coco Wheats cereal

1. Place all the ingredients into the Vitamix container in the order listed and secure the lid. Select Variable 1. Turn the machine on and slowly increase the speed to Variable 10, then to High. Blend for 1 minute, using the tamper to press the ingredients into the blades. The consistency should be thick like dough. If it is too thick, adjust by adding more milk.

2. Form into 1-inch (2.5-cm) balls and freeze.

AMOUNT PER TRUFFLE: calories 60, total fat 3 g, saturated fat 0 g, cholesterol 0 mg, sodium 0 mg, total carbohydrate 8 g, dietary fiber 1 g, sugars 5 g, protein 2 g

Pumpkin Pudding

This cozy pumpkin pudding has all of the flavors of classic pumpkin pie without the bother of making a crust or turning on the oven. The pudding base is heated in the Vitamix—use a thermometer to make sure the mixture has reached 180°F (85°C)—and then thickened with a slurry made with potato starch and water. Delicious served either warm or cold.

PREPARATION: **15 minutes**   PROCESSING: **7 minutes**   YIELD: **4¼ cups (1 liter)**

1 cup (240 ml) reduced-fat (2%) milk, at room temperature

½ cup (120 ml) plain 0% Greek yogurt, stirred, at room temperature

3 tablespoons firmly packed (41 g) dark brown sugar

2 pitted dates

2 large eggs

1 cup (240 ml) canned unsweetened pumpkin puree, or preferably homemade (page 55)

½ teaspoon ground cinnamon

¼ teaspoon pumpkin pie spice

⅛ teaspoon sea salt

2 teaspoons potato starch

1. Place the milk, yogurt, brown sugar, dates, eggs, pumpkin puree, cinnamon, pumpkin pie spice, and salt into the Vitamix container in the order listed and secure the lid. Select Variable 1. Turn the machine on and slowly increase the speed to Variable 10, then to High. Blend for 6 minutes, or until the temperature reaches 180°F (85°C).

2. Meanwhile, stir together the potato starch and 2 tablespoons (30 ml) water in a small bowl to make a slurry.

3. Reduce the speed to Variable 5 and remove the lid plug. Pour the slurry in through the lid plug opening. Replace the lid plug. Slowly increase the speed to Variable 10, then to High. Blend for an additional 1 minute.

4. Serve warm or chill before serving.

AMOUNT PER ½ CUP (120 ML) SERVING: calories 70, total fat 2 g, saturated fat 0.5 g, cholesterol 45 mg, sodium 75 mg, total carbohydrate 11 g, dietary fiber 1 g, sugars 9 g, protein 4 g

Mixed Berry Puree

Frozen fruit, lemon juice, water, and a little granulated sugar come together to make a bright, flavorful berry sauce. Spoon it over a frozen dessert such as Coconut-Pineapple Sherbet (page 277) or use it to dress up a simple cake like the gluten-free Cornmeal Honey and Date Cake (page 262).

PREPARATION: **10 minutes**   PROCESSING: **3 minutes**   YIELD: **3½ cups (840 ml)**

1½ cups (168 g) frozen unsweetened red raspberries

1½ cups (210 g) frozen unsweetened strawberries

1 cup (155 g) frozen unsweetened blueberries

1 cup (240 ml) water

1 tablespoon fresh lemon juice

¼ cup (50 g) sugar

1. Let the berries sit at room temperature for 10 minutes to partially thaw.

2. Place the water, lemon juice, berries, and sugar into the Vitamix container in the order listed and secure the lid. Select Variable 1. Turn the machine on and slowly increase the speed to Variable 10, then to High. Blend for 3 minutes, using the tamper to press the ingredients into the blades.

AMOUNT PER ¼ CUP (60 ML) SERVING: calories 30, total fat 0 g, saturated fat 0 g, cholesterol 0 mg, sodium 0 mg, total carbohydrate 8 g, dietary fiber 1 g, sugars 6 g, protein 0 g

Apple Pie Ice Cream

This simple, delicious dessert is apple pie à la mode in ice cream form! Real apple pie should be this easy.

PREPARATION: **10 minutes**   PROCESSING: **30 seconds**   YIELD: **3 cups (720 ml)**

3 ounces (90 ml) frozen apple juice concentrate

¼ cup (60 ml) vanilla low-fat yogurt

½ medium apple, cored and quartered

1 tablespoon vanilla extract

¼ teaspoon ground cinnamon

½ ripe banana

3 cups (720 ml) ice cubes

Place all the ingredients into the Vitamix container in the order listed and secure the lid. Select Variable 1. Turn the machine on and slowly increase the speed to Variable 10, then to High. Use the tamper to press the ingredients into the blades. In about 30 seconds, the sound of the motor will change and 4 mounds should form in the mixture. Stop the machine. Do not overmix or melting will occur. Serve immediately.

AMOUNT PER ½ CUP (120 ML) SERVING: calories 60, total fat 0 g, saturated fat 0 g, cholesterol 0 mg, sodium 10 mg, total carbohydrate 12 g, dietary fiber 1 g, sugars 10 g, protein 1 g

Papaya Tropical Dessert

Curious about papaya and guava but not sure how to serve them? Use one or a combination of both to make this delicious frozen dessert. Greek yogurt and banana give the dessert a creamy texture while the papaya or guava gives it a tropical flavor.

PREPARATION: **10 minutes**   PROCESSING: **30 to 45 seconds**   YIELD: **4½ cups (1 liter)**

½ cup (120 ml) plain 0% Greek yogurt, stirred

1½ cups (250 g) fresh papaya or guava chunks

1 banana, peeled, quartered, and frozen

1 orange, peeled and halved

½ lemon, peeled

1 tablespoon honey or agave nectar

3 cups (720 ml) ice cubes

Place all the ingredients into the Vitamix container in the order listed and secure the lid. Select Variable 1. Turn the machine on and slowly increase the speed to Variable 10, then to High, using the tamper to press the ingredients into the blades. In 30 to 45 seconds, the sound of the motor will change and 4 mounds should form in the mixture. Stop the machine. Do not overmix or melting will occur. Serve immediately.

AMOUNT PER ½ CUP (120 ML) SERVING: calories 45, total fat 0 g, saturated fat 0 g, cholesterol 0 mg, sodium 10 mg, total carbohydrate 10 g, dietary fiber 1 g, sugars 7 g, protein 2 g

Frozen Bananas Foster

All of the deliciousness of traditional Bananas Foster without making caramel or setting rum ablaze. Both the cinnamon and the pecans balance the sweetness in this decadent dessert.

PREPARATION: **15 minutes**   PROCESSING: **45 to 55 seconds**   YIELD: **4½ cups (1 liter)**

5 large bananas, peeled, halved, and frozen

1⅓ cups (320 g) plain low-fat yogurt

2 teaspoons rum extract (optional)

2 tablespoons (30 ml) caramel sauce

1 teaspoon honey

1 teaspoon ground cinnamon

½ cup (50 g) unsalted roasted pecans

1. Let the bananas sit at room temperature for 15 minutes to soften.

2. Place the yogurt, bananas, rum extract (if using), caramel sauce, honey, cinnamon, and pecans into the Vitamix container in the order listed and secure the lid. Select Variable 1. Turn the machine on and slowly increase the speed to Variable 10, then to High, using the tamper to press the ingredients into the blades. In 45 to 55 seconds, the sound of the motor will change and 4 mounds should form in the mixture. Stop the machine. Do not overmix or melting will occur. Serve immediately.

AMOUNT PER ½ CUP (120 ML) SERVING: calories 140, total fat 5 g, saturated fat 1 g, cholesterol 0 mg, sodium 35 mg, total carbohydrate 22 g, dietary fiber 2 g, sugars 13 g, protein 3 g

Coconut-Pineapple Sherbet

Simple ingredients—light coconut milk, agave nectar, vanilla, and frozen pineapple—are quickly transformed into something quite special. Garnish with fresh fruit or a sprinkle of toasted unsweetened coconut if desired.

PREPARATION: **10 minutes**   PROCESSING: **35 to 45 seconds**   YIELD: **3½ cups (840 ml)**

1 cup (240 ml) canned light coconut milk

1 teaspoon agave nectar

¼ teaspoon vanilla extract

1 pound (454 g) frozen unsweetened pineapple chunks

Fresh mint, for garnish (optional)

Place all the ingredients into the Vitamix container in the order listed and secure the lid. Select Variable 1. Turn the machine on and slowly increase the speed to Variable 10, then to High, using the tamper to press the ingredients into the blades. In 35 to 45 seconds, the sound of the motor will change and 4 mounds should form in the mixture. Stop the machine. Do not overmix or melting will occur. Serve immediately. Garnish with fresh mint if desired.

AMOUNT PER ½ CUP (120 ML) SERVING: calories 60, total fat 2.5 g, saturated fat 2 g, cholesterol 0 mg, sodium 5 mg, total carbohydrate 10 g, dietary fiber 1 g, sugars 2 g, protein 0 g

Berry Sorbet with Mixed Spices

Adding aromatic spices—cinnamon, cloves, allspice, and nutmeg—and vanilla to this sublime sorbet makes it taste like a baked dessert, almost cookie-like, but without masking the bright fruit flavor. The gentle spice of the fresh ginger keeps the fruits' sweetness from being overbearing.

PREPARATION: **25 minutes**   PROCESSING: **1 minute 15 seconds**   YIELD: **4½ cups (1.1 liters)**

1 cup (150 g) frozen unsweetened strawberries

1 cup (140 g) frozen unsweetened blueberries

1 cup (140 g) frozen unsweetened blackberries

1 cup (140 g) frozen unsweetened red raspberries

2 cups (300 g) frozen pitted Bing cherries

One 1-inch (2.5-cm) cube fresh gingerroot (0.5 oz / 15 g)

¼ cup (50 g) sugar

1 cup (240 ml) cold water

½ cup (13 g) fresh mint leaves

½ teaspoon ground cinnamon

¼ teaspoon ground nutmeg

⅛ teaspoon ground allspice

⅛ teaspoon ground cloves

1 teaspoon vanilla extract

1. Let the frozen fruit sit at room temperature for 20 minutes to partially thaw.

2. Place the ginger, sugar, and water into the Vitamix container and secure the lid. Select Variable 1. Turn the machine on and slowly increase the speed to Variable 8. Blend for 20 seconds, or until the ginger is finely chopped.

3. Stop the machine and remove the lid. Add the fruit, mint, spices, and vanilla to the container and secure the lid. Select Variable 1. Turn the machine on and slowly increase the speed to Variable 10, then to High, using the tamper to press the ingredients into the blades. In 45 to 55 seconds, the sound of the motor will change and 4 mounds should form in the mixture. Stop the machine. Do not overmix or melting will occur. Serve immediately.

AMOUNT PER ½ CUP (120 ML) SERVING: calories 70, total fat 0 g, saturated fat 0 g, cholesterol 0 mg, sodium 0 mg, total carbohydrate 19 g, dietary fiber 3 g, sugars 14 g, protein 1 g

Orange Sorbet

A wonderful whole-fruit dessert bursting with flavor! Drizzle it with Mixed Berry Puree (page 272) or serve a scoop alongside Batter Cake with Bing Cherries (page 260).

PREPARATION: **10 minutes**   PROCESSING: **30 to 40 seconds**   YIELD: **3½ cups (840 ml)**

1 teaspoon grated orange
zest

2 medium oranges, peeled
and halved

2 tablespoons (30 ml)
honey

1 tablespoon frozen orange
juice concentrate

5 cups (1.2 liters) ice cubes

Place all the ingredients into the Vitamix container in the order listed and secure the lid. Select Variable 1. Turn the machine on and slowly increase the speed to Variable 10, then to High, using the tamper to press the ingredients into the blades. In 30 to 40 seconds, the sound of the motor will change and 4 mounds should form in the mixture. Stop the machine. Do not overmix or melting will occur. Serve immediately.

AMOUNT PER ½ CUP (120 ML) SERVING: calories 40, total fat 0 g, saturated fat 0 g, cholesterol 0 mg, sodium 0 mg, total carbohydrate 10 g, dietary fiber 1 g, sugars 9 g, protein 0 g

Pink Grapefruit Granita

Most granita recipes instruct you to freeze the combined ingredients and then stir every thirty minutes or so to create a flaky texture. In our recipe, you freeze this no-sugar-added mixture until it is hard and then quickly pulse it in the Vitamix to create the finished dessert.

PREPARATION: **3 to 4 hours**   PROCESSING: **pulsing**   YIELD: **3 cups (720 ml)**

2½ cups (600 ml) fresh pink grapefruit juice

4 teaspoons stevia blend

1 cup (240 ml) water

1. Combine the juice, stevia, and water in a bowl and whisk until the stevia has dissolved. Pour the liquid into a baking pan and freeze until hard, 3 to 4 hours.

2. With a fork, break the granita into large chunks. Transfer the chunks to the Vitamix container and secure the lid. Select Variable 4. Use the On/Off switch to quickly pulse the mixture while using the tamper to press the ingredients into the blades. Continue pulsing until the mixture is smooth. Do not overmix or melting will occur.

3. Serve immediately.

AMOUNT PER ½ CUP (120 ML) SERVING: calories 45, total fat 0 g, saturated fat 0 g, cholesterol 0 mg, sodium 0 mg, total carbohydrate 11 g, dietary fiber 1 g, sugars 7 g, protein 1 g

Peach Soy Sorbet

A creamy, dairy-free sorbet for a hot summer day or a midwinter ice cream craving. Scoop this sweet treat into a cone or serve in a dish with sliced fruit and toasted sliced almonds.

PREPARATION: **10 minutes**   PROCESSING: **45 seconds**   YIELD: **5 cups (1.2 liters)**

1 pound (680 g) frozen unsweetened peach slices

1 cup (240 ml) plain soy yogurt

1 teaspoon vanilla extract

1½ tablespoons (45 ml) honey

1. Let the peaches sit at room temperature for 15 minutes to soften slightly.

2. Place the yogurt, vanilla, peaches, and honey into the Vitamix container in the order listed and secure the lid. Select Variable 1. Turn the machine on and slowly increase the speed to Variable 10, then to High, using the tamper to press the ingredients into the blades. In about 45 seconds, the sound of the motor will change and 4 mounds should form in the mixture. Stop the machine. Do not overmix or melting will occur. Serve immediately.

AMOUNT PER ½ CUP (120 ML) SERVING: calories 70, total fat 1 g, saturated fat 0 g, cholesterol 0 mg, sodium 0 mg, total carbohydrate 13 g, dietary fiber 1 g, sugars 11 g, protein 2 g

A Burst of Fruit Frozen Dessert

With six varieties of fruit, yogurt, wheat germ, flax seeds, and herbs, you may be tempted to eat this delicious frozen dessert for breakfast as well as after dinner.

PREPARATION: **10 minutes**   PROCESSING: **45 to 60 seconds**   YIELD: **5 cups (1.2 liters)**

1 cup (240 ml) coconut water

½ cup (120 ml) vanilla 0% Greek yogurt, stirred

½ medium banana, peeled and frozen

6 pitted dates

1 teaspoon flax seeds

1 teaspoon toasted wheat germ

2 fresh basil leaves

3 fresh mint leaves

¾ cup (105 g) frozen mixed berries (strawberries, blackberries, blueberries, red raspberries)

2 cups (480 ml) ice cubes

Place all the ingredients into the Vitamix container in the order listed and secure the lid. Select Variable 1. Turn the machine on and slowly increase the speed to Variable 10, then to High, using the tamper to press the ingredients into the blades. In 45 seconds to 1 minute, the sound of the motor will change and 4 mounds should form in the mixture. Stop the machine. Do not overmix or melting will occur. Serve immediately.

AMOUNT PER ½ CUP (120 ML) SERVING: calories 40, total fat 0 g, saturated fat 0 g, cholesterol 0 mg, sodium 5 mg, total carbohydrate 9 g, dietary fiber 1 g, sugars 6 g, protein 1 g

Ginger Peach Tea Ice

The perfect dessert for a sweltering summer afternoon when you crave a tall glass of sweet tea. Cold green tea and fresh ginger pair wonderfully with the peaches and honey in this refreshing dessert.

PREPARATION: **10 minutes**   PROCESSING: **1 minute 45 seconds**   YIELD: **4½ cups (1 liter)**

1 pound (454 g) frozen unsweetened peach slices

1 cup (240 ml) brewed green tea, cold

1 teaspoon honey

¾ teaspoon vanilla extract

1 teaspoon grated fresh gingerroot

2 to 2½ cups (480 to 600 ml) ice cubes

1. Let the peaches sit at room temperature for 10 minutes to soften slightly.

2. Place the tea, honey, vanilla, ginger, peaches, and ice cubes into the Vitamix container in the order listed and secure the lid. Select Variable 1. Turn the machine on and slowly increase the speed to Variable 10, then to High, using the tamper to press the ingredients into the blades. In about 1 minute 45 seconds, the sound of the motor will change and 4 mounds should form in the mixture. Stop the machine. Do not overmix or melting will occur. Serve immediately.

AMOUNT PER ½ CUP (120 ML) SERVING: calories 20, total fat 0 g, saturated fat 0 g, cholesterol 0 mg, sodium 0 mg, total carbohydrate 6 g, dietary fiber 1 g, sugars 5 g, protein 0 g

Goji and Strawberry Frozen Dessert

If you are struggling to get your nine servings of fruits and vegetables every day, consider adding this dessert to your repertoire. Frozen strawberries, fresh spinach, pitted dates, and dried goji berries pack nutrients into a cold, sweet, spoonable treat that you will find yourself making again and again.

PREPARATION: **10 minutes**   PROCESSING: **30 to 60 seconds**   YIELD: **3 cups (720 ml)**

1¼ cups (300 ml) unsweetened almond milk

2 teaspoons fresh lemon juice

1 teaspoon vanilla extract

¼ cup (22 g) dried goji berries

6 large pitted dates

1¼ cups (1.5 oz / 43 g) baby or regular spinach

2½ cups (350 g) frozen unsweetened strawberries

Place all the ingredients into the Vitamix container in the order listed and secure the lid. Select Variable 1. Turn the machine on and slowly increase the speed to Variable 10, then to High, using the tamper to press the ingredients into the blades. In 30 to 60 seconds, the sound of the motor will change and 4 mounds should form in the mixture. Stop the machine. Do not overmix or melting will occur. Serve immediately.

AMOUNT PER ½ CUP (120 ML) SERVING: calories 50, total fat 0.5 g, saturated fat 0 g, cholesterol 0 mg, sodium 55 mg, total carbohydrate 11 g, dietary fiber 2 g, sugars 6 g, protein 1 g

Green Tea Fruit Freeze

Drinking a lot of sweetened beverages has been shown to have a negative impact on health, in part because it is easy to consume a lot of calories quickly. If you like sweetened green tea, consider making this dessert when you get a craving. Full of whole fruits, it has a wonderful tea flavor, sweetness without refined sugar, and fiber, too.

PREPARATION: **10 minutes**   PROCESSING: **45 seconds**   YIELD: **2½ cups (600 ml)**

½ cup (120 ml) cold brewed green tea, or ½ teaspoon matcha green tea powder stirred into ½ cup (120 ml) water

¼ cup (60 ml) plain or vanilla low-fat yogurt

2 tablespoons (30 ml) honey or agave nectar

1 banana, peeled and frozen

½ cup (55 g) frozen cranberries

1 cup (160 g) frozen pineapple chunks

½ cup (75 g) frozen unsweetened strawberries

Place all the ingredients into the Vitamix container in the order listed and secure the lid. Select Variable 1. Turn the machine on and slowly increase the speed to Variable 10, then to High, using the tamper to press the ingredients into the blades. In about 45 seconds, the sound of the motor will change and 4 mounds should form in the mixture. Stop the machine. Do not overmix or melting will occur. Serve immediately.

AMOUNT PER ½ CUP (120 ML) SERVING: calories 80, total fat 0 g, saturated fat 0 g, cholesterol 0 mg, sodium 10 mg, total carbohydrate 19 g, dietary fiber 2 g, sugars 14 g, protein 1 g

Banana Freeze

When frozen and blended, bananas have a wonderfully creamy texture that is very similar to ice cream. This delicious banana freeze comes together in under ten minutes and is the perfect dessert for a hot summer's day or whenever the ice cream craving strikes.

PREPARATION: **5 minutes**   PROCESSING: **30 seconds**   YIELD: **5 cups (1.2 liters)**

1 cup (240 ml) skim milk

3 ripe bananas

1 tablespoon sugar

5 cups (1.2 liters) ice cubes

Place all the ingredients into the Vitamix container in the order listed and secure the lid. Select Variable 1. Turn the machine on and slowly increase the speed to Variable 10, then to High. Use the tamper to press the ingredients into the blades. In about 30 seconds, the sound of the motor will change and 4 mounds should form in the mixture. Stop the machine. Do not overmix or melting will occur. Serve immediately.

AMOUNT PER ½ CUP (120 ML) SERVING: calories 45, total fat 0 g, saturated fat 0 g, cholesterol 0 mg, sodium 10 mg, total carbohydrate 11 g, dietary fiber 1 g, sugars 7 g, protein 1 g

Strawberry Tofu Freeze

A delicious, creamy, vegan dessert! A teaspoon of vanilla extract takes this deeply fruity treat and makes it taste much like old-fashioned strawberry ice cream.

PREPARATION: **15 minutes**   PROCESSING: **1 minute**   YIELD: **5 cups (1.2 liters)**

1½ pounds (680 g) frozen unsweetened strawberries

12 ounces (340 g) extra-firm silken tofu

¼ cup (60 ml) fresh orange juice (see page 301)

½ orange, peeled and halved

1 teaspoon vanilla extract

1. Let the strawberries sit at room temperature for 10 minutes to soften slightly.

2. Place the tofu, orange juice, orange, vanilla, and strawberries into the Vitamix container in the order listed and secure the lid. Select Variable 1. Turn the machine on and slowly increase the speed to Variable 10, then to High, using the tamper to press the ingredients into the blades. In about 1 minute, the sound of the motor will change and 4 mounds should form in the mixture. Stop the machine. Do not overmix or melting will occur. Serve immediately.

AMOUNT PER ½ CUP (120 ML) SERVING: calories 40, total fat 0 g, saturated fat 0 g, cholesterol 0 mg, sodium 35 mg, total carbohydrate 8 g, dietary fiber 2 g, sugars 4 g, protein 3 g

Strawberry Yogurt Freeze

This delightful, two-ingredient dessert can be whipped up in under ten minutes. And since it is just yogurt and strawberries, you could even serve it for breakfast!

PREPARATION: **10 minutes**   PROCESSING: **30 to 60 seconds**   YIELD: **3¼ cups (780 ml)**

1 cup (240 ml) vanilla low-fat yogurt

1 pound (454 g) frozen unsweetened strawberries

Place all the ingredients into the Vitamix container in the order listed and secure the lid. Select Variable 1. Turn the machine on and slowly increase the speed to Variable 10, then to High, using the tamper to press the ingredients into the blades. In 30 to 60 seconds, the sound of the motor will change and 4 mounds should form in the mixture. Stop the machine. Do not overmix or melting will occur. Serve immediately.

AMOUNT PER ½ CUP (120 ML) SERVING: calories 60, total fat 0.5 g, saturated fat 0 g, cholesterol 0 mg, sodium 25 mg, total carbohydrate 13 g, dietary fiber 2 g, sugars 9 g, protein 3 g

Pineapple Freeze

If you have the three ingredients for this dessert on hand, you can go from an empty dish to a sweet treat in just five minutes. The soft tofu gives this freeze a creamy full flavor without any dairy.

PREPARATION: **5 minutes**   PROCESSING: **30 seconds**   YIELD: **2 cups (480 ml)**

¾ cup (158 g) soft tofu

1¾ cups (260 g) frozen pineapple chunks

½ teaspoon fresh lime juice

Place all the ingredients into the Vitamix container in the order listed and secure the lid. Select Variable 1. Turn the machine on and slowly increase the speed to Variable 10, then to High, using the tamper to press the ingredients into the blades. In about 30 seconds, the sound of the motor will change and 4 mounds should form in the mixture. Stop the machine. Do not overmix or melting will occur. Serve immediately.

AMOUNT PER ½ CUP (120 ML) SERVING: calories 70, total fat 1.5 g, saturated fat 0 g, cholesterol 0 mg, sodium 0 mg, total carbohydrate 11 g, dietary fiber 1 g, sugars 2 g, protein 4 g

Tropical Freeze

This tasty tropical dessert is perfect for serving after a meal of Fish Tacos with Slaw (page 195) or Spicy Jerk Chicken (page 197). Cool, creamy, and tangy, this frozen dessert can be garnished with extra fresh fruit or scooped into ice cream cones.

PREPARATION: **10 minutes**   PROCESSING: **35 to 40 seconds**   YIELD: **3½ cups (840 ml)**

1 cup (186 g) frozen mango pieces

1 cup (240 ml) pineapple juice

1 medium banana

½ cup (120 ml) plain 0% Greek yogurt, stirred

½ teaspoon grated lemon zest

3 fresh mint leaves

¾ cup (180 ml) ice cubes

1. Let the mango sit at room temperature for 5 minutes to soften slightly.

2. Place the pineapple juice, banana, yogurt, lemon zest, mint, mango, and ice cubes into the Vitamix container in the order listed and secure the lid. Select Variable 1. Turn the machine on and slowly increase the speed to Variable 10, then to High, using the tamper to press the ingredients into the blades. In 35 to 40 seconds, the sound of the motor will change and 4 mounds should form in the mixture. Stop the machine. Do not overmix or melting will occur. Serve immediately.

AMOUNT PER ½ CUP (120 ML) SERVING: calories 60, total fat 0 g, saturated fat 0 g, cholesterol 0 mg, sodium 10 mg, total carbohydrate 13 g, dietary fiber 1 g, sugars 10 g, protein 2 g

Tropical Mango Freeze

Once you get the hang of making delicious frozen desserts in your Vitamix blender, you may hesitate to buy ice cream or frozen yogurt at the store. The key is to not overmix the ingredients, or you will end up with a very cold smoothie instead of a spoonable dessert.

PREPARATION: **10 minutes**   PROCESSING: **1 minute**   YIELD: **3 cups (720 ml)**

8 ounces (227 g) frozen unsweetened mango chunks

8 ounces (227 g) frozen unsweetened pineapple chunks

1 cup (240 ml) plain 0% Greek yogurt, stirred

1 teaspoon vanilla extract

1. Let the frozen fruit sit at room temperature for 10 minutes to soften slightly.

2. Place the yogurt, vanilla, and fruit into the Vitamix container in the order listed and secure the lid. Select Variable 1. Turn the machine on and slowly increase the speed to Variable 10, then to High, using the tamper to press the ingredients into the blades. In about 1 minute, the sound of the motor will change and 4 mounds should form in the mixture. Stop the machine. Do not overmix or melting will occur. Serve immediately.

AMOUNT PER ½ CUP (120 ML) SERVING: calories 70, total fat 0 g, saturated fat 0 g, cholesterol 0 mg, sodium 15 mg, total carbohydrate 13 g, dietary fiber 1 g, sugars 8 g, protein 4 g

WHOLE FOODS SUCCESS STORY

Pamela Flemming

Bill and Ruth Barnard's children learned about the importance of health and good nutrition around their own kitchen table and through their work with the Vitamix business. As the years went by, subsequent generations inherited and expanded this legacy of health. Meanwhile, in an entirely different family, Pamela Flemming was learning about good nutrition from a beloved aunt.

As a child, Pamela would travel from her home in Brooklyn, New York, to spend her summers in the Poconos in Pennsylvania with her aunt Wini. As a child, Wini had rheumatic fever, and as a young adult was plagued by health problems. One day she wandered into a health food store—a relative rarity in the 1950s—and the proprietor told her about the Vitamix product and how she could address her health problems through her diet. Wini bought a Vitamix and began blending fruit, vegetables, and nuts into healthy drinks. Her subsequent transformation, Pamela recalls, was apparent. "[Our] family remarked that she was an ugly duckling that had become a swan."

Convinced by her own success, Wini became the manager of a health food store and, later, a holistic nutritionist. When Pamela would visit, they picked produce in Wini's organic garden for their smoothies, Wini would talk to young Pamela about the importance of good nutrition and avoiding pesticides. Back in Brooklyn, Pamela remembers, "I would try and lecture all of my friends and family [about] holistic health, but it was a strange concept back then."

Flash-forward to 2009. Inspired by years of gentle encouragement from Wini, Pamela purchased a Vitamix. Pamela enjoys whipping up "health drinks, smoothies, soups, even healthy frozen yogurt for my grandkids." Pamela also carries on Aunt Wini's legacy, teaching friends and family about good nutrition and health. "Nearly every day of my life, I find myself quoting my aunt Wini, or silently thanking her for her wisdom and generosity in sharing her knowledge. I consider myself an advocate of good nutrition, and feel I am indeed carrying Aunt Wini's torch. When Pamela sees a Vitamix demonstration at Costco, she likes to offer her encouragement to the crowd. Pamela says her friends often say that she work for Vitamix, and she says, "In a way, I do. It's a product I truly believe in."

Not unlike the Barnards, Pamela's family now has a strong legacy of achieving better health and wellness by using their Vitamix machines to eat more whole foods. What sort of healthy life legacy do you hope to share with your friends and family?

Clockwise from top:
Nourishing Beets (page 340),
Carrot-Apple Juice Blend (page 305),
Spinach Sparkler (page 335)

Chapter 8

Drinks

As you can imagine, I learned the breadth of uses for the Vitamix very early on. It was the family business, after all! Some I learned probably sooner than I should have. When I was growing up, my parents' favorite party drink was the blended whiskey sour. I will admit that we kids would hide under the table, and when the party moved to the other room, we would sneak out and share the few drops that remained in the Vitamix container. This may be how I came up with the idea of serving my husband smoothies with a shot of vodka after a long day at the office. I quickly weaned him off the vodka, and it took a while before he thought to even ask. Now it is a straight smoothie—no chaser!

Spiked or not, smoothies are now a part of the American culinary landscape. Perhaps because smoothies are quick to prepare and easy to drink in the flurry of our morning routine, lunch, or workout routine, Americans drink a lot of them. Our research team at Vitamix tells us that, between April 2014 and March 2015, Americans whipped up 3.76 *billion* homemade smoothies, a jaw-dropping number and an increase of almost 16 percent from the previous year.

Blended drinks encompass a much wider range of drinks than smoothies, of course. Blended tea and coffee drinks pop up more and more and in an expanding range of flavors. Juice, also a blended drink depending on how it is produced, has come to include a staggering range of ingredients, too. Americans can now buy or make a wide range of juices with fruits, vegetables, and other healthy ingredients. And nut milks? A quick internet search shows that lots of us are interested in drinking, and making, nondairy milks too, and we are using our Vitamix blenders to do it.

Does this explosion of interest in blended drinks translate into a healthier America? While there is never a silver bullet, we can hope for positive change. If by drinking smoothies and whipping up nut milks and fresh juices, we are eating more whole foods, then we are on the right track. If by making these drinks and snacks at home, Americans are consuming less sodium and sugar, then that is also good, even if the transformation is not yet dramatic.

Small simple steps toward increasing your health and vitality are absolutely worth taking. In this chapter we will look at the different ways you can use your Vitamix machine to make drinks that contain whole foods and avoid lots of extra salt and sugar. Let's raise a glass to our health!

Smoothies

According to research that we mentioned above, 25 percent of Vitamix owners add kale to their smoothies. We love our green smoothies here at Vitamix! Several of the recipes in this chapter—Basil Romaine Boost (page 320), Fresh Mint with Sprouts Beverage (page 348), Kale-Flax Smoothie with Pear (page 339), Going Green Smoothie (page 330), and Greens Juice Blend (page 307), to name just a few—give you new and creative ways to add fruits and leafy green vegetables to your diet.

Of course, whole vegetable juices and drinks aren't just about greens. Salsa in a Glass (page 336) and Spicy Tomato Drink (page 308) offer two ways to enjoy whole food tomato juice with much less sodium than many packaged varieties. Nourishing Beets (page 340) pairs deeply purple and naturally sweet beets and apples with chile pepper, garlic, celery, and ginger for a delicious and slightly unconventional whole-vegetable drink. Spinach Sparkler (page 335) combines greens, celery, cucumber, a whole lemon, a splash of pineapple juice, and sparkling water for a fresh, effervescent drink that would delight Popeye and Olive Oyl alike.

Many smoothies, even vegetable-based ones, benefit from fresh, dried, or frozen fruit to add a little sweetness. Banana Boost (page 321), Cherry Red Smoothie (page 325), Fig Smoothie with Goji Berries and Chia Seeds (page 326), Purple Fruit Smoothie (page 319), and Tofu Tropic Smoothie (page 343) will give you new and delicious ways to work more fruits into your breakfasts and afternoon snacks.

Whole Food Juicing

What, you might ask, is the difference between whole food smoothies and whole food juices? Here at Vitamix, our chef and manager of recipe development, Bev Shaffer, says smoothies have a silky smooth texture of varying thicknesses while juices tend to be thinner and may or may not retain some of the texture of the fruits and vegetables.

Whole food juices, like smoothies, contain all of the fiber and nutrients that you would get from eating the fruit or vegetable on its own. Whole food juices can be made quite thin, but because of the fiber, they will tend to have a thicker texture than a drink made with a juicer / juice extractor. If you want your drink to be more like the liquid produced by a juicer, you can strain the liquid through a fine-mesh sieve before you drink it.

You can make delicious juices with both fruits and vegetables. Recipes for Apple Juice (page 302), Berry Veggie Juice Blend (page 309), Cherry Anise Juice Blend (page 312), Greens Juice Blend (page 307), and Tart Citrus Juice Blend (page 311), among others, will show you how. You can also make your own Orange Juice (page 301) and either drink it on its own or use it in a smoothie or as part of a juice blend.

Nondairy Milks

If you want milk but are avoiding dairy, your options are increasing quickly these days. Milks made from hemp seeds, soy, rice, and a wide variety of nuts abound. However, packaged nondairy milks often contain thickeners, sweeteners, and additives. Thankfully these milks are easy to make at home with a few simple ingredients and the amazing Vitamix machine. Not only can you adjust the sweetness and the texture to your own preferences, but the fresh flavor is pretty unbeatable. Explore the do-it-yourself nondairy milk options with recipes such as Almond Milk (page 354), Sweet Almond Cinnamon Milk (page 356), and Soy Milk (page 353). Once made, these milks will keep in the refrigerator for about a week.

Caffeinated Drinks

A green smoothie may give you a boost, but few things can compete with the eye-opening powers of coffee or green tea. Heavily sweetened blended coffee and tea drinks are widely available, but they are easier, cheaper, and often healthier to make at home. Try a Mocha Cooler (page 360), a Tea of Green Smoothie (page 362), or an Espresso Banana Drink (page 359) the next time you need a caffeine boost. Loyal Vitamix owner Janice Summers (read more about her on page 254) says she started blending her own coffee drinks because she wanted an all-organic drink, and now she prefers her home-blended coffees. "Now that I make my own, they are so much better than what I get when out, that even if I could get organic I wouldn't choose to, since I like the creaminess and taste of mine better!"

Techniques for the Best Results

Here are a couple of quick tips to ensure that you make the best smoothies, juices, and other blended drinks.

- Put the ingredients in the Vitamix container in the order that they are listed. In general, liquids go in first, then dry goods, leafy greens, fruits and veggies, and, last, any frozen ingredients. Why, you might ask? Because the heavier frozen ingredients help push everything into the blades.
- Start the machine slowly—this helps the blades "grab" the ingredients—but then quickly switch to a higher speed. Using the top speeds is actually easier on the motor, so increase the speed as directed.
- If needed, add a little more liquid or use the tamper to help the ingredients circulate fully and blend more completely.
- As we say in our *Personal Blending* book, "Perfection cannot be rushed. Blend for the full processing time suggested in the recipe at least the first time you make it." If you prefer to shorten the blend time in the future, your drink may not be quite as smooth, but it is all about preference.

CHEERS!

Orange Juice

You are just minutes away from fresh, delicious orange juice! Enjoy this drink on its own or add it to any recipe in this book that calls for orange juice.

PREPARATION: **10 minutes**   PROCESSING: **1 minute**   YIELD: **4 cups (960 ml)**

½ cup (120 ml) water

4 large oranges, peeled and halved

½ cup (120 ml) ice cubes

Place all the ingredients into the Vitamix container in the order listed and secure the lid. Select Variable 1. Turn the machine on and slowly increase the speed to Variable 10, then to High. Blend for 1 minute, or until the desired consistency is reached.

AMOUNT PER ½ CUP (120 ML) SERVING: calories 45, total fat 0 g, saturated fat 0 g, cholesterol 0 mg, sodium 0 mg, total carbohydrate 11 g, dietary fiber 2 g, sugars 9 g, protein 1 g

Apple Juice

This refreshing cider-like drink tastes wonderfully and simply of apples. It is sure to be a hit with young and old alike!

PREPARATION: **10 minutes**   PROCESSING: **45 seconds**   YIELD: **2 servings**

¼ cup (60 ml) water

1½ pounds (680 g) apples, quartered and seeded

1. Place all the ingredients into the Vitamix container in the order listed and secure the lid. Select Variable 1. Turn the machine on and slowly increase the speed to Variable 10, then to High. Blend for 45 seconds, using the tamper to press the ingredients into the blades.

2. Transfer the puree to a bowl lined with 4 layers of cheesecloth and twist until the juice is extracted.

AMOUNT PER SERVING: calories 60, total fat 0 g, saturated fat 0 g, cholesterol 0 mg, sodium 15 mg, total carbohydrate 15 g, dietary fiber 0 g, sugars 13 g, protein 0 g

Apple Pear Fruit Juice

Save a little homemade apple juice (page 302) and make this flavor-packed whole fruit juice. Fresh ginger and a little cinnamon balance out the natural sweetness of the apples, pears, and green grapes.

PREPARATION: **10 minutes**   PROCESSING: **1 minute**   YIELD: **4 to 5 servings**

¾ cup (180 ml) unsweetened apple juice

½ cup (75 g) green grapes

2 apples (13.5 oz / 382 g), halved and seeded

2 pears (1 pound / 454 g), halved and seeded

One ½-inch (1.3-cm) cube fresh gingerroot, peeled

½ teaspoon ground cinnamon

Place all the ingredients into the Vitamix container in the order listed and secure the lid. Select Variable 1. Turn the machine on and slowly increase the speed to Variable 10, then to High. Blend for 1 minute, or until the desired consistency is reached, using the tamper to press the ingredients into the blades.

AMOUNT PER 1 CUP (240 ML) SERVING: calories 140, total fat 0 g, saturated fat 0 g, cholesterol 0 mg, sodium 5 mg, total carbohydrate 38 g, dietary fiber 6 g, sugars 27 g, protein 1 g

Carrot-Apple Juice Blend

This lip-smacking juice blend takes a little more planning than some of the other drinks. Carrots, steamed and cooled before blending or left over from another meal, give this drink a delightfully smooth texture. The basil might seem out of place but don't skip it. The herby, anise flavor balances the sweetness of the apple, apple juice, and carrots.

PREPARATION: **15 minutes**   PROCESSING: **1 minute**   YIELD: **2 to 3 servings**

½ cup (120 ml) water

½ cup (120 ml) unsweetened apple juice

4 medium carrots (½ pound / 227 g), peeled, cut into pieces, steamed until tender, and cooled

1 tablespoon chopped fresh basil

1 small apple, halved and seeded

½ cup (120 ml) ice cubes

Place all the ingredients into the Vitamix container in the order listed and secure the lid. Select Variable 1. Turn the machine on and slowly increase the speed to Variable 10, then to High. Blend for 1 minute, or until the desired consistency is reached, using the tamper to press the ingredients into the blades.

AMOUNT PER 1 CUP (240 ML) SERVING: calories 80, total fat 0 g, saturated fat 0 g, cholesterol 0 mg, sodium 55 mg, total carbohydrate 20 g, dietary fiber 4 g, sugars 13 g, protein 1 g

Mango Carrot Juice Blend

Marigold-hued and bursting with flavor, this mango carrot blend may replace plain orange juice as your morning beverage. There is still some naturally occurring sugar in this whole foods juice (19 grams versus 22 grams for a cup of orange juice), but along with that sugar, you get 4 grams of fiber. You also get a greater variety of fruits and veggies in a cup of this juice blend. And is variety not the spice of life?

PREPARATION: **15 minutes**   PROCESSING: **1 minute**   YIELD: **4 servings**

¾ cup (180 ml) water

½ cup (120 ml) no-sugar-added mango nectar

1 teaspoon grated orange zest

1 orange, peeled and halved

1 small apple, halved and seeded

3 carrots (6 oz / 170 g), quartered

1 cup (186 g) frozen mango chunks

1 cup (240 ml) ice cubes

Place all the ingredients into the Vitamix container in the order listed and secure the lid. Select Variable 1. Turn the machine on and slowly increase the speed to Variable 10, then to High. Blend for 1 minute, or until the desired consistency is reached, using the tamper to press the ingredients into the blades.

AMOUNT PER 1 CUP (240 ML) SERVING: calories 90, total fat 0 g, saturated fat 0 g, cholesterol 0 mg, sodium 35 mg, total carbohydrate 24 g, dietary fiber 4 g, sugars 19 g, protein 1 g

Greens Juice Blend

Juicing whole foods allows you to keep the fiber and nutrients that the ingredients contain, but the resulting drink is thicker, more smoothie-like. Here we use equal parts water and ice to give this juice blend a thinner, more juice-like quality without sacrificing any nutritional benefits.

PREPARATION: **15 minutes**   PROCESSING: **35 seconds**   YIELD: **3 to 4 servings**

1 cup (240 ml) water

1 cup (70 g) broccoli florets

½ cup (83 g) fresh pineapple chunks

½ apple, halved and seeded

½ banana

1 cup (28 g) baby spinach

½ cup (15 g) chopped kale leaves

¼ cup (15 g) fresh flat-leaf parsley leaves

2 fresh basil leaves

1 cup (240 ml) ice cubes

Place all the ingredients into the Vitamix container in the order listed and secure the lid. Select Variable 1. Turn the machine on and slowly increase the speed to Variable 10, then to High. Blend for 35 seconds, or until the desired consistency is reached, using the tamper to press the ingredients into the blades.

AMOUNT PER 1 CUP (240 ML) SERVING: calories 60, total fat 0 g, saturated fat 0 g, cholesterol 0 mg, sodium 30 mg, total carbohydrate 14 g, dietary fiber 3 g, sugars 7 g, protein 2 g

Spicy Tomato Drink

Make this bright, zippy drink when tomatoes are in season for the best flavor. Consider serving it with a cheese sandwich on whole-grain bread for a summertime twist on the classic tomato soup and grilled cheese pairing.

PREPARATION: **10 minutes**   PROCESSING: **20 seconds**   YIELD: **3 to 4 servings**

1½ pounds (680 g) tomatoes, quartered (about 4 cups)

1 lemon, peeled and halved

2 tablespoons (20 g) chopped yellow onion

6 dashes of hot sauce

½ cup (120 ml) ice cubes

Place all the ingredients into the Vitamix container in the order listed and secure the lid. Select Variable 1. Turn the machine on and slowly increase the speed to Variable 10, then to High. Blend for 20 seconds, or until the desired consistency is reached.

AMOUNT PER 1 CUP (240 ML) SERVING: calories 40, total fat 0 g, saturated fat 0 g, cholesterol 0 mg, sodium 15 mg, total carbohydrate 10 g, dietary fiber 3 g, sugars 6 g, protein 2 g

Berry Veggie Juice Blend

Pairing naturally sweet, nutrient-rich vegetables like corn, carrots, and roasted beets with frozen berries creates a delicious, flavorful smoothie. If you are trying to add (or sneak!) more veggies into your daily diet, this tasty drink is a great way to do it.

PREPARATION: **10 minutes plus roasting**   PROCESSING: **1 minute**   YIELD: **4 to 5 servings**

1¼ cups (300 ml) water

1 cup (150 g) fresh or thawed frozen strawberries

1 cup (112 g) frozen unsweetened red raspberries

1 medium red beet, roasted, peeled, and quartered

2 carrots, quartered

1 cup (145 g) fresh or thawed frozen corn kernels

1 cup (240 ml) ice cubes

Place all the ingredients into the Vitamix container in the order listed and secure the lid. Select Variable 1. Turn the machine on and slowly increase the speed to Variable 10, then to High. Blend for 1 minute, or until the desired consistency is reached, using the tamper to press the ingredients into the blades.

AMOUNT PER 1 CUP (240 ML) SERVING: calories 60, total fat 0.5 g, saturated fat 0 g, cholesterol 0 mg, sodium 40 mg, total carbohydrate 15 g, dietary fiber 3 g, sugars 7 g, protein 2 g

Digestive Juice Drink

Move over, salty vegetable juices, there is a new, healthier drink in town! A great way to get your veggies on the go, this whole foods juice is packed with tomatoes, carrots, fennel, beets, celery, garlic, herbs, and spices. Take it with you for a healthy lunch or snack.

PREPARATION: **15 minutes**   PROCESSING: **1 minute**   YIELD: **4 to 5 servings**

½ cup (120 ml) water

2 medium tomatoes, quartered

2 carrots, cut into pieces

¼ fennel bulb, cut into chunks

1 garlic clove, peeled

4 fresh basil leaves

1 tablespoon fresh dill

½ teaspoon fresh thyme leaves

2 celery stalks

1 small/medium red beet, quartered

¼ teaspoon ground turmeric

¼ teaspoon dry mustard

¼ teaspoon ground cumin

1 cup (240 ml) ice cubes

Place all the ingredients into the Vitamix container in the order listed and secure the lid. Select Variable 1. Turn the machine on and slowly increase the speed to Variable 10, then to High. Blend for 1 minute, or until the desired consistency is reached, using the tamper to press the ingredients into the blades.

AMOUNT PER 1 CUP (240 ML) SERVING: calories 45, total fat 0 g, saturated fat 0 g, cholesterol 0 mg, sodium 65 mg, total carbohydrate 10 g, dietary fiber 3 g, sugars 5 g, protein 2 g

Tart Citrus Juice Blend

This zippy, bright juice blend will really get your eyes open in the morning! Full of whole citrus fruits, this drink has a little honey for sweetness as well as whole cranberries for color and extra pucker. Cut the juice with club soda for a bubbly treat or use as a base for a whole fruit margarita.

PREPARATION: **10 minutes**   PROCESSING: **1 minute**   YIELD: **3 to 4 servings**

½ cup (120 ml) water

2 oranges, peeled and halved

1 grapefruit, peeled and halved

1 lime, peeled

½ cup (65 g) cranberries, fresh or frozen

1 teaspoon honey

½ cup (120 ml) ice cubes

Place all the ingredients into the Vitamix container in the order listed and secure the lid. Select Variable 1. Turn the machine on and slowly increase the speed to Variable 10, then to High. Blend for 1 minute, or until the desired consistency is reached, using the tamper to press the ingredients into the blades.

AMOUNT PER 1 CUP (240 ML) SERVING: calories 80, total fat 0 g, saturated fat 0 g, cholesterol 0 mg, sodium 0 mg, total carbohydrate 21 g, dietary fiber 4 g, sugars 10 g, protein 1 g

Cherry Anise Juice Blend

The subtle licorice flavor of fennel complements the sweetness of the cherries in this drink. Don't worry if you are not ordinarily a licorice fan; the taste of fennel is more vegetable and less assertive than your average black licorice whip. Adding this delicious vegetable and a whole peeled lime gives this whole juice bright flavor and fiber without adding a lot of extra calories.

PREPARATION: **15 minutes**   PROCESSING: **40 seconds**   YIELD: **2 servings**

½ cup (120 ml) water

1 cup (150 g) green grapes

½ lime, peeled

¼ fennel bulb, cut into pieces

1 cup (140 g) frozen pitted dark cherries

Place all the ingredients into the Vitamix container in the order listed and secure the lid. Select Variable 1. Turn the machine on and slowly increase the speed to Variable 10, then to High. Blend for 40 seconds, or until the desired consistency is reached, using the tamper to press the ingredients into the blades.

AMOUNT PER SERVING: calories 110, total fat 0 g, saturated fat 0 g, cholesterol 0 mg, sodium 20 mg, total carbohydrate 29 g, dietary fiber 4 g, sugars 21 g, protein 2 g

Breakfast Shake

The King of Shake (Rattle and Roll, that is), Elvis Presley may have preferred his banana and peanut butter fried in a sandwich with bacon, but perhaps he would have enjoyed his favorite flavors in this breakfast drink, too (minus the bacon!). Easily put together with pantry staples, it is a crowd—and specifically a kid—pleaser!

PREPARATION: **10 minutes**   PROCESSING: **15 to 20 seconds**   YIELD: **2 servings**

⅓ cup (80 ml) skim milk

¾ cup (180 ml) plain nonfat yogurt

1 teaspoon vanilla extract

1 teaspoon honey

1 medium banana

1 tablespoon peanut butter

Place all the ingredients into the Vitamix container in the order listed and secure the lid. Select Variable 1. Turn the machine on and slowly increase the speed to Variable 10, then to High. Blend for 15 to 20 seconds, until the desired consistency is reached.

AMOUNT PER 1 CUP (240 ML) SERVING: calories 190, total fat 6 g, saturated fat 1.5 g, cholesterol 5 mg, sodium 110 mg, total carbohydrate 27 g, dietary fiber 2 g, sugars 19 g, protein 9 g

Wake Up Breakfast Smoothie

Need to dash out the door but still want a healthy breakfast? Take traditional breakfast fixings—milk, yogurt, strawberries, banana, wheat germ, and maple syrup—and blend them into a tasty, nutritious, and entirely portable meal. Really pressed for time? Whip this smoothie up the night before for a truly grab-and-go breakfast.

PREPARATION: **15 minutes**   PROCESSING: **30 seconds**   YIELD: **5 servings**

½ cup (120 ml) skim milk

1½ cups (360 ml) plain nonfat yogurt

½ teaspoon vanilla extract

2 cups (332 g) sliced fresh strawberries

1 small banana halved

2 tablespoons (15 g) wheat germ

1 tablespoon maple syrup

1½ cups (360 ml) ice cubes

Place all the ingredients into the Vitamix container in the order listed and secure the lid. Select Variable 1. Turn the machine on and slowly increase the speed to Variable 10, then to High. Blend for 30 seconds, or until the desired consistency is reached, using the tamper to press the ingredients into the blades.

AMOUNT PER 1 CUP (240 ML) SERVING: calories 110, total fat 0.5 g, saturated fat 0 g, cholesterol 0 mg, sodium 65 mg, total carbohydrate 20 g, dietary fiber 2 g, sugars 15 g, protein 6 g

Banana Apple Oatmeal Smoothie

Vanilla yogurt, banana, apple, and two tablespoons of quick-cooking oats work together to give this smoothie a thick, creamy texture. Dried cranberries add a bit of tartness to balance out the sweet, and cinnamon adds the gentlest bit of spice. A wonderful drink to start your day or give you a late-afternoon boost!

PREPARATION: **10 minutes**   PROCESSING: **45 seconds**   YIELD: **2 servings**

1 cup (240 ml) water

¼ cup (60 ml) vanilla low-fat yogurt

½ banana

2 tablespoons (10 g) quick-cooking oats

½ medium apple, halved and seeded

¼ cup (30 g) dried unsweetened cranberries

⅛ teaspoon ground cinnamon

Place all the ingredients into the Vitamix container in the order listed and secure the lid. Select Variable 1. Turn the machine on and slowly increase the speed to Variable 10, then to High. Blend for 45 seconds, or until the desired consistency is reached.

AMOUNT PER 1 CUP (240 ML) SERVING: calories 140, total fat 1 g, saturated fat 0 g, cholesterol 0 mg, sodium 30 mg, total carbohydrate 32 g, dietary fiber 3 g, sugars 24 g, protein 3 g

Raspberry Oatmeal Smoothie

The most delicious and drinkable oatmeal you have ever had! This smoothie is full of fiber, protein, and a gentle sweetness from the raspberries and the honey. Feel free to try this smoothie with other fruits and berries too, adjusting the honey depending on the sweetness of the fruit.

PREPARATION: **10 minutes**   PROCESSING: **20 seconds**   YIELD: **1 serving**

1½ tablespoons quick-cooking oats

½ cup (120 ml) boiling water, plus ¼ cup (60 ml) cold water

1 cup (125 g) fresh or frozen red raspberries, partially thawed if frozen

1 teaspoon honey

3 tablespoons (45 ml) plain 0% Greek yogurt, stirred

1. Soak the oats in the boiling water for 10 minutes.

2. Place the cold water, the oat mixture with any remaining liquid, the raspberries, honey, and yogurt into the Vitamix container in the order listed and secure the lid. Select Variable 1. Turn the machine on and slowly increase the speed to Variable 10, then to High. Blend for 20 seconds.

AMOUNT PER SERVING: calories 130, total fat 0.5 g, saturated fat 0 g, cholesterol 0 mg, sodium 25 mg, total carbohydrate 30 g, dietary fiber 9 g, sugars 7 g, protein 6 g

Almond Milk Banana Smoothie

This delicious smoothie, great for breakfast or an afternoon pick-me-up, is a great way to use homemade almond milk. Two ounces of slivered almonds add an extra nutty flavor, and the vanilla extract makes the drink taste almost dessert-like.

PREPARATION: **10 minutes**   PROCESSING: **25 seconds**   YIELD: **3 to 4 servings**

2 cups (480 ml) unsweetened almond milk, preferably homemade (page 354), cold

2 ounces (57 g) slivered almonds

2 ripe small bananas, halved

1½ teaspoons vanilla extract

½ cup (120 ml) ice cubes

Place all the ingredients into the Vitamix container in the order listed and secure the lid. Select Variable 1. Turn the machine on and slowly increase the speed to Variable 10. Blend for 25 seconds, or until the desired consistency is reached.

AMOUNT PER 1 CUP (240 ML) SERVING: calories 160, total fat 9 g, saturated fat 0.5 g, cholesterol 0 mg, sodium 95 mg, total carbohydrate 17 g, dietary fiber 4 g, sugars 7 g, protein 5 g

Purple Fruit Smoothie

Unsweetened cranberry juice contains 13 micrograms of vitamin K (14% of the daily value for women, 10% for men), but many of us find it too tart to drink on its own. Blend it with a nondairy milk, blueberries, cherries, and a banana, however, and you get all of the nutrition in a sweeter, purple-hued drink that is much less tart.

PREPARATION: **10 minutes**   PROCESSING: **30 seconds**   YIELD: **2 servings**

¼ cup (60 ml) unsweetened cranberry juice

½ cup (120 ml) unsweetened soy milk or nut milk, preferably homemade (pages 353 and 354)

½ cup (74 g) fresh or frozen blueberries

½ cup (70 g) fresh or frozen pitted cherries

1 banana, halved

½ cup (120 ml) ice cubes

Place all the ingredients into the Vitamix container in the order listed and secure the lid. Select Variable 1. Turn the machine on and slowly increase the speed to Variable 10, then to High. Blend for 30 seconds.

AMOUNT PER 1 CUP (240 ML) SERVING: calories 140, total fat 2 g, saturated fat 0 g, cholesterol 0 mg, sodium 0 mg, total carbohydrate 30 g, dietary fiber 3 g, sugars 19 g, protein 4 g

Basil Romaine Boost

Vibrantly green and lightly sweet, greens in the morning (or the afternoon or the evening) have never tasted so good! Make this smoothie the night before you want to drink it, if you like. Simply stir the smoothie to reemulsify it before you enjoy it.

PREPARATION: **10 minutes**   PROCESSING: **45 seconds**   YIELD: **3 to 4 servings**

1 cup (240 ml) water

1 pear, quartered and seeded

1 orange, peeled and halved

½ cup (3 oz / 45 g) chopped broccoli

2 cups (3 oz / 85 g) baby romaine lettuce mix

½ cup (16 g) fresh basil leaves

1 cup (240 ml) ice cubes

Place all the ingredients into the Vitamix container in the order listed and secure the lid. Select Variable 1. Turn the machine on and slowly increase the speed to Variable 10, then to High. Blend for 45 seconds, or until the desired consistency is reached, using the tamper to press the ingredients into the blades.

AMOUNT PER 1 CUP (240 ML) SERVING: calories 45, total fat 0 g, saturated fat 0 g, cholesterol 0 mg, sodium 20 mg, total carbohydrate 11 g, dietary fiber 3 g, sugars 7 g, protein 1 g

Banana Boost

Americans love bananas: We eat more bananas than apples and oranges combined. Why not boost the creamy sweet flavor of the banana with other whole fruits? Here a peeled and halved lemon, pitted dates, and half a pineapple, core and all, are blended with banana and soy milk for a tasty drink that is sure to give your day a lift!

PREPARATION: **10 minutes**   PROCESSING: **30 seconds**   YIELD: **4 servings**

1¼ cups (300 ml) unsweetened soy milk, cold, preferably homemade (page 353)

1 lemon, peeled and halved

1 small ripe banana (fresh or frozen), peeled

4 to 5 pitted dates

½ pineapple (18 oz / 511 g), cut into pieces, core included

Place all the ingredients into the Vitamix container in the order listed and secure the lid. Select Variable 1. Turn the machine on and slowly increase the speed to Variable 10, then to High. Blend for 30 seconds, or until the desired consistency is reached.

AMOUNT PER 1 CUP (240 ML) SERVING: calories 230, total fat 2 g, saturated fat 0 g, cholesterol 0 mg, sodium 0 mg, total carbohydrate 54 g, dietary fiber 4 g, sugars 41 g, protein 6 g

Berry Beet Blast

A half cup of roasted beets, deeply purple and with an earthy sweetness, blends beautifully with orange and lemon juices, a little honey, and mixed berries to create a delicious juice. The beet combines so seamlessly with the berries; you may forget you are drinking a vegetable!

PREPARATION: **10 minutes**   PROCESSING: **45 seconds**   YIELD: **1¾ cups (420 ml)**

¼ cup (60 ml) water

1 tablespoon fresh lemon juice

½ cup (120 ml) fresh orange juice (see page 301)

1 teaspoon honey

½ cup (91 g) roasted beet chunks

½ cup (80 g) frozen mixed berries

½ cup (120 ml) ice cubes

Place all the ingredients into the Vitamix container in the order listed and secure the lid. Select Variable 1. Turn the machine on and slowly increase the speed to Variable 10, then to High. Blend for 45 seconds, or until the desired consistency is reached, using the tamper to press the ingredients into the blades.

AMOUNT PER 1 CUP (240 ML) SERVING: calories 90, total fat 0 g, saturated fat 0 g, cholesterol 0 mg, sodium 40 mg, total carbohydrate 22 g, dietary fiber 3 g, sugars 17 g, protein 2 g

Fruit Nut Shake

Adding protein, healthy fats, and fiber to your shakes can help them keep you full longer. Here pecans, skim milk, and Greek yogurt give a protein boost to blueberries and peaches and create a drink that will help you power through your busiest days.

PREPARATION: **10 minutes**   PROCESSING: **30 seconds**   YIELD: **2 servings**

1 cup (140 g) frozen unsweetened peach slices

½ cup (120 ml) skim milk

1 cup (240 ml) plain 0% Greek yogurt, stirred

1 tablespoon pecan pieces

½ teaspoon vanilla extract

¼ cup (37 g) fresh or frozen blueberries

1. Let the peaches sit at room temperature for 15 minutes to thaw slightly.

2. Place the milk, yogurt, pecans, vanilla, peaches, and blueberries into the Vitamix container in the order listed and secure the lid. Select Variable 1. Turn the machine on and slowly increase the speed to Variable 10, then to High. Blend for 30 seconds, or until the desired consistency is reached.

AMOUNT PER 1 CUP (240 ML) SERVING: calories 140, total fat 3 g, saturated fat 0 g, cholesterol 0 mg, sodium 70 mg, total carbohydrate 17 g, dietary fiber 2 g, sugars 15 g, protein 13 g

Cherry Red Smoothie

Combining unsweetened cherry juice—made from tart cherries—and frozen Bing cherries gives you a bright, sweet taste without refined sugar. Vanilla extract and 0% Greek yogurt lend a creamy, almost ice cream–like flavor.

PREPARATION: **10 minutes**　　PROCESSING: **45 seconds**　　YIELD: **3 to 4 servings**

1 cup (240 ml) unsweetened cherry juice

1²/₃ cups (400 ml) plain 0% Greek yogurt, stirred

1 teaspoon vanilla extract

1 cup (166 g) frozen pitted Bing cherries

½ cup (120 ml) ice cubes

Place all the ingredients into the Vitamix container in the order listed and secure the lid. Select Variable 1. Turn the machine on and slowly increase the speed to Variable 10, then to High. Blend for 45 seconds, or until the desired consistency is reached, using the tamper to press the ingredients into the blades.

AMOUNT PER 1 CUP (240 ML) SERVING: calories 120, total fat 0 g, saturated fat 0 g, cholesterol 0 mg, sodium 45 mg, total carbohydrate 20 g, dietary fiber 1 g, sugars 16 g, protein 10 g

Fig Smoothie with Goji Berries and Chia Seeds

This super-tasting, superfood-packed smoothie has *a lot* going on: a whopping 7 grams of fiber, 90% of the daily value for vitamin A, and 15% of the daily value for iron and calcium. You get two kinds of greens, chia seeds, walnuts, and dried goji berries and figs too. Thanks to the power of the Vitamix, all of these hearty ingredients can be blended into a smooth, delicious drink.

PREPARATION: **10 minutes**   PROCESSING: **1 minute**   YIELD: **4 to 5 servings**

2 cups (480 ml) water

1 cup (240 ml) pomegranate juice

⅔ cup (100 g) dried figs

1 cup (67 g) kale, torn

1 cup (28 g) spinach leaves

¼ cup (42 g) chia seeds

¼ cup (25 g) walnuts

½ cup (45 g) dried goji berries

½ cup (120 ml) ice cubes

Place all the ingredients into the Vitamix container in the order listed and secure the lid. Select Variable 1. Turn the machine on and slowly increase the speed to Variable 10, then to High. Blend for 1 minute, or until the desired consistency is reached, using the tamper to press the ingredients into the blades.

AMOUNT PER 1 CUP (240 ML) SERVING: calories 220, total fat 7 g, saturated fat 0.5 g, cholesterol 0 mg, sodium 30 mg, total carbohydrate 37 g, dietary fiber 7 g, sugars 26 g, protein 4 g

Ginger Smoothie

Used in Ayurvedic and traditional Chinese medicines for hundreds of years, ginger has been the subject of more modern research, some of which suggests it may have anti-inflammatory properties. Regardless of what the scientists conclude about its benefits, we can confidently say that ginger is delicious! Paired with pears, cucumbers, and kale, ginger lends a bright, slightly spicy flavor to this delicious drink.

PREPARATION: **10 minutes**   PROCESSING: **1 minute**   YIELD: **5 servings**

2 cups (480 ml) water

½ cucumber (4 oz / 114 g), cut into large pieces

2 pears, quartered and seeded

One ½-inch (1.3-cm) cube fresh gingerroot, peeled

6 Tuscan (black/lacinato) kale leaves

½ cup (120 ml) ice cubes

Place all the ingredients into the Vitamix container in the order listed and secure the lid. Select Variable 1. Turn the machine on and slowly increase the speed to Variable 10, then to High. Blend for 1 minute, or until the desired consistency is reached, using the tamper to press the ingredients into the blades.

AMOUNT PER 1 CUP (240 ML) SERVING: calories 50, total fat 0 g, saturated fat 0 g, cholesterol 0 mg, sodium 10 mg, total carbohydrate 13 g, dietary fiber 3 g, sugars 7 g, protein 1 g

Blackberry-Pear Smoothie

If you like something sweet in the morning, even if it is a glass of orange juice or a cup of sweetened yogurt, consider whipping up this flavorful drink instead. Lightly sweet and packed with naturally occurring nutrients and fiber, this creamy smoothie is sure to please!

PREPARATION: **10 minutes**   PROCESSING: **45 seconds**   YIELD: **4 to 5 servings**

²/₃ cup (160 ml) water

1 cup (240 ml) plain low-fat yogurt

2 bananas, halved

1 pear, halved and seeded

1 apple, halved and seeded

2 cups (280 g) frozen blackberries

Place all the ingredients into the Vitamix container in the order listed and secure the lid. Select Variable 1. Turn the machine on and slowly increase the speed to Variable 10, then to High. Blend for 45 seconds, or until the desired consistency is reached, using the tamper to press the ingredients into the blades.

AMOUNT PER 1 CUP (240 ML) SERVING: calories 140, total fat 2 g, saturated fat 1 g, cholesterol 5 mg, sodium 25 mg, total carbohydrate 31 g, dietary fiber 6 g, sugars 21 g, protein 3 g

Cinnapeach Smoothie

Trying to convert a spinach-skeptic into a Popeye-esque enthusiast? This tasty drink has two cups of nutrient-packed spinach, but the flavors of peaches, rice or almond milk, vanilla, and cinnamon dominate. A quick, delicious way to add greens to anyone's diet!

PREPARATION: **10 minutes**   PROCESSING: **25 seconds**   YIELD: **2 to 3 servings**

1 cup (240 ml) unsweetened almond or rice milk, preferably homemade (page 354)

1 cup (140 g) peach slices, fresh or thawed frozen

½ teaspoon ground cinnamon

½ teaspoon vanilla extract

2 cups (2.15 oz / 62 g) spinach leaves

3 mint leaves

½ cup (120 ml) ice cubes

Place all the ingredients into the Vitamix container in the order listed and secure the lid. Select Variable 1. Turn the machine on and slowly increase the speed to Variable 10, then to High. Blend for 25 seconds, or until the desired consistency is reached, using the tamper to press the ingredients into the blades.

AMOUNT PER 1 CUP (240 ML) SERVING: calories 60, total fat 1 g, saturated fat 0 g, cholesterol 0 mg, sodium 105 mg, total carbohydrate 13 g, dietary fiber 3 g, sugars 8 g, protein 2 g

Going Green Smoothie

A pretty pale green and full of delicious fruit flavor, this smoothie is a terrific place to start if you are new to green smoothies. Fresh spinach blends with fruit, ice, and water to create a refreshing smoothie that even the most vegetable-wary kid can enjoy.

PREPARATION: **10 minutes**   PROCESSING: **30 seconds**   YIELD: **2½ cups (600 ml)**

½ cup (120 ml) water

1 cup (150 g) green grapes

½ cup (75 g) fresh pineapple chunks

½ medium banana

2 cups lightly packed (60 g) spinach

½ cup (120 ml) ice cubes

Place all the ingredients into the Vitamix container in the order listed and secure the lid. Select Variable 1. Turn the machine on and slowly increase the speed to Variable 10, then to High. Blend for 30 seconds, or until the desired consistency is reached.

AMOUNT PER 1 CUP (240 ML) SERVING: calories 90, total fat 0 g, saturated fat 0 g, cholesterol 0 mg, sodium 40 mg, total carbohydrate 23 g, dietary fiber 2 g, sugars 15 g, protein 1 g

Silky Green Smoothie

Avocados (botanically speaking a fruit) have a mild, creamy texture that blends as easily into a smoothie as a banana would. Here vanilla almond milk and plain nonfat yogurt play up the avocado's creamy side, while two cups of spinach highlight its savory qualities. Dates, lemon juice, and a splash of vanilla transform this diverse group of ingredients into something truly delicious and nutritious.

PREPARATION: **15 minutes**   PROCESSING: **35 seconds**   YIELD: **2 servings**

1 cup (240 ml) unsweetened almond milk, preferably homemade (page 354)

2 teaspoons fresh lemon juice

½ cup (120 ml) plain nonfat yogurt

½ teaspoon vanilla extract

6 pitted dates

½ avocado, pitted and peeled

2 cups lightly packed (85 g) spinach

½ cup (120 ml) ice cubes

Place all the ingredients into the Vitamix container in the order listed and secure the lid. Select Variable 1. Turn the machine on and slowly increase the speed to Variable 10, then to High. Blend for 35 seconds, or until the desired consistency is reached.

AMOUNT PER 1 CUP (240 ML) SERVING: calories 190, total fat 7 g, saturated fat 0.5 g, cholesterol 0 mg, sodium 180 mg, total carbohydrate 29 g, dietary fiber 6 g, sugars 19 g, protein 5 g

Very Citrus Slushy

Better than lemonade, this vibrantly flavorful slushy will help you cool down on the very hottest afternoon. Drink through a curly straw if you like.

PREPARATION: **15 minutes**   PROCESSING: **1 to 2 minutes**   YIELD: **6 cups (1.4 liters)**

1½ pounds (680 g) pink grapefruit (2 or 3 medium), peeled and quartered

1 tablespoon grated orange zest

1 orange, peeled and quartered

1 lime, peeled and halved

1 tablespoon honey

3 to 4 cups (720 to 960 ml) ice cubes, more for a slushier consistency

Place all the ingredients into the Vitamix container in the order listed and secure the lid. Select Variable 1. Turn the machine on and slowly increase the speed to Variable 10, then to High. Blend for 1 to 2 minutes, until the desired consistency is reached, using the tamper to press the ingredients into the blades.

AMOUNT PER ½ CUP (120 ML) SERVING: calories 60, total fat 0 g, saturated fat 0 g, cholesterol 0 mg, sodium 0 mg, total carbohydrate 15 g, dietary fiber 2 g, sugars 5 g, protein 1 g

Green Goodness

Green smoothies often contain leafy greens, but some, like this one, can make delicious use of green fruits. Complete with fiber and vitamin C, green Bartlett pears are delicious and widely available. Blend skin and all, with green grapes, soy milk, wheat germ, and a pinch of nutmeg for a tasty and nutritious drink.

PREPARATION: **10 minutes**   PROCESSING: **30 seconds**   YIELD: **2 servings**

¼ cup (60 ml) unsweetened soy milk

1¼ cups (188 g) green grapes

1 tablespoon wheat germ

¼ teaspoon ground nutmeg

1 large Bartlett pear, quartered and seeded

¾ cup (180 ml) ice cubes

Place all the ingredients into the Vitamix container in the order listed and secure the lid. Select Variable 1. Turn the machine on and slowly increase the speed to Variable 10, then to High. Blend for 30 seconds, or until the desired consistency is reached, using the tamper to press the ingredients into the blades.

AMOUNT PER 1 CUP (240 ML) SERVING: calories 160, total fat 1.5 g, saturated fat 0 g, cholesterol 0 mg, sodium 5 mg, total carbohydrate 37 g, dietary fiber 5 g, sugars 27 g, protein 4 g

Spinach Sparkler

Bright green and delightfully bubbly, this sparkler gives you a new and enchanting way to drink your vegetables. Using almost all of a lemon here—the zest and the fruit, but not the bitter pith—gives you bright citrus flavor.

PREPARATION: **15 minutes**   PROCESSING: **45 seconds**   YIELD: **3 servings**

¼ cup (60 ml) still water

1 medium cucumber, cut into pieces

1 celery stalk, halved

2½ cups (70 g) spinach leaves

2 tablespoons (7 g) fresh flat-leaf parsley leaves

Grated zest of 1 lemon

1 lemon, peeled and halved

1 tablespoon pineapple juice

⅓ cup (120 ml) ice cubes

⅓ to ⅔ cup (80 to 160 ml) sparkling water

1. Place all the ingredients except the sparkling water into the Vitamix container in the order listed and secure the lid. Select Variable 1. Turn the machine on and slowly increase the speed to Variable 10, then to High. Blend for 45 seconds, using the tamper to press the ingredients into the blades.

2. Divide among 3 glasses and top with sparkling water.

AMOUNT PER 1 CUP SERVING: calories 35, total fat 0 g, saturated fat 0 g, cholesterol 0 mg, sodium 55 mg, total carbohydrate 10 g, dietary fiber 3 g, sugars 3 g, protein 2 g

Salsa in a Glass

Bright, spicy, and full of fresh vegetable flavor, this juice really ought to be garnished with a celery stick or wedge of lime. The perfect on-the-go, veggie-packed snack! Having friends over for brunch? Add vodka and transform this drink into a whole food Bloody Mary.

PREPARATION: **15 minutes**   PROCESSING: **40 seconds**   YIELD: **3 to 4 servings**

½ cup (120 ml) water

1 pound (454 g) tomatoes, quartered

1 jalapeño pepper, halved and seeded

2 tablespoons (20 g) chopped yellow onion

6 cilantro sprigs

½ lime, peeled

½ cup (120 ml) ice cubes

Place all the ingredients into the Vitamix container in the order listed and secure the lid. Select Variable 1. Turn the machine on and slowly increase the speed to Variable 8. Blend for 40 seconds, or until the desired consistency is reached.

AMOUNT PER 1 CUP (240 ML) SERVING: calories 30, total fat 0 g, saturated fat 0 g, cholesterol 0 mg, sodium 10 mg, total carbohydrate 7 g, dietary fiber 2 g, sugars 4 g, protein 1 g

Velvet Smoothie

Part of the value of a Vitamix is its ability to create silky smooth purees. Some ingredients, like avocado and banana, can create an extra-velvety smoothie, even when chewy dates and crunchy sunflower seeds are added.

PREPARATION: **10 minutes**   PROCESSING: **25 seconds**   YIELD: **3 to 4 servings**

1½ cups (360 ml) unsweetened rice milk, preferably homemade (page 355)

½ avocado, pitted and peeled

½ banana

¼ teaspoon grated lemon zest

¼ lemon, peeled

1 tablespoon chopped pitted dates

1 teaspoon clover honey

1 tablespoon sunflower seeds

1 cup (240 ml) ice cubes

Place all the ingredients into the Vitamix container in the order listed and secure the lid. Select Variable 1. Turn the machine on and slowly increase the speed to Variable 10, then to High. Blend for 25 seconds, or until the desired consistency is reached.

AMOUNT PER 1 CUP (240 ML) SERVING: calories 120, total fat 6 g, saturated fat 0.5 g, cholesterol 0 mg, sodium 60 mg, total carbohydrate 17 g, dietary fiber 3 g, sugars 6 g, protein 1 g

Banana Chia Smoothie

You might not want a bowl of kale, chia seeds, and almond butter for breakfast. But if you buzz these nutritious ingredients in a Vitamix with dates, fresh blueberries, and frozen bananas, you will have a drink that you will want to make again and again. With 7 grams of fiber, 6 grams of protein, and healthy fats from the almond butter and chia seeds, this drink will really stick to your ribs too.

PREPARATION: **15 minutes**   PROCESSING: **1 minute**   YIELD: **4 servings**

1¾ cups (420 ml) water

¼ cup (64 g) almond butter

2 tablespoons (21 g) chia seeds

5 large pitted dates

½ cup (74 g) fresh blueberries

6 kale leaves

2 large bananas, peeled and frozen

Place all the ingredients into the Vitamix container in the order listed and secure the lid. Select Variable 1. Turn the machine on and slowly increase the speed to Variable 10, then to High. Blend for 1 minute, or until the desired consistency is reached, using the tamper to press the ingredients into the blades.

AMOUNT PER 1 CUP (240 ML) SERVING: calories 230, total fat 11 g, saturated fat 1.5 g, cholesterol 0 mg, sodium 45 mg, total carbohydrate 31 g, dietary fiber 7 g, sugars 17 g, protein 6 g

Kale-Flax Smoothie with Pear

Grinding flax seeds makes their nutritional benefits—including omega-3 fatty acids and fiber—more accessible. (Whole flax seeds may pass through your body more or less undigested.) Thanks to the Vitamix blender, you can add ground flax seeds to this tasty smoothie. Like many of the recipes in this chapter, fresh vegetables like kale are blended with whole fruits to create delicious results. Encouraging people to improve their vitality is central to Vitamix's mission, and if adding pears and half a banana to a drink helps you eat more greens, we are all for it!

PREPARATION: **15 minutes**   PROCESSING: **30 seconds**   YIELD: **3 to 4 servings**

1 cup (240 ml) no-sugar-added pear nectar

½ cup (120 ml) vanilla rice milk or soy milk, preferably homemade (pages 355 and 353

2 Bartlett or Forelle pears, cut into large chunks and seeded

½ medium banana (fresh or frozen), peeled

2 tablespoons (18 g) flax seeds

2 fresh mint leaves

2 cups lightly packed (150 g) torn kale leaves

½ cup (120 ml) ice cubes

Place all the ingredients into the Vitamix container in the order listed and secure the lid. Select Variable 1. Turn the machine on and slowly increase the speed to Variable 10, then to High. Blend for 30 seconds, or until the desired consistency is reached.

AMOUNT PER 1 CUP (240 ML) SERVING: calories 200, total fat 3 g, saturated fat 0 g, cholesterol 0 mg, sodium 45 mg, total carbohydrate 42 g, dietary fiber 7 g, sugars 15 g, protein 5 g

Nourishing Beets

Many purchased vegetable juices feature tomatoes, but when you make your own, you can move purple-hued, nutrient-packed beets to center stage. (And unlike many of its bottled counterparts, this drink has no added salt.) Apples complement the beet's natural sweetness, while the fresh chile, a chunk of fresh ginger, and garlic lend spice. The vegetable flavor of celery keeps the overall taste more savory than sweet.

PREPARATION: **15 minutes**   PROCESSING: **2 minutes**   YIELD: **7 servings**

2 cups (480 ml) water

3 small/medium beets (1¼ pound / 570 g), tops intact, cut into pieces

One ½-inch (1.3-cm) cube fresh gingerroot, peeled

1 fresh chile pepper

2 small apples, quartered

1 garlic clove, peeled

2 celery stalks, cut into pieces

1 cup (240 ml) ice cubes

1. Place 1 cup (240 ml) of the water into the Vitamix container, then add the beets, ginger, chile, apples, garlic, and celery and secure the lid. Select Variable 1. Turn the machine on and slowly increase the speed to Variable 10, then to High. Blend for 1 minute 30 seconds, using the tamper to press the ingredients into the blades.

2. Stop the machine and remove the lid. Add the remaining water and the ice cubes to the Vitamix container and secure the lid. Select Variable 1. Turn the machine on and slowly increase the speed to Variable 10, then to High. Blend for 30 additional seconds.

AMOUNT PER 1 CUP (240 ML) SERVING: calories 60, total fat 0 g, saturated fat 0 g, cholesterol 0 mg, sodium 75 mg, total carbohydrate 15 g, dietary fiber 4 g, sugars 10 g, protein 2 g

The Vitamix Cookbook

Liquid Apple Pie

Why drink plain old apple juice when you can sip apple pie instead? Cinnamon, nutmeg, vanilla, and maple syrup pack classic apple pie flavors into a delicious, slushy drink.

PREPARATION: **10 minutes**   PROCESSING: **15 to 20 seconds**   YIELD: **1 serving**

¼ cup (60 ml) water

½ cup (120 ml) unsweetened apple juice

¼ cup (60 ml) unsweetened soy milk, preferably homemade (page 353)

1 teaspoon maple syrup

¼ teaspoon vanilla extract

⅛ teaspoon ground cinnamon

⅛ teaspoon ground nutmeg

½ cup (120 ml) ice cubes

Place all the ingredients into the Vitamix container in the order listed and secure the lid. Select Variable 1. Turn the machine on and slowly increase the speed to Variable 10. Blend for 15 to 20 seconds, until the drink has a slightly slushy consistency. Serve immediately.

AMOUNT PER 1¼ CUP (300 ML) SERVING: calories 110, total fat 2 g, saturated fat 0 g, cholesterol 0 mg, sodium 10 mg, total carbohydrate 20 g, dietary fiber 1 g, sugars 17 g, protein 3 g

Tofu Tropic Smoothie

Soft, silken tofu has a rich, creamy texture that blends beautifully into this tropical-flavored smoothie. Partially defrosted fruit seems to have a fuller flavor, which is why we suggest that you thaw the mango for 10 minutes before blending.

PREPARATION: **10 minutes**   PROCESSING: **45 seconds**   YIELD: **4 servings**

½ cup (120 ml) water

2 cups (373 g) frozen mango chunks

1¼ cups (300 ml) pineapple juice

6 ounces (170 g) light, soft silken tofu

Grated zest of 1 lime

1 lime, peeled and halved

1. Let the mango sit at room temperature for 10 minutes to thaw slightly.

2. Place all the ingredients into the Vitamix container in the order listed and secure the lid. Select Variable 1. Turn the machine on and slowly increase the speed to Variable 10, then to High. Blend for 45 seconds, or until the desired consistency is reached, using the tamper to press the ingredients into the blades.

AMOUNT PER 1 CUP (240 ML) SERVING: calories 140, total fat 1.5 g, saturated fat 0 g, cholesterol 0 mg, sodium 25 mg, total carbohydrate 29 g, dietary fiber 3 g, sugars 22 g, protein 4 g

Tropical Shake

Kids (and the kid in all of us) love slurping up a sweet shake through a straw. Vegan and bursting with zippy fresh fruit flavor, this shake will be a hit with young and old alike.

PREPARATION: **15 minutes**   PROCESSING: **40 seconds**   YIELD: **3¼ cups (780 ml)**

1 cup (240 ml) pineapple juice

¾ cup (180 ml) soy milk

½ lemon, peeled

1 banana, peeled and frozen

1 cup (187 g) frozen mango chunks

Place all the ingredients into the Vitamix container in the order listed and secure the lid. Select Variable 1. Turn the machine on and slowly increase the speed to Variable 10, then to High. Blend for 40 seconds.

AMOUNT PER 1 CUP (240 ML) SERVING: calories 150, total fat 1 g, saturated fat 0 g, cholesterol 0 mg, sodium 35 mg, total carbohydrate 35 g, dietary fiber 3 g, protein 3 g

Mango Freeze Drink

Cultivated since about 2000 BC, mangoes give us vitamins A and C as well as fiber, magnesium, and potassium. Blend this healthy fruit with a little peach nectar and ice on a hot summer's day for a refreshing treat. Garnish with a lime wedge if you like.

PREPARATION: **15 minutes**   PROCESSING: **1 minute**   YIELD: **5 to 6 servings**

1½ cups (360 ml) no-sugar-added peach nectar, chilled

3 medium mangoes, peeled, seeded, and cut into chunks

2½ cups (600 ml) ice cubes

Place all the ingredients into the Vitamix container in the order listed and secure the lid. Select Variable 1. Turn the machine on and slowly increase the speed to Variable 10, then to High. Blend for 1 minute, or until the desired consistency is reached, using the tamper to press the ingredients into the blades.

AMOUNT PER 1 CUP (240 ML) SERVING: calories 190, total fat 1 g, saturated fat 0 g, cholesterol 0 mg, sodium 5 mg, total carbohydrate 47 g, dietary fiber 3 g, sugars 3 g, protein 0 g

Melon Madness

Our tasty Melon Madness is the perfect drink to whip up when the stores and markets are full of ripe melons. Skim milk and Greek yogurt add calcium and protein to this wonderfully fruit-filled drink.

PREPARATION: **15 minutes**   PROCESSING: **25 seconds**   YIELD: **4 to 5 servings**

1 cup (140 g) frozen peach slices

1 cup (240 ml) skim milk

¼ cup (60 ml) water

¾ cup (180 ml) peach 0% Greek yogurt, stirred

½ teaspoon vanilla extract

½ cup (78 g) cantaloupe pieces

½ cup (85 g) honeydew melon pieces

½ cup (70 g) watermelon pieces

⅓ cup (80 ml) ice cubes

1. Let the frozen peaches sit at room temperature for 10 minutes to thaw slightly.

2. Place the milk, water, yogurt, vanilla, melon pieces, peaches, and ice cubes into the Vitamix container in the order listed and secure the lid. Select Variable 1. Turn the machine on and slowly increase the speed to Variable 10, then to High. Blend for 25 seconds, or until the desired consistency is reached.

AMOUNT PER 1 CUP (240 ML) SERVING: calories 80, total fat 0 g, saturated fat 0 g, cholesterol 0 mg, sodium 45 mg, total carbohydrate 15 g, dietary fiber 1 g, sugars 14 g, protein 6 g

Drinks

Fresh Mint with Sprouts Beverage

You may eat your greens most days, but sometimes you may want or need to drink them, too! This vibrant, minty drink combines the green goodness of kiwi, broccoli, kale, mint, and sprouts with almond milk, dates, and a little vanilla. Sweet enough to be totally slurpable but not so sweet that the flavor of the greens is hidden.

PREPARATION: **15 minutes**   PROCESSING: **40 seconds**   YIELD: **2 to 3 servings**

1 cup (240 ml) unsweetened almond milk, preferably homemade (page 354)

2 kiwi fruit, peeled and halved

¼ cup (22 g) chopped broccoli florets, fresh or frozen

2 pitted dates

1 cup (19 g) torn kale leaves

1 cup (13 g) fresh mint leaves

½ cup (16 g) alfalfa sprouts or broccoli sprouts, rinsed and patted dry

1 teaspoon vanilla extract

½ cup (120 ml) ice cubes

Place all the ingredients into the Vitamix container in the order listed and secure the lid. Select Variable 1. Turn the machine on and slowly increase the speed to Variable 10, then to High. Blend for 40 seconds, or until the desired consistency is reached, using the tamper to press the ingredients into the blades.

AMOUNT PER 1 CUP (240 ML) SERVING: calories 80, total fat 1.5 g, saturated fat 0 g, cholesterol 0 mg, sodium 80 mg, total carbohydrate 15 g, dietary fiber 3 g, sugars 9 g, protein 2 g

Nuts and Seeds Smoothie

Not just for the birds anymore, nuts and seeds can be a good way to add protein, omega-3 fatty acids, fiber, calcium, and iron to your diet. While absolutely nutrient-dense and a source of healthy fats, nuts and seeds also pack a bigger caloric punch, so enjoy them in moderation.

PREPARATION: **15 minutes**   PROCESSING: **1 minute**   YIELD: **3 servings**

1½ cup (360 ml) water

⅓ cup (43 g) unsalted sunflower seeds

⅓ cup (48 g) blanched almonds

1 tablespoon chia seeds, soaked in 3 tablespoons water until a gel is formed

½ cup (60 g) dried apricots

½ avocado, pitted and peeled

2 cups (3 oz / 85 g) spring greens mix

½ teaspoon ground cinnamon

¼ teaspoon ground nutmeg

1 teaspoon vanilla extract

1¾ cups (420 ml) ice cubes

Place all the ingredients into the Vitamix container in the order listed and secure the lid. Select Variable 1. Turn the machine on and slowly increase the speed to Variable 10, then to High. Blend for 1 minute, or until the desired consistency is reached, using the tamper to press the ingredients into the blades.

AMOUNT PER 1 CUP (240 ML) SERVING: calories 300, total fat 20 g, saturated fat 2 g, cholesterol 0 mg, sodium 40 mg, total carbohydrate 26 g, dietary fiber 9 g, sugars 9 g, protein 8 g

Soy Fruit Splendor

Not only do dried figs lend a caramel-like sweetness to this vegan drink, but they also add calcium. A half cup of dried figs contains about the same amount of calcium as a half cup of low-fat (1%) milk: 133 milligrams versus 142 milligrams.

PREPARATION: **10 minutes**   PROCESSING: **1 minute**   YIELD: **3 to 4 servings**

¾ cup (180 ml) fresh orange juice (see page 301)

¼ cup (60 ml) unsweetened soy milk

1½ apples (14 oz / 398 g), quartered and seeded

5 dried figs, pitted

1 cup (240 ml) ice cubes

Place all the ingredients into the Vitamix container in the order listed and secure the lid. Select Variable 1. Turn the machine on and slowly increase the speed to Variable 10, then to High. Blend for 1 minute, or until the desired consistency is reached, using the tamper to press the ingredients into the blades.

AMOUNT PER 1 CUP (240 ML) SERVING: calories 130, total fat 1 g, saturated fat 0 g, cholesterol 0 mg, sodium 5 mg, total carbohydrate 33 g, dietary fiber 4 g, sugars 24 g, protein 2 g

B-Smoothie

This simple smoothie gives you a delicious way to add the nutrient-packed goodness of wheat germ, flaxseed, and hemp seeds into your diet. Chia seeds contain omega-3 fatty acids, fiber (10 grams per two tablespoons), iron, calcium, and more. Hemp seeds contribute omega-3 and omega-6 fatty acids, magnesium, fiber (2 grams per three tablespoons), and protein (10 grams per three tablespoons) to your diet. Good old wheat germ gives this drink an extra boost of magnesium, fiber, and vitamins B5 and E. This smoothie is delicious and nutritious. What could be better?

PREPARATION: **10 minutes**   PROCESSING: **40 seconds**   YIELD: **2 to 3 servings**

½ cup (120 ml) pineapple juice

¼ cup (60 ml) unsweetened almond milk, preferably homemade (page 354)

1 small ripe banana

1 cup (165 g) pineapple chunks, fresh or frozen

1 tablespoon wheat germ

2 teaspoons flax seeds

½ teaspoon hemp seeds

½ cup (120 ml) ice cubes

Place all the ingredients into the Vitamix container in the order listed and secure the lid. Select Variable 1. Turn the machine on and slowly increase the speed to Variable 10, then to High. Blend for 40 seconds, or until the desired consistency is reached.

AMOUNT PER 1 CUP (240 ML) SERVING: calories 120, total fat 2 g, saturated fat 0 g, cholesterol 0 mg, sodium 20 mg, total carbohydrate 26 g, dietary fiber 2 g, sugars 16 g, protein 2 g

Soy Milk

Once your dried soybeans are soaked and steamed, this preservative- and additive-free fresh soy milk comes together in a flash. If you are going to use the milk in smoothies, don't worry about straining it. If you want to stir it into your coffee or pour it over cereal, you might want to use either a nut milk bag or a fine-mesh strainer to get an end product that is even creamier.

PREPARATION: **8 hours**   PROCESSING: **1 minute**   COOK TIME: **15 minutes**
YIELD: **4 cups (960 ml) unstrained or 3 cups (720 ml) strained**

1 cup (200 g) dried soybeans

3½ cups (840 ml) water

1 tablespoon sugar

1. Rinse the dried soybeans and pick over for debris. Place in a bowl and add water to cover by 3 inches. Soak for 4 to 8 hours.

2. Steam for about 15 minutes. Transfer the soybeans to a bowl and let cool. Measure out 1½ cups (258 g) cooked beans. Reserve any leftover soybeans in the refrigerator for another use.

3. Place the water in the Vitamix container, then add the cooked beans and the sugar and secure the lid. Select Variable 1. Turn the machine on and slowly increase the speed to Variable 10, then to High. Blend for 1 minute, or until your desired consistency—thin, thick, or coarse—is reached.

4. To obtain commercial-style soy milk, strain the milk through a nut milk bag or let it drain through a fine-mesh sieve.

For a refreshing flavor, add a 1-inch (2.5-cm) cube of gingerroot before blending.

AMOUNT PER 1 CUP (240 ML) SERVING (UNSTRAINED): calories 120, total fat 6 g, saturated fat 1 g, cholesterol 0 mg, sodium 10 mg, total carbohydrate 10 g, dietary fiber 4 g, sugars 5 g, protein 11 g

Almond Milk

You can purchase almond milk, but you will often be buying stabilizers, added sugar, and preservatives along with the convenience. Once you have a Vitamix blender, you can blend your own almond milk and add as much or as little sweetness as you like. (A few pitted dates can be added in lieu of sugar.) The resulting nut milk is fresh and delicious, and it will keep in the refrigerator for 3 to 4 days.

PREPARATION: **8 hours**   PROCESSING: **45 seconds**

YIELD: **4½ cups (1 liter) unstrained or 2¾ cups (660 ml) strained**

1 cup (140 g) raw almonds, soaked at least 8 hours, drained

3 cups (720 ml) water

Sugar or other sweetener, to taste (optional)

1. Place the almonds in a bowl. Cover with 1 inch (2.5 cm) water and let sit for 8 hours to soak. Drain well.

2. Place all the ingredients into the Vitamix container in the order listed and secure the lid. Select Variable 1. Turn the machine on and slowly increase the speed to Variable 10, then to High. Blend for 45 seconds. Add sugar to taste, if desired.

3. To obtain commercial-style almond milk, strain the milk through a nut milk bag or let it drain through a fine-mesh sieve.

AMOUNT PER 1 CUP (240 ML) UNSTRAINED SERVING: calories 180, total fat 16 g, saturated fat 1 g, cholesterol 0 mg, sodium 5 mg, total carbohydrate 7 g, dietary fiber 4 g, sugars 1 g, protein 7 g

The Vitamix Cookbook

Rice Milk

Purchased rice milk, just like most nondairy milks, can contain a lot of preservatives, thickeners, and sweeteners. By blending your own fresh rice milk, you skip the additives and focus on the flavor, adding sweeteners and vanilla to taste.

PREPARATION: **10 minutes**   PROCESSING: **1 minute**   YIELD: **2¼ cups (540 ml)**

2 cups (480 ml) water

½ cup (100 g) cooked brown rice, cooled

½ tablespoon brown sugar or other sweetener, or more to taste

½ teaspoon vanilla extract (optional)

Place all the ingredients into the Vitamix container in the order listed and secure the lid. Select Variable 1. Turn the machine on and slowly increase the speed to Variable 10, then to High. Blend for 1 minute, or until the desired consistency is reached.

AMOUNT PER 1 CUP (240 ML) SERVING: calories 60, total fat 0 g, saturated fat 0 g, cholesterol 0 mg, sodium 10 mg, total carbohydrate 13 g, dietary fiber 1 g, sugars 3 g, protein 1 g

Sweet Almond Cinnamon Milk

Purchased almond milk's flavor pales in comparison to the fresh, nutty flavor of the real deal. Dates give the nut milk a rich, almost brown-sugar-like sweetness and the cinnamon complements this taste. Our sweet almond milk tastes amazing plain, blended into a smoothie, or poured over cereal.

PREPARATION: **10 minutes**   PROCESSING: **45 seconds**   YIELD: **4½ cups (1 liter)**

1 cup (150 g) raw almonds

3 cups (720 ml) water

½ teaspoon ground cinnamon

4 pitted dates

1. Place the almonds in a bowl with water to cover by 4 inches (10 cm) and let soak for at least 8 hours. Drain.

2. Place the water, drained almonds, cinnamon, and dates into the Vitamix container and secure the lid. Select Variable 1. Turn the machine on and slowly increase the speed to Variable 10, then to High. Blend for 45 seconds. To obtain commercial-style almond milk, strain the milk through a nut milk bag or let it drain through a fine-mesh sieve.

AMOUNT PER 1 CUP (240 ML) SERVING: calories 200, total fat 16 g, saturated fat 1 g, cholesterol 0 mg, sodium 10 mg, total carbohydrate 12 g, dietary fiber 5 g, sugars 6 g, protein 7 g

Iced Frappe

Coffee and chocolate: a great combination or the *greatest* combination? Regardless of your answer, this iced frappe will help you power through your day, and for much cheaper than the usual coffee shop prices.

PREPARATION: **10 minutes**   PROCESSING: **15 seconds**   YIELD: **3 to 4 servings**

1 cup (240 ml) strong brewed coffee, cold

½ cup (120 ml) skim milk

1 teaspoon honey

2 pitted dates

2 tablespoons (18 g) chopped semisweet chocolate

½ cup (120 ml) ice cubes

Place all the ingredients into the Vitamix container in the order listed and secure the lid. Select Variable 1. Turn the machine on and slowly increase the speed to Variable 8. Blend for 15 seconds. Serve immediately.

AMOUNT PER 1 CUP (240 ML) SERVING: calories 60, total fat 2 g, saturated fat 1 g, cholesterol 0 mg, sodium 25 mg, total carbohydrate 10 g, dietary fiber 1 g, sugars 8 g, protein 2 g

Espresso Banana Drink

Do you love the icy cold, blended coffee drinks sold at coffee shops but wish they were healthier? Our espresso banana drink will remind you of your favorite sweet, smooth iced coffee, but with only 7 grams of sugar per serving. Sweet, creamy bananas, eye-opening espresso, soy milk, and ice whir together to make a treat that can start the morning or perk up the most sluggish afternoon.

PREPARATION: **10 minutes**   PROCESSING: **20 seconds**   YIELD: **1 serving**

¼ cup (60 ml) brewed espresso, cold

½ small ripe banana

½ cup (120 ml) unsweetened soy milk, preferably homemade (page 353)

½ cup (120 ml) ice cubes

Place all the ingredients into the Vitamix container in the order listed and secure the lid. Select Variable 1. Turn the machine on and slowly increase the speed to Variable 10, then to High. Blend for 20 seconds, or until the desired consistency is reached.

AMOUNT PER 1 CUP (240 ML) SERVING: calories 110, total fat 3.5 g, saturated fat 0.5 g, cholesterol 0 mg, sodium 15 mg, total carbohydrate 15 g, dietary fiber 2 g, sugars 7 g, protein 7 g

Mocha Cooler

The mellow, creamy flavor of banana and the deeper and more caramel-like sweetness of dates pair beautifully with the natural bitterness of espresso and cocoa powder. Together with ice, some fat-free milk, and a splash of vanilla, these ingredients make a refreshing and indulgent-tasting mocha.

PREPARATION: **10 minutes**   PROCESSING: **15 seconds**   YIELD: **2 servings**

1 cup (240 ml) skim milk

1 medium banana

1 large pitted date

2 teaspoons unsweetened cocoa powder

1 teaspoon instant espresso powder

½ teaspoon vanilla extract

½ cup (120 ml) ice cubes

Place all the ingredients into the Vitamix container in the order listed and secure the lid. Select Variable 1. Turn the machine on and slowly increase the speed to Variable 10, then to High. Blend for 15 seconds, or until the desired consistency is reached.

AMOUNT PER 1 CUP (240 ML) SERVING: calories 160, total fat 0 g, saturated fat 0 g, cholesterol 0 mg, sodium 55 mg, total carbohydrate 36 g, dietary fiber 3 g, sugars 27 g, protein 6 g

Tea of Green Smoothie

Brewing your own green tea delivers far more of its naturally occurring antioxidants than purchased iced tea. In some cases, you would have to drink almost twenty bottles of the purchased stuff to get the same benefits present in one homemade cup. Here, homemade iced green tea is blended with four different fruits to create a refreshing smoothie without any refined sugar.

PREPARATION: **10 minutes**   PROCESSING: **40 seconds**   YIELD: **3 servings**

1 cup (240 ml) freshly brewed green tea, chilled

1 small banana, peeled

2 cups (340 g) honeydew melon chunks

2 pitted dates

1 kiwi fruit, peeled and sliced

Place all the ingredients into the Vitamix container in the order listed and secure the lid. Select Variable 1. Turn the machine on and slowly increase the speed to Variable 10. Blend for 40 seconds, or until the desired consistency is reached.

AMOUNT PER 1 CUP (240 ML) SERVING: calories 100, total fat 0 g, saturated fat 0 g, cholesterol 0 mg, sodium 20 mg, total carbohydrate 25 g, dietary fiber 3 g, sugars 18 g, protein 1 g

Thai Eye Opener

A splash of creamy coconut milk, fresh pineapple, carrots, apple, and fresh ginger are blended together to create a vibrant, Thai-inspired juice. When you are cutting up your pineapple, you only need to cut away the thinnest layer of the skin. The "eyes" of the pineapple and the fibrous core will be pureed to silky perfection in your Vitamix machine!

PREPARATION: **20 minutes**   PROCESSING: **1 minute**   YIELD: **2 to 3 servings**

¼ cup (60 ml) coconut milk

¼ cup (40 g) fresh pineapple chunks

2 carrots, halved

1 medium apple, quartered and seeded

¼ teaspoon chopped fresh gingerroot

1 cup (240 ml) ice cubes

Place all the ingredients into the Vitamix container in the order listed and secure the lid. Select Variable 1. Turn the machine on and slowly increase the speed to Variable 10, then to High. Blend for 1 minute, or until the desired consistency is reached, using the tamper to press the ingredients into the blades.

AMOUNT PER 1 CUP (240 ML) SERVING: calories 100, total fat 4 g, saturated fat 3.5 g, cholesterol 0 mg, sodium 40 mg, total carbohydrate 17 g, dietary fiber 3 g, sugars 12 g, protein 1 g

Brad and Alyson Shedd

Countless articles have been devoted to getting wary children to eat their vegetables. Scanning the literature, several trends emerge. First, you have to set a good example. It's a challenge to get kids to eat their veggies if the adults around them don't. Another frequently heard theme is the importance of including your children in preparing food. Kids, in theory, are often more apt to enjoy a salad that they helped prepare. But think of it this way. Most adults eat the same foods they were exposed to as a child. So the key may be as simple as exposing them to the flavors of fruits and vegetables in a way that is delicious as early as you can. Put a green smoothie in a sippy cup, and most kids will cry for more.

For parents who did not start their kids out young, persuading one or maybe two children to eat vegetables can be a seemingly impossible task. But eight? It is a challenge that Brad and Alyson Shedd handle with great grace. And, perhaps, with a little help from their Vitamix blender, a gift for Alyson's birthday in 2010. Do they set a good example? Yes!

"We have lots of fruit and vegetables throughout the day—usually a huge salad each evening—but the Vitamix helps us get started right with fruits and vegetables at the very beginning of the day! We all have started craving it," says Brad. They created a delicious Shedd-family formula for their morning smoothies—yogurt, spinach, frozen fruit, and apple juice—that they enjoy right along with their kids. "We mix up smoothies for all ten of us (we just about go over-capacity on the machine!) each morning!" Brad says. He and Alyson use kid-friendly ingredients like yogurt and fruit to make it nutritious and delicious.

And do they involve their kids? Yes! Brad says his daughter Laura, now eight years old, is his primary smoothie assistant. In fact Laura, who has been helping Brad for the past two years, can assemble all of the ingredients herself and just needs help operating the machine.

When asked if he had any advice for someone considering buying a Vitamix blender, Brad had this to say: "Start with some of the simple recipes included with the package, and begin to experiment and branch out from there. There's no rush. You're going to be using this tool pretty much the rest of your life!"

Acknowledgments

This book started as a desire to share the story of my ancestors and how their commitment to whole food blending and health created a legacy that I have the honor of stewarding for the next generation. The number of people involved and the work they did to take it from a desire to a reality are impressive. I want to thank our friends at Falls Communications and the numerous Vitamix employees, with a special shout-out to our talented chefs who developed the delicious recipes: Bev Shaffer and Anne Thacker.

Thank you to all of my family who made our story possible, and especially to those who helped tell the story and verify the details—it was truly a multigenerational project: my father, John Barnard; my cousin Loree Connors; my sister, Beth McBride; and my niece Robin Dieterich. Thank you, Heather Gaynor, for keeping the project on track, and Beth McBride, for bringing our family story to life.

UNIVERSAL CONVERSION CHART

OVEN TEMPERATURE EQUIVALENTS

250°F = 120°C   400°F = 200°C

275°F = 135°C   425°F = 220°C

300°F = 150°C   450°F = 230°C

325°F = 160°C   475°F = 240°C

350°F = 180°C   500°F = 260°C

375°F = 190°C

MEASUREMENT EQUIVALENTS

Measurements should always be level unless directed otherwise.

⅛ TEASPOON = 0.5 ML

¼ TEASPOON = 1 ML

½ TEASPOON = 2 ML

1 TEASPOON = 5 ML

1 TABLESPOON = 3 TEASPOONS = ½ FLUID OUNCE = 15 ML

2 TABLESPOONS = ⅛ CUP = 1 FLUID OUNCE = 30 ML

4 TABLESPOONS = ¼ CUP = 2 FLUID OUNCES = 60 ML

5⅓ TABLESPOONS = ⅓ CUP = 3 FLUID OUNCES = 80 ML

8 TABLESPOONS = ½ CUP = 4 FLUID OUNCES = 120 ML

10⅔ TABLESPOONS = ⅔ CUP = 5 FLUID OUNCES = 160 ML

12 TABLESPOONS = ¾ CUP = 6 FLUID OUNCES = 180 ML

16 TABLESPOONS = 1 CUP = 8 FLUID OUNCES = 240 ML

Index

NOTE: Page references in *italics* refer to photos of recipes.